The Pocket Mentor

Mentor

A Handbook for Teachers

Chris Niebrand
Elizabeth Horn
Robin Holmes

J. Weston Walch, Publisher
Portland, Maine

1   2   3   4   5   6   7   8   9   10

0-8251-2123-X

Copyright © 1992
J. Weston Walch, Publisher
P.O. Box 658 • Portland, Maine 04104-0658

Printed in the United States of America

This book is dedicated to
Brent, Gary, and Mike

Contents

Chapter 5: Curriculum-Based Problems 115

Chapter 6: Record-Keeping 149

Chapter 7: Legal Considerations 159

Chapter 8: Administration 170

Chapter 9: Ancillary Personnel 180

Acknowledgments

As with any major production, *The Pocket Mentor* was made possible by many players behind the scenes. We'd like to say thank you to a few.

To Ken Anderson, assistant principal, who, in spite of a schedule that would overwhelm Superman, finds the time to prove he's still a master teacher.

To Robert Auth, master teacher, retired administrator, and Chris's father, whose wisdom and advice planted the seeds for this book.

To Dr. Pete Bailey, an administrator and master teacher whose keen sense of organization helped us focus on our priorities.

To Jim Coughlin, master teacher, whose ability to mentor extends beyond the schoolhouse, to the community, and even into the legislature.

To Dean Hamilton, a master teacher who acknowledges that mentoring goes beyond the first years of teaching.

To Dr. David Lachiondo, principal, counselor, master teacher, and educational law professor, who offered us his own version of Perry Mason.

To Dian Liles, R.N, who is certainly a relative of Mother Teresa.

To Merlin Lords, Boise City Police Department, who demonstrates that law enforcement can be synonymous with diplomacy.

To Al Musser, administrator, who has the monumental task of ensuring the mentoring of tomorrow's master teachers.

To Gary Slee, principal, counselor, and master teacher, whose dedication to young people and "at risk" students illustrates that "tough love" is not an oxymoron.

To Dr. Blossom Turk, principal, counselor, and master teacher, whose newspaper columns, books, and seminars represent her tireless quest for student success.

To the countless new teachers we've worked with over the years.

—Thank you.

xi

The Faculty

Mike
Kindergarten

Mary
Secondary
Reading

Barbara
Language Arts
Junior High

Bill
Spanish
High School

Marc
Math
Junior High

Gary
Humanities
High School

Tami
Science
High School

Nick
Band
High School

Allen
Math
Junior High

Kathy
6th Grade

Brian
Social Studies
High School

Ellen
4th Grade

Robert	Betty	Gerry	Jeff
2nd/3rd Grade	*Language Arts* *High School*	*Vocal Music* *High School*	*Science/Coach* *High School*

Katie	Sharon	Melanie	Angie
P.E. *Junior High*	*Media Specialist* *Middle School*	*History/Coach* *Secondary*	*School Secretary* *Elementary*

Your Authors

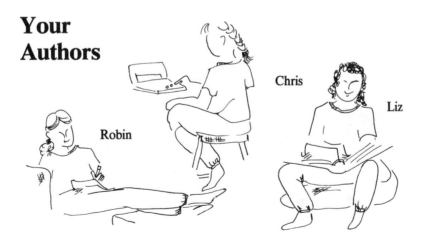

Introduction: Why This Book?

Like weddings, funerals, and graduation, first days of school are milestones that conjure memories of warm fuzziness or goose-pimply horror. How you deal with this day is critical to you and your students and, most importantly, to how the rest of the year will unfold. You set the tone.

Even if you are a veteran teacher, a change in building, curriculum, room, or class represents starting over. Changes require preparation. Although these alterations in your career may be exciting and challenging, they do represent new problems and frustrations. This is all the more reason to establish an appropriate learning environment from the beginning.

As students and teachers, we have all suffered through awkward beginnings. The year we (Chris and Liz) met proved to be the toughest we'd encountered before or since. Although there were several reasons for this, we traced much of that grim experience back to the first day of class in a different school. It was a nightmare.

Because we shared similar plights, we became kindred spirits. Both of us had transferred from junior highs and were facing a new environment, new curricula, and a new administration.

Chris was replacing a well-liked veteran teacher of an accelerated class. She faced many hostile juniors who were afflicted with a severe case of teacher loyalty—to the old teacher. As a result, Chris's new students entered the class as reluctant learners, doubting the credibility of anyone replacing the previous instructor.

Liz faced five classes of "at-risk" students. The classes were large, ranging in size from 32 to 38 of the most notorious young characters in the community. The students were challenge enough, but our classrooms presented even more of a challenge in those first weeks of school.

We'd received our schedules for adjoining rooms—which evolved into a blessing— in a remodeled wing of an ancient building. Desks were "on order." Shadeless windows faced a southern exposure. The scarred hardwood floor, freckled with paint, resembled a Jackson Pollock canvas. Carpeting, too, was due to arrive "any day." We were told not to put anything on the walls until the room renovation was complete. Consequently, students had a difficult time establishing a feeling of community and belonging. A few folding chairs and tired, graffiti-covered desks were clumped in the hot little rooms which faced a hectic downtown street. We were often party to the traffic and shrieks of the YMCA playground across the street. On Mondays garbage was collected; Tuesdays were lawn-mowing days. Chris especially remembers reading Dylan Thomas's "Do Not Go Gentle Into That Good Night" to the accompaniment of a leaf blower. So much for tone.

A couple of colleagues took pity. With their help and the detective work of the custodians, we eventually obtained teacher-sized desks. The middle drawer of Chris's was broken and frequently fell out, resulting in a floor strewn with staples, pens, and pencils; eventually, she and the students got used to that. We were able to scavenge cinder blocks and boards for shelves; cardboard boxes or plastic milk cartons served as temporary file cabinets. In time, all this equipment trickled in, but the first weeks of class were an experience that we'd equate with frequent trips to the dentist for root canal work.

Robin's case was entirely different. Right after student teaching, she was fortunate enough to simply slide into her supervising teacher's position. Everything was familiar; the climate had been established, the rules had been presented, and the parents and students had already accepted her. Robin knew her way around the school. This situation would be any beginning teacher's dream come true.

Twelve years later, Robin transferred to a new school in a larger district. Even though Robin was a veteran teacher, she found herself in the same frightening predicament as a novice teacher—alone, needing materials and friendly colleagues. Her teaching assignment was a combined second/third-grade classroom in a school serving an affluent section of the city. Parents were immediately concerned that their third graders would not be challenged enough in the combined class. The second-graders' parents worried that their children were being taught material beyond their abilities. Robin not only had to get used to a new school and class but also had to demonstrate her competency to the parents.

During the second week of school, a local television crew interviewed Robin about how a mixed class functions. Robin handled the interview like a professional, educated parents, and got to the business of teaching her class with aplomb. However, she is a master teacher.

But if you are not a master teacher, whom do you trust? Where do you find answers? How can you identify what you need to know? Who cares enough to help you?

The story of Odysseus tells of his wife, Penelope, and son, Telemachus, who were left on the island of Ithaca while Odysseus was fated to wander for ten years. Because of the hero's lengthy absence, the people of Ithaca assumed that Odysseus was dead. Rude, greedy men spent days in his great hall, slaughtering livestock, consuming his food and wine, and tormenting his family. Frustrated with the intrusions, Penelope and Telemachus felt helpless. The goddess Athena took pity on Telemachus. In the guise of the great Ithacan Mentor, she visited him and offered comfort and encouragement. Inspired by her guidance, Odysseus' son found the inner strength to embark on the journey that would bring him to his father and restore the family's house to peace.

Ideally, a guardian angel figure will appear miraculously at your side—a mentor who will nurture you and tell you how to handle discipline. This mentor will tell you where to find a copy of the curriculum, the library, or even the restroom. How nice it would be to know that you should take your grade book along during fire drills, that you must write progress reports, and that you must keep accurate daily records.

We wish we had known what to do about cheating, make-up work, or procedures for admitting new students to classes. We wish someone had told us what to do when a fight breaks out in the classroom or what to do about a student who comes consistently late to class. We wish that we, like Telemachus, had had a mentor to offer encouragement and advice as we began our teaching odyssey.

After that first nightmarish year, we made a pact to offer other teachers the guidance we'd never had. We came to the realization that all teachers, regardless of grade level or assignment or years of experience, need mentoring. So in *The Pocket Mentor*, we've attempted to ease the way for those teachers who need help with curriculum decisions, discipline problems, and the daily routines that govern the business of teaching.

This is not a book of statistics; it is an anecdotal handbook based on battle scars acquired during 50 years of combined teaching experience from kindergarten to college. It represents years of graduate work, articles written and published, grants, seminars, workshops taken and presented, and trial and error.

This is not a book of hard and fast rules, either. To be effective, you must teach, inspire, and keep order in the ways that work best for *you*. That's why we offer suggestions and personal anecdotes rather than prescriptions for procedures.

To help you find the guidance you need for a particular situation, we've included a comprehensive index. Using the Index, you should be able to find several different approaches for dealing with the situation you're facing. In addition, when we mention a book in the text, you'll find complete information about that book in the Bibliography at the end of this text.

As we were writing, we often discussed whether there was a need to separate sections dealing with elementary and secondary strategies. We found we had, in most cases, common concerns and common solutions.

This handbook offers advice for all levels and disciplines. We believe that teaching is a universal process with universal goals. Teaching can be difficult and stressful, yet many days offer successes and rewards.

We intend that this book serve as your mentor until you locate that guardian angel in your profession who will answer all your questions before you know enough to ask them. *The Pocket Mentor* can assist you in establishing goals and priorities. This book plus a healthy sense of humor will launch you on your journey as a beginning teacher or smooth your voyage as an experienced teacher.

CHAPTER 1

Professionalism

Don't ever say you've never taught before. If students ask if this is your first year, just say no. (after all, you've student taught!)
— Catherine, Grade 12

Ryan   grade 9
Be nice and understanding
    to a person haveing a hard time

On the first day of a new school year, be assertive and somewhat stern.
— Molly C. 12

Beginning teachers need to show their class that they are self confident and comfortable with their position. there is nothing worse than having a nervous teacher who seems flustered on the first day of class.
    Marianne K.

Teachers are professional people who both work in the public arena and live in the community. The people in your community will perceive you as a teacher both in and out of school. For better or worse, this means you have to be aware of the impression you make, in school and in your community. So while the remainder of this book is devoted to advice about teaching itself, this opening chapter offers you tips on professionalism and living your private life that we hope will be helpful.

Experienced teachers may recognize some of these situations and groan, "How well I know." Beginning teachers may gasp, "I never would have thought of *that*—now at least I'm prepared for it."

Dressing for the Job

One fall day a student in Marc's junior high math class asked Marc, "Why do you always wear a suit and tie? My history teacher doesn't." The question caught Marc off guard, and his immediate reply was, "Because I'm a professional." Thinking about it later, Marc realized that there was more to it than that. He recognized that dressing up each day added to his self-confidence, established a difference between him and his students, and conveyed a message that said, "I value myself, what I do, and how others perceive me."

Especially if you are a beginning teacher, you need to understand the reasons for establishing your role as teacher and professional. If you are young and within ten years of the ages of your students, one of the most challenging tasks ahead of you will be defining your role as the teacher and person in charge. If you dress, talk, and act like your students, they will see you as a peer or as someone trying to be their peer, and you will embark on a frustrating journey to self-destruction.

Two Teachers
Two Professional Dressers?

If you are a beginning teacher, you will probably not possess an extensive professional wardrobe. The important point is that you should look like an adult in a professional situation. Numerous books and magazines address this subject. John T. Molloy's books on dressing for success—if taken with a grain of salt—are good sources for the professional man or woman. Numerous magazines offer advice and photographs. *Gentleman's Quarterly, Glamour, Vogue, Working Woman,* and *Self* are among the many you can refer to. *Instructor, Teacher,* and *NEA Today* show photographs of teachers at work.

No one expects teachers to wear three-piece suits each day. If your day will involve sitting on a floor or using finger paints, you'll adjust accordingly. If you're being formally evaluated, meeting with parents or colleagues, or attending conferences, you'll want to appear as professional as possible. Your dress will depend on the climate and mores of your community. If your administration expects ties and jackets for men and nylons for women, comply. Even if your school doesn't have this kind of dress code, keep in mind that you are representing a profession and, most importantly, establishing yourself as your students' teacher and model.

Language and the Classroom

Professional educators do not use obscene language in their classroom, nor should they permit their students to do so. Profanity debases the educational situation and the people involved. Swearing at a class is condescending to your students and sets a poor example. Even if you're thinking vile things, don't say them. Part of what teachers are trying to convey is respect for self and others. The use of appropriate language models speech patterns that students can adopt for lifetime use. Students need to learn that there is a time and place for appropriate behavior; the school is such a place.

Dealing with Questions

Students, like most people, are curious. In the beginning, while you are establishing your credibility, your students will attempt to find out things about you. Some will ask personal questions very politely, while others, if permitted, will blurt a question out during a lecture when you least expect it: "Ms. Jones, are you married?" or, "Mr. Thomas, how many kids do ya have?" Some students have few "positive" adult role models in their lives. You may be their only example, and they will be eager to see what makes you tick. Sometimes this is a ploy to divert your attention from the lesson.

If the question is blurted out but is one that you'd feel comfortable answering,, remind the student that interrupting is not appropriate at that time, but that if he or she asks you again at the end of class, you'll respond then. If the question is rudely stated and makes you uncomfortable, simply statte that you'll see the student after class and proceed with the lesson. After class, discuss with the student the inappropriateness of asking personal questions. You might ask the student how he or she would feel about being asked such a question in front of a group of people.

Sometimes during a discussion, students will ask your opinion on a highly controversial topic, such as abortion, capital punishment, or a political candidate. Many teachers in a situation like this employ the strategy of Socrates, questioning the students in return. If you choose to share your opinion, be sure you state that this is simply your opinion and *not a fact*. Even so, stating your opinion may arouse the wrath of parents, who may start a crusade about town that you are, for instance, a professed "abortionist." Marc approaches such questions by stating that his role is not to influence but to present both sides as objectively as possible. He will steer the class into a discussion among students that may present opposing sides. His purpose is to instigate thinking so that students may explore thier personal values and come to their own conclusions.

If a student asks a general question in a way and at a time that you feel is appropriate, feel free to answer if you wish to. "Yes, I'm married." "No, I don't have children. Why would I want children when I have 150 sweet ones here at school?" Do not give any response you wouldn't want to see in print on a billboard. Definitely do not answer anything that might get you fired. You can be confident that anything you say will be repeated at one or more family dinner tables.

If you don't know an answer, it's better to say you don't know than to get caught in a lie. Lying to students is one of the quickest ways to lose your credibility with them. Keep appointments with them. Be honest about mistakes, evaluations, and their progress.

Professionalism and Your Colleagues

Giving Support

A term that's often tossed around in the work force is "team player." While logic might dictate that such a person is perceived as a helper, how do you know the difference between being a team player and being a doormat?

Team players can be counted on to help, yet not be taken advantage of. If an emergency requires that a colleague leave school and you're asked to cover a class, do so if possible. There may be a time when you'll have such a request. If a coach is short on timers for a track meet and you have no other obligations, it's a good idea to help out. Teaching is an isolated profession; it's easy to remain in your own comfortable niche. Helping in other departments or buildings gives you a broader perspective on your school.

However, if the same people keep asking, and you seem to be the only person sacrificing prep time, evenings, or weekends, don't be afriad to say "no." Your own stress level is critical. The important thing is to participate to the extent that you meet other people and to help out when you can.

In the turmoil of the work day, people often forget to thank their fellow workers. Many people in a school building work to make our jobs easier. Don't forget these people. Say "thank you." An occasional card or small gift will be appreciated. The day after Mary, a secondary reading teacher, covered a class for a colleague, she arrived at school to find a rose on her desk with a brief note of thanks. Her considerate neighbor had not only remembered to express his gratitude, he had also given Mary a lovely reminder that brightened her classroom the whole day.

Colleagues' Perceptions

A strong correlation exists between how your colleagues perceive you and how your students do. The whiner who perpetually complains to coworkers is often the dark cloud in a student's day. If your fellow teachers regard you as a competent professional, they will treat you with respect. Students will notice this and will be inclined also to treat you respectfully.

Life in the Public Eye

Private vs. Public Life

Kathy, a sixth-grade teacher, tells a story about a Saturday years ago after she'd been teaching for two years. She'd been scrambling that day, like most people who work outside the home, to grocery shop, pick up her prescription from the pharmacy, and grab clothes from the cleaners.

While rolling her cart down the aisle at the supermarket, Kathy encountered one of her sixth-graders, his younger brother, and his mother. She'd met this mother before in conferences, but suddenly Kathy panicked. First, she quickly did what many of us do when caught off guard; she thought about how she was dressed. She was wearing faded jeans and her sorority sweatshirt; her hair was carelessly pulled into a ponytail. Next, she became acutely aware of the contents of her cart: two six-packs of beer and a box of wine. She noticed her student, his brother, and his mother eyeing those contents. Kathy didn't think about the chicken, bread, aluminum foil, or canned corn that were also in the cart; her thoughts focused solely on the beer and wine.

She chatted a few moments with the family, but remained uncomfortably aware of the cart's contents and berated herself for not being better dressed. The real embarrassment occurred when Kathy later handed her prescription note for birth-control pills to the pharmacist. As the pharmacist typed the label for the pills, he began to make conversation. "It's great that your class did so well in the city spelling bee. Janie's been so excited since she practiced every night at home with us. You should really be proud." In a wave of cold realization, Kathy recognized the father of one of her students.

It took that one Saturday for Kathy to realize that teachers live in a fishbowl. Even though she knew she'd done nothing wrong, she still felt uncomfortable about what the parents might have assumed. She knew that if she wanted to stay in teaching, she either needed to adjust to the reality of living in her community as a semi-public figure or find other ways to deal with her private life.

Similarly, if you choose to become active in a community group, you must never lose sight of your image as a professional educator in the community. The general public is all too quick to find fault with teachers and to use a single instance to condemn us. Anything we do publicly that meets with community disapproval or notice risks being repeated in newspapers and described in flyers for the world to read while other people expressing the same ideas may remain anonymous. Because we are entrusted with the minds of youngsters, we often have to present public profiles that are on the squeaky-clean side.

If you visit the corner bar with some frequency, even if you are only imbibing a soft drink with friends, you can be perceived as an alcoholic by outsiders who wish you evil, had bad school experiences, or habitually jump to conclusions and are quick to condemn. Cruel gossip can be very damaging. A few years ago, a television crew was interviewing students about drug abuse and drug availability in schools. A flippant young man, thrilled to be momentarily famous, announced that he could get drugs from his science teacher. He never mentioned a name, but at 8:00 the next morning his teacher, who had a spotless reputation, was being investigated by the school administration. The student appeared on television the next night, without prompting, and admitted that he had been lying for no reason at all. However, the ghost of that implication remains like a poorly erased word over that teacher's head. An accusation never seems to be forgotten once it is aimed, however falsely.

Even though teachers, like everyone else, have private lives away from their jobs, what they believe and how they act is an integral part of the professional image of a teacher. You certainly have every right to your own style of private life. But living in the public eye does come with the job.

Therefore, our unanimous advice is to live your life in and out of the classroom discreetly. Try to avoid any public actions or activities that could give rise to gossip. Although you may not like it, when you choose to be a teacher, you also choose to represent the public's image of a good (not perfect, though) teacher.

Working Hours

Another aspect of life in the public eye is your working hours. The public knows you work during school hours. But the public doesn't see you grading papers and preparing lessons until the wee hours or spending weekends doing more of the same. Many people are not aware that in the summer, teachers are employed, pursue their own education, and travel or study to enhance their curricula.

If you work in a district where you leave school before 4:00, do not apologize or engage in a debate justifying yourself. Conversely, you don't want to be perceived by your staff or students as someone who beats the kids out the door. Fortunately, many people are finally realizing that a teacher's work day doesn't end at 3:30.

Professional Organizations and Conferences

Professional organizations are groups of teachers who associate for the purpose of improving teaching.

A great many teachers choose to join a general teachers' association. These organizations are usually structured to include a local, state, and national affiliation. Two examples are the National Education Association and the American Federation of Teachers. A teachers' association can provide a wide variety of services to its members. It may engage in collective bargaining to obtain a suitable master contract covering all teachers in the district. It may also research to provide you with the best possible insurance packages, provide legal support if you are sued, and advise you if you feel your contractual rights are not being respected. The national association may offer additional insurance coverage at reduced rates and publish research materials and periodicals of interest to educators.

Whether or not you join is a personal preference in most districts, and membership is not cheap. However, you will probably find that the benefits are worth the price. A foreign language teacher was sued recently in a neighboring district over a conflict with a senior who had cheated on her semester exam. The parents said that the teacher had destroyed their daughter's perfect 4.0 grade-point average, thereby ruining her reputation for life. The association lawyer was in this teacher's room in less than an hour. The ensuing litigation did not cost the teacher a penny.

Another type of teaching organization is the subject-area group. These associations function on the local, state, national, and international levels to advance members' knowledge and teaching expertise in a particular subject area. Membership usually includes a subscription to a magazine in that subject area that features articles on current teaching philosophies and how-to articles written by teachers about successful classroom assignments. These fresh ideas can provide real boosts to your teaching when you are feeling overwhelmed by your workload. The articles explain the process step by step and usually include warnings about mistakes the authors made. Subject-area association memberships are worth every penny just to get these new ideas.

Subject-area associations also sponsor yearly, state, regional, national, and international conventions. Make an effort to attend any in your area. The conventions include publisher and supplier displays, seminar meetings, and often well-known speakers. It is a chance to see what is new on the market or what might be that perfect supplement to your present supplies. You will get a chance to attend workshops and seminars on topics that interest or trouble you. Not only will you gather information, but also you will get to meet and talk to people with similar interests. You will also discover that other teachers in other districts suffer the same problems as you. Perhaps talking together will generate possible solutions. Costs you incur while attending these conventions are tax-deductible.

A recent National Science Teachers Association convention featured a session expressly for new teachers to gather and talk about what was happening to them that year. One young man said he had found his first year of teaching physics mind-boggling and had pretty much decided to give up teaching science. However, after coming to the convention, meeting people, and gathering new ideas, he felt enthused, regenerated, and eager to teach physics again in the fall.

These association memberships also offer you reduced prices on professional books that might be unavailable elsewhere. These memberships also offer reduced rates on travel packages, hotel rooms, and car rentals.

Local organizations may also exist in your subject area. These small local groups are cheaper to join, provide programs by local experts whom you could contact later for more ideas, and give you a chance to meet other local teachers with common interests outside your building.

We all remember that the first years of teaching are lean times burdened by college debts, low salaries, and family obligations. However, we still recommend joining at least one professional organization of your choice. Over the years each of us may have said, "I never have time to keep up with my journal reading," but none of us has said, "I am sorry I joined."

Professional Journals

Subscribing to professional journals is easy. Finding time to read them is the hard part. Arrange specific time for reading. You might bring your lunch to your room once a week (lock the door or students will cheerfully join and annoy or distract you) and read. You might put aside onne morning a week to read. Many states and districts sponsor professional days for subject-area meetings. Take your stack of magazines along to read during slack times.

When a magazine first arrives in the mail, page through it, read the jokes, and note the emphasis of the articles. If there is an article about the unit you are currently teaching, read it immediately. (Most of the time the articles are on the unit you just finished.) If you are really pressed for time, read just the articles that pertain to your subject area. If you find an article you really like, underline or highlight pertinent points, rip it out of the magazine, clearly label it in a folder, and put it into your file cabinet at the beginning of the related unit so you will reread it the next year before you begin the unit.

When you do have time, read the articles about other grade levels and areas that you don't teach. You may get ideas for techniques you can use in your own classes as well as an overview of your subject area.

Whether you choose to read every word of a professional magazine or just those articles immediately helpful to your teaching, remember that you must deliberately schedule reading time or you will end up putting that magazine under your pillow, hoping that the information will enter your head by osmosis.

Research

What?! On top of coping with curriculum, discipline, parents, colleagues, administrators, reports, and playground duty, this book *dares* to talk about research? Unbelievable! You probably won't have time to do much educational research—especially if you have to plan or "steal" time to read professional articles. Maybe that reading will be all the research you have time to do in your first year or two of teaching. However, if you are working on a pet project or a night class, or just need more information on a method of effective teaching, others in the school might prove a good resource.

Your school librarian can tell you what books your school presently has on your topic. Your principal, counselor, psychologist, or social worker might have articles you need. If you are completing research in order to defend a thesis or dissertation during your first year of teaching, then you probably don't even have time to be reading this book.

Conclusion

Professionalism is demonstrated in dress, attitude, and communication. Maintaining this image requies common sense and discretion, both in and out of school.

You enhance your professional growth when you join organizations, attend conferences, and *read.* A list of the names and addresses of professional education associations appears at the end of this book. Write to those that interest you, inquiring about membership benefits and journals published.

CHAPTER 2

Classroom Management, Behavior, Discipline

<u>My Advice To Teachers</u>
I think teachers need to give discipline. 3rd
Bret B.

The most disastrous thing that can happen to a beginning teacher is to lose control of the class. A beginning teacher must assert him/her self and establish discipline in the classroom.

Dan Z.
10th

Mary, a secondary reading teacher, still remembers that tall, lanky troublemaker all these years later. Tom was towering past six feet and still growing, with a cheerful, teddy-bear face. He wasn't a bad kid—he just worked hard at constantly avoiding work that might accidentally result in learning. He was a low achiever and definitely not interested in taking a chance on being successful. The year seemed to stretch forever. Mary looked forward to the day when this nagging, whining senior would graduate.

Over the months, Mary had talked to Tom quietly, spoken sharply, yelled, threatened, nagged—all the usual techniques. One normal morning everyone needed her simultaneously. Tom appeared at her desk again with yet another work-avoiding request. Mary found herself doing what education professors advise against: She raised an accusing finger between them and started to shake it for emphasis. However, since Mary is 5 feet 6 inches, and Tom had long passed the 6-feet-6-inch mark, her imperious finger punctuated the air somewhere not too far above the belt buckle. Suddenly she stood outside herself, saw the ludicrous situation in progress, and instinctively made the right decision.

Mary said, "Hey, wait a minute. This isn't working." She pulled over her desk chair, climbed on the seat, and was a head *above* Tom. She waggled a finger down at his face. They broke into friendly laughter, both seeing the ridiculousness of the whole scene. Somehow that laughter created a feeling of mutual respect. From that day forward, Tom worked hard on every assignment. He brought Mary two yellow roses when he graduated.

Effective Discipline for a Tall Student

Discipline is the scariest unknown for teachers. Discipline plans need to have three main focus points. The plan must:

1. Address the safety and well-being of every student.
2. Teach respect for self and others.
3. Help students establish self-discipline.

Ultimately, all students can develop self-discipline. Classroom procedures should be structured to achieve these goals.

You must make the final decision about which of the techniques discussed in this book suit your teaching style and personality. Every teaching decision that you make in regard to discipline needs to be consistent and compassionate.

All teachers arrive in the classroom with a knowledge base, teaching materials, and a sense of curriculum expectations, but with little or no clear idea about the personalities of the students and how they will mold into a functioning learning group. Getting to know those who will shortly occupy the desks is a monumental, creative job. Students will express their needs and deliberately or accidentally create the most unexpected dilemmas at the most unexpected times. The only guarantee is that the unexpected *will* happen—unexpectedly. Unfortunately, this beginning-of-the-year concern does not disappear after the first years of teaching. The first day with a classroom full of new students and all the accompanying stress never changes. You just become more adept at the process of creating a positive learning climate. However, even as a first-year teacher, there are things you can do to create the classroom atmosphere you want right from the beginning.

Before the First Day of School—General Standards for Discipline

Before you step into your classroom, you'll want to have a clear idea in your mind about how you will approach discipline problems generally. The following ideas can help you do this.

The Administrative Process   Have clear knowledge of the administrative process at either the building or district level for dealing with a disruptive student. If no one covers this specific topic in the first days before school begins, ask. Keep a copy of the written policy in your desk. Ideally, you will want to handle all discipline problems yourself. By handling these conflicts in a timely manner, you retain control of the situation and consistently demonstrate your leadership role in the classroom. This adds to your teaching credibility. Students will respect your consistent, compassionate classroom management skills. This active role as the in-class disciplinarian is appropriate in the eyes of your administrators. They are there to support you if you need their help. Sending a student to an administrator should only be a last resort when the problem has escalated past what you feel capable of dealing with, you have already exhausted all other avenues of discipline, and the student's behavior has not changed.

Voice Control   Mentally put yourself through the discipline process. Think about what you will say and not say to a student. Rehearse saying these phrases in a low-pitched, calm voice. When your voice indicates you are angry, the student gains control. By keeping your voice low and slow, you will appear calm. Don't allow your voice to rise in pitch at the end of a statement.

Classroom Rules   Set up clear classroom rules and consequences. You might consult other teachers before school begins and ask what basic rules they use. The next section of this chapter deals more with setting up classroom rules and gives examples.

Consistency   Be consistent. This is the key to discipline. In the beginning of the year you don't know the personality nuances of your charges. Use that to your advantage. Apply all the rules to all the students. You cannot be arbitrary in discipline. If a rule has been established and a student violates it, impose the consequences and then get on with the lesson. The trick is not to get furious. Shrug your shoulders and keep your face benign while your body language and voice imply, "You broke the rule; you accept the consequence." Then continue teaching. The message is that the lesson is more important and draws the focus back to you and away from the class clown or problem. You probably should rehearse the classic shrug-with-body-language in front of a mirror. You'll make Broadway yet! The neutral-but-bored-with-the-interruption facial expression is also useful.

Firmness   Be firm when disciplining. If a student comes tearfully to your desk after class with extenuating circumstances that explain the class disruption, you might say, "I understand your situation and am glad to know about it. However, when you break a class-established rule you will have to accept the penalty." This will convey the message that you care, but you will continue applying rules consistently to the whole class.

No Academic Penalties   Do not use academic penalties for behavior problems. Nothing turns kids off to writing more quickly than the 5,000-word essay on "Why I Shouldn't Misbehave in Class." Language arts teachers invest a great deal of time in making writing a positive experience. Essay penalties not only cause the students to dislike writing but also rarely solve problems.

Reasonable Consequences   If you've set up your expectations in the beginning and students know the consequences for their actions, you have an advantage. Punishments should be reasonable and fit the offense. Having a student clean his or her desk after writing on it is a good example of this. However, students need to know these consequences from the beginning of the year.

Special Services   Start learning about the special services your school might provide for students with problems. Read the chapters in this book on ancillary personnel, record-keeping, parents, and administration.

Classroom Rules

Students need clear perimeters. You may feel most comfortable determining these perimeters yourself. Another alternative is to allow your students the opportunity to help develop a set of rules that all can live with. This gives your students power over their own behavior and is a big step toward maturity. Be clear about your own needs and expectations.

How to Use Classroom Rules

Here are some helpful suggestions about classroom rules.

1. Keep the rules simple.
2. Create rules and logical, enforceable consequences. For example, if a student writes on a desk, she or he must take time to clean the desk.
3. Post the rules and the consequences. After the rules have been established, a committee of students could prepare a poster listing the rules and consequences.
4. Read and review the posted rules several times at the beginning of the semester. Some teachers include questions about the rules in the first quiz.
5. You may need to repeat some rules, such as those pertaining to food and drink in the classroom or continual use of inappropriate language. Repeat the rule calmly, impose the consequences, and get on with the lesson.

Brian, a social studies teacher, acknowledges to his classes that since students usually want to prove their maturity to the world, his class is a perfect place to start. He goes on to explain that swearing is inappropriate. Class is an opportunity to stretch language. "We all know what *those* words mean,'" he drawls in his sagest tone, "but in this class we will practice speaking and writing about those feelings using subtle, more appropriate, tasteful words. That will drive your enemies crazy because they won't know if you are complimenting them or insulting them."

Methods of Establishing Classroom Rules

Teacher-Established Rules You may decide on your rules before your students arrive. Three general rules that work well might be:

1. Follow all published school rules. (This covers all the rules the administration needs enforced to maintain a safe, positive school climate.)
2. Arrive in class on time and prepared to work. (This covers all the nitty-gritty requirement stuff like pens, paper, and assignments the dog didn't chew.)
3. Treat all class members with respect and expect it in return. (This rule says that teacher and student deserve equal consideration. It also covers the student who sleeps in class, because sleeping is definitely disrespectful.)

Student-Established Rules You might decide to involve students in establishing rules. It's a good idea to begin your lesson on classroom rules by discussing where society's laws, codes of behavior, and etiquette come from and why we have them. With this background information, your students will have a better feeling for the reason behind classroom rules. On the first day of class, Brian assigns the following homework: "For tomorrow write down five appropriate classroom rules on notebook paper and be ready to turn them in." Because it is the beginning of the year and everyone is still excited about school, most students come with the homework. This affords Brian a chance to award each student a good homework grade and sends a strong message about success and student participation, making the class a positive learning place for everyone. The class period is used to discuss the suggested rules, and the class reaches consensus on a list of rules. The rules are generally consistent from class to class and the consequences often more severe than Brian would have planned, but the students follow the rules because they made them.

Safety Rules   If you are responsible for a class using a laboratory setting (science, home economics, industrial arts, art, or physical education), you need to establish specific safety-related rules in order to teach. While students may help establish policies about getting along, rules concerning safety must be established by the teacher and must be strictly enforced.

Middle-School Rules   If you are a middle school teacher, you might select several important rules and allow a class to select the rest. For example, you could list ten classroom rules and have the students debate and choose the five they wanted to live with.

A junior high math teacher who is easygoing in his approach to students uses the following poem:

CLASSROOM RULES

> No snacks,
> No hats,
> No violent acts.
>
> No skip,
> No lip,
> No tardyship.

Elementary Rules   Grade school classrooms use similar rules. You might see them listed as:

1. Show respect
2. Practice good conversation skills:

   - Listen when others speak.
   - Let people speak without interruption.
   - Respond politely.
   - Respect others' ideas.

3. Keep your hands and feet to yourself.
4. Take care of your possessions.

Kathy, who teaches sixth grade, has her students gather in a class meeting to establish their own classroom rules. She thinks the process

Classroom Policies

I. Classroom Rules

1. All the rules stated in the student handbook apply in this room.
2. You are required to bring a notebook and a pen or a pencil to class every day.
3. You are required to be in the room when the bell rings.
4. At the end of the class period, you will be dismissed by your teacher, not by the bell.
5. All students are responsible for leaving their desk, chair, and lab area clean, dry, and straightened at the end of each class period.
6. Never take any chemicals or other laboratory materials out of the room unless you are given permission by your teacher.
7. Never touch or handle projects, demonstrations, or experiments that are set up in the room.

II. Attendance Policy

1. You are required to be in class.
2. If you are absent, have your parents call the school to verify your absence. The number to call is 939-1416.
3. If you are going on a school-excused absence or a planned trip, your work is due before you go unless special arrangements are made in advance.
4. When you are absent, you have two (2) days for each day you were absent to make up any work that you missed. An extension can be obtained if you make prior arrangements with your teacher.
5. When you are absent, it is your responsibility to find out what work you have missed.
6. The work you have missed can be made up before school, after school, or during some time arranged by you and your teacher.

(continued)

7. Tests or quizzes that are missed during an absence can be made up before school, after school, or duing some time set up by you and your teacher. Failure to make up a test or a quiz will result in a zero (0) on that test or quiz.
8. If you are truant, you will receive a zero (0) on all work done while truant.

III. Tardies

1. If you are not in the room when the bell rings, you are tardy.
2. When you are tardy, you must sign the tardy sheet. It is located in the back of the room by the door.
3. You are considered absent if you are more than 15 minutes late.
4. The consequences for tardies are explained in your student handbook.

IV. Assignments

1. Written work must be submitted by the end of the day that it is due. You will receive a zero (0) on all assignments not turned in.
2. Late work will be accepted up to two (2) days after the due date for half (½) credit.
3. No work will be accepted after the two- (2) day grace period unless prior arrangements are made with your teacher.
4. You will put your name, the date, the period, and what the assignment is in the upper right-hand corner of your paper.

V. Grading Policy

1. Your grade will be calculated from your achievement in the following areas: tests, quizzes, lab work, and assignments.

(continued)

2. The following scale will be used:

$$90\%-100\% = A$$
$$80\%-89\% = B$$
$$70\%-79\% = C$$
$$60\%-69\% = D$$
$$0\%-59\% = E$$

3. Your quarter grade will be determined by averaging all your grades from that quarter.
4. Your semester grade will be determined by averaging your quarter grades.

—Centennial High School
Boise, Idaho

Bill of Rights and Responsibilities

1. I have the right to learn.

   I have the responsibility to listen, ask questions, follow directions, and participate.

2. I have the right to be accepted for who I am as an individual.

   I have the responsibility to accept others for who they are and to be sensitive to their feelings.

3. I have the right to be safe.

   I have the responsibility to act in a way that is safe to those around me.

4. I have the right to my own opinion and to express my thoughts.

   I have the responsibility to be respectful of the opinions of others and to express myself in an appropriate manner.

5. I have the right to make mistakes.

   I have the responsibility to learn from my mistakes and to help others learn from their mistakes.

6. I have the right to my own space, possessions, and privacy.

   I have the responsibility to respect others' space, possessions, and privacy.

7. I have the right to grow up in a clean world.

   I have the responsibility to keep our environment healthy through recycling, reducing, and reusing.

—Highlands Elementary School
Boise, Idaho

teaches important communication skills while also giving the students power and control over their behavior. Kathy then adds the reminder, "You made the rule; you are expected to live with it."

Class Expectations   You might hand out and discuss a class expectations sheet.

Verbal and Written Presentation   Present the rules both verbally and in writing.

Mutual Respect Role-Play   You might choose to invest class time discussing or writing about the rules, especially the topic of mutual respect. Have students role-play, practicing how to care for others' belongings, how to work together, and how to express feelings when they feel they've been treated unfairly.

Divide the class into groups of twos or threes. Give each group a different situation dealing with respect. Plan an impromptu skit which includes all group members. Give the groups a limited time to plan a class presentation. Because each group has a different task, other class members will watch with interest. Their perception of respect may please and surprise you.

Besides involving students in discussing and demonstrating correct classroom behavior, these presentations will provide an interesting opportunity for you to observe how your students work together.

Sample Task Cards for Skits on Respect

Your group needs to discuss the following topic. Talk about how to solve the problem being respectful toward everyone involved. Plan a skit to present to the class illustrating this topic. Each group member must have a part.

YOU ARE BLAMED BY THE VICE-PRINCIPAL FOR SOMETHING YOU DIDN'T DO.

Your group needs to discuss the following topic. Talk about how to solve the problem being respectful toward everyone involved. Plan a skit to present to the class illustrating this topic. Each group member must have a part.

YOUR BEST FRIEND ASKS THE BOY/GIRL YOU HAVE A CRUSH ON TO THE HOLIDAY DANCE.

Your group needs to discuss the following topic. Talk about how to solve the problem being respectful toward everyone involved. Plan a skit to present to the class illustrating this topic. Each group member must have a part.

YOU ARE HARASSED IN THE HALLWAY AT SCHOOL.

These and related ideas can be found in *Building a Positive Self-Concept* (see Bibliography).

Elementary students are often uncomfortable discussing their personal behavior but can deal with discussing the behavior of a character in a book. Fourth-grade teacher Ellen reads *Best Friends for Frances* or *I'm Terrific* (see Bibliography). She then leads her students into a discussion about what happened in the book and how the characters handled the situation.

Administering Consequences

The following is a **sample** of a possible discipline policy. Become aware of the discipline steps established by your school or district. If you don't follow the procedure, you may find that legally your administration will not be able to support you. You will be instructed to return to Step 1 and document the process from the beginning.

A Sample Six-Step Procedure

We have found the following six-step procedure to be an effective way to deal with students who break classroom rules and otherwise need some disciplinary action.

1. *First offense: Issue a nonverbal warning.* This might be in the form of a meaningful look, a tapping on the student's desk, or a cocked eyebrow. When you are lecturing or giving directions and off-topic conversation continues between students, you might move between the talkers. Proximity is an excellent classroom management technique. You might stop mid-sentence and stare passively (the passive, nonjudgmental stare is more effective than anger) until the talking stops. Then continue your sentence. Other students will usually be quick to hush the offenders. In turn, do not interrupt when a student is speaking! If the chatter resumes, stop again and go to Step 2.

2. *Second offense: Issue a verbal warning.* You might couple a simple "Enough, Tom!" with a nonverbal action and return to the lesson quickly. Depending on the student, this contact could be made quietly, one-on-one. This shows that you expect compliance. If the student still misbehaves, go to Step 3.

3. *Third offense: Have a conference after class.* "Tom, I said enough. Please see me after class," and continue the lesson. It is crucial that you not argue the point with Tom in front of the class. Doing so will allow the conflict to overshadow the learning objective for the day. Your unspoken message is "This is not up for discussion at this time."

   Begin the conference conversation with a statement like "I'm glad we could get together to talk now. It was not appropriate at the time to discuss what happened." Think about where you and the student will sit. If you remain at your desk and the student chooses a student desk, the implication of authority remains. You might both sit in student desks. This tells the student, "Since this is just a discussion between you and me about what happened, we can sit here and not play the teacher-student roles at our usual desks."

   If a student refuses to sit, accept that and either casually stand yourself or sit on the desktop so you still occupy the same level of space.

   Give the student an opportunity to express his or her version. When the student finishes, pause a few seconds thoughtfully. Then paraphrase the essence of the student's response and say, "I can see how the misunderstanding happened. You saw . . . , but I saw . . . ," and make one statement. If the student interrupts you, wait politely. Then, quietly and in a low, calm voice say, "I didn't interrupt when you were giving your version. I need the same respect from you. May I finish?"

Mutually decide on new behavior expectations and make sure the student understands the consequence if the misbehavior continues. End the conference with a statement of your confidence in the student's ability to improve. You will usually not have to go beyond this step. If Tom continues to misbehave, though, you will have to go to Step 4.

4. ***Inform the parent(s).*** This can be done through a phone call, a note, or a conference. State the facts. Tell the parent the steps you have taken so far. "Andy is in my U.S. History class and I called because I need you to know about the situation . . . ." Ask for the parent's support in reinforcing the correct behavior. You need to follow up this call a few weeks later with a call to the same parent to compliment the student on improved behavior. This will be the best reinforcement of all and help maintain that improved behavior.

You'll find more discussion on parent phone calls in Chapter 10. Keep a written record of the contact. If needed, proceed to Step 5.

5. ***Inform the counselor.*** The counselor might be able to provide insights into the behavior of this student. A meeting between the counselor and student may or may not include you and might result in increased understanding on both sides. This same counselor is also the person who initiates testing for special services. Depending on your school policy, you may need to go to Step 6.

6. ***Write a referral to the vice-principal or other person responsible for discipline.*** In this referral, state the problem clearly and list the steps you have taken to change the behavior. If you have to write a document like a discipline referral when you are seething with anger, use short sentences and include the student's exact words. Report, don't editorialize. If you keep part of your mind focused on the grammar and sentence structure, you will help yourself calm down. Next, recopy the referral to improve your handwriting and the general spacing. Rip up the first copy and dispose of it where other students can't dig it out. The administrator may meet with the student, plan a behavior modification program, and inform you and the parents about the results of this conference.

Repeated problems might result in the student being removed from your class or taking part in a support program where she or he can function successfully.

If you must work through these steps with a student, keep written records of the process. Check Chapter 6 about keeping appropriate records.

Extreme Violations

District policies are generally in place to support the teacher after all discipline strategies have been utilized and found ineffective. Examples of extreme disciplinary violations might include continuous insubordination, verbal or physical abuse of teacher or students, or possession of a weapon or controlled substance.

Steps in a disciplinary process for extreme violations might include:

1. First violation: The student is sent to an administrator for a conference, and the parents are notified in writing. The teacher submits paperwork on the incident. Some form of suspension might be initiated.
2. Second violation: The parents of the student are called into school for a conference with the administrator. The teacher and student might or might not be at the meeting. Many teachers prefer having the student at the conference because the student is then able to hear all points of view firsthand. This keeps the student responsible for his or her own behavior. Written records of the conference are sent to all parties concerned, and some form of suspension might be initiated.
3. Third and subsequent violations: If this is the student's third offense in a semester, a formal suspension might be initiated and the student might be removed from your class if all parties deem that there has been no attempt at improvement. The student is often referred to the hearing panel of the school district and may face suspension for the remainder of the semester or the rest of the school year.

Elementary School—Special Considerations

Since elementary teachers enjoy the luxury of having the same students all day, there are more opportunities for teacher-student discussion about behavior. It is important to establish eye contact. Explain, "I need to look at your eyes." Frequently, a young child in tears over a situation needs to gain control before you can talk. You may need to leave the child alone. You might offer comfort, but don't allow the child to work into a frenzy.

When the child is ready to talk, use *I* statements: "I feel . . . when you . . . because . . . " State that the inappropriate behavior does not show self-respect. "I want you to talk about your problems, not what Bob did to you." Don't let the child reduce the situation to "but she told

me to . . . ." Don't allow the blame to be passed to another: "Tell me
what you did. How did you behave? We're talking about you."

Elementary teacher Robert relates a story about a group of five girls
in his second/third-grade class. Because there was an odd number, one
was always left out. The left-out girl (not always the same one) would
come to Robert in tears, complaining. The girls were often upset; mean
words were exchanged. Even though the class held several meetings
about friendship, the problem remained unsolved.

One recess, Robert kept all five girls in the room. He reminded
them that each had had her feelings hurt that fall, yet they all wanted to
be friends. He asked them to think about the discussions they'd had in
class and what they were going to do to spare other people's feelings. He
told them to talk about their problem. He said, "Let me know what you
decide." Later, they told Robert that they had talked about whining and
feeling left out and decided that each girl had only to join rather than
complain. When she joined and stated her needs, her friends could help
her feel better. The girls have been good, mutually supporting friends
ever since.

Later in the year, a school counselor was talking with the least
secure of those five girls and remarked that her friendships seemed
stronger that year. That girl said that the meeting the girls had had was
most important to her. The girls had learned to respect the individual
and make statements such as, "I'm so glad that you . . . "

Avoiding Discipline Problems

Most of the discipline problems that rear their ugly heads in a
classroom stem from a student's need for attention. This is universal in
all grades. You can reduce these problems.

1. Give lots of individual attention. The easiest way to accomplish this is
   to be at your door when your students arive. Do this whenever you can.
   It seems simple, but it produces great results. Barbara, a junior high
   English teacher, began greeting her students by name as they entered
   her classroom. The next test scores were 10 points higher even though
   she had done nothing else differently—she had only recognized each
   student individually.
2. When a student needs your attention, make it undivided. Hold up a
   hand, make quick eye contact, or give some other form of

acknowledgement to the waiting student, and remain attentive to the first. When that student no longer needs you, turn to the second child and say, "Thank you for being patient. Now *you* can have my undivided attention." You might sometimes laugh and suggest taking numbers. Students will usually wait patiently if they know they will also get your attention.

3. When students are working at their desks, wander between the rows watching them work. Point out a phrase you like, answer questions, mutter a quiet "Good job, Carl," or even ask, "Are you doing okay? Do you understand the assignment?" Every student can be confident that you will come by his or her desk several times. Students don't waste time by waving arms. Students keep working, knowing you will be there soon. This is another way to use proximity as a classroom management technique. Moving closer to a developing problem, reinforcing the academic work being done, and giving suggestions for getting started give the message that the learning is important and negative behavior is *not* the way to get attention.

4. Know that this positive attention is one of the easiest preventive measures you can practice in your classroom. Students need lots of positive, consistent attention. As you get to know your students, tailor your attention to individual needs. Some students need more reassurance than others.

5. Don't give false praise. Do recognize improvements. If the effort is still unsatisfactory, don't say it's wonderful. Acknowledge that the student is trying, and ask what the student will work to improve next.

6. Engage students before and after class in conversation. "So what did the Bounding Baby Basset do last night?" This question opened so much conversation between an extremely shy, handicapped young-ster and his teacher that Brutus the Basset seemed like a class member. Mention student activities as well. "Good game last night, Sally. How many points did you score?"

Kathy returned to teaching after raising her family. She encountered an especially incorrigible child. She knew the child was acting out because of deeply rooted home problems, but the disruptions hindered the other students, and this little girl was constantly being moved away from the group. Out of desperation, Kathy moved Wendy's desk against hers so the little girl would cause less interruption. Whenever Kathy had the opportunity, she either acknowledged a correct answer she saw on Wendy's paper, smiled at the child, or praised quiet work.

At the end of two weeks, Kathy realized that this little girl had not acted out once during this time and pointed it out to Wendy. The child then worked even harder to improve. Kathy next noticed that when Wendy worked with the math groups at the other side of the room, she would act out again. Kathy asked Wendy if she would feel more comfortable nearer Kathy's desk, thus giving Wendy control of the decision. Wendy made the move, and the acting-out stopped again.

Wendy's case illustrates the point that some children require a lot of teacher support and attention to avert or end discipline problems. Other students will require this degree of teacher interaction only at vulnerable times in their lives.

One difficulty with handling discipline problems in the classrooom is that a minor irritation can mutate into a

A quiet discussion with a student

major difficulty before a teacher—especially a new teacher—even realizes something is going wrong. Eventually, however, you will become adept at spotting trouble before it happens. Your students will ask you if you are psychic. Don't answer. Only smile benevolently and knowingly.

Individual Discipline Problems

When a discipline problem does occur in your classroom, remember that the student is usually not making a personal attack on you. These kinds of problems often arise from frustration caused by difficulty with the learning task or stress induced by an out-of-class conflict, a family problem, or fatigue. The problem may simply be a need for attention. Over the years you will develop a thick skin an elephant would envy.

When a discipline problem does occur—and it will—stay calm. This will take practice. Most of the time you will be able to follow a standard procedure like the six-step one outlined above. However, you need to recognize all students as individuals, and you may need to expand on some of the steps for some students. You could try these steps:

1. Don't act without thinking.
2. Take a deep breath and exhale slowly. It will help you regain control of

your emotions and will show your students that you are dealing with the problem rationally.

3. Keep your voice pitch low and speak slowly.
4. The first time a student presents a problem, begin following your standard procedure, like the six-step process previously mentioned. Issuing a nonverbal warning is usually the best first step.
5. Avoid reprimanding a student in front of classmates. This creates a power struggle.
6. Consistently follow your discipline procedure. Failure to do so will damage your credibility.

Recently, a colleague who teaches slow learneers did not follow this advice. What she did do is an example of what *won't* work. It was early in the year, and the teacher did not know the students well. They were writing. As the instructor walked around the room, supervising and offering individual praise and encouragement, she discovered one young man slouched at his desk, arms crossed, staring into space. She asked him calmly to get to work. He didn't. After several requests and no action, she changed her request to a choice: "You can get to work or you can go to the office." She offered the choice several times in as calm a voice as she could muster. Eventually, the student used abusive language, and the teacher had to withdraw her choices and send him to the office. By this time, the entire class was focused on the conflict and not on the assignment.

This teacher made the following errors:

1. She had not followed standard discipline procedure. Sending the boy to the office had not solved the in-class problem. The assignment was never completed, and the boy slumped in class the following day.
2. The student had been put on the defensive. She had given him an impossible choice without providing a chance to explain his side of the story or show improvement.
3. She had also put him on the spot in front of his peers. Everyone in this situation lost.

Instead, this teacher could have done the following:

1. She could have quietly asked the student if there was anything she could do to help or why the student was not working.
2. She could have listened, then suggested the student stop by and talk further after class.

3. She could have reminded the student of the assignment and the amount of time left in class to work.
4. As soon as the student began to work, she could have immediately recognized the effort.
5. If this procedure didn't work, she could have moved the student away from the other students.
6. After the student had ten minutes by himself to calm down, the teacher probably could have talked with him and they might have reached a compromise. This compromise would have been preferable to pushing each other beyond reasonable behavior.

This incident is an example of expanding the verbal warning step to accommodate individual needs. If the problem is one you feel a support person can solve, solicit help. Chapter 9 further explains the role of these support staff personnel.

Your job is to teach your students, not solve their personal problems. That sounds hard-hearted, but all too often teachers who genuinely care get entangled in the personal lives of students and end up in ethically awkward or legally difficult positions. Students will use your compassion to enable their own inappropriate behaviors. Discipline them with consistency or send them to personnel trained in student advocacy.

Group Discipline Problems

If the problem is affecting the entire class, you could try these steps.

1. Stop the lesson and name the problem. If it is something that you can deal with, do so: The room may be too stuffy, the overhead is not focused, or the class did not understand the directions.
2. If the problem is major, you might call a class meeting to deal with the conflict. "What can we do about people blurting out their ideas and not letting others participate?" When the problem is solved, restart the lesson.
3. If the problem affecting the class is out of your control and doesn't affect your class (across the hall, Mr. M—— has a dog in his room), shut your door, lead the students in a few relaxation exercises, and then repeat part of the lesson to help them focus.

Fights

If a confrontation between students had escalated into a full-fledged fight, you need to be ready to make some fast decisions. These decisions depend on your school policy concerning fights. This policy will address the specific age level and needs of your district. When a fight begins outside your classroom:

1. Send a student for administrative support.
2. Request help from your neighboring teachers.
3. Think carefully of the consequences *if* and *before* you wade into the melee. A lot depends on how big the combatants are, who they are, and if they are armed.

If the fight is in your classroom:

1. Don't leave!
2. Try to separate the fighters by verbal persuasion. Remain calm. The other students may be frightened or excited. Say, "Tony, please come with me." Repeat this until you get a response.
3. Again, think carefully of the consequences before you wade into the melee. Do not step between fighters. A lot depends on how big the combatants are, who they are, and if they are armed.
4. Your proximity is critical, but you do not want to endanger yourself. Speak clearly and calmly, using the students' names if possible. (Other students might help with identification.) Keep repeating statements that discourage fighting: "Chris, break it up!" or "Pat, this is not going to solve the problem!"
5. If no help arrives, send another student.

Laughter/Humor

Teaching with Humor

Laughter is a highly desirable part of positive discipline, but it is elusive, difficult to use, and fragile. There is the laughter that ripples through a classroom when everyone shares a pun or a joke that reinforces the learning. There is the laughter elicited when a teacher uses a well-chosen joke to focus a topic or complete an idea. A teacher exercising a good sense of humor can adjust to all the unexpected changes that occur in a school day. Don't let all the interruptions, stacks of record-keeping, forms, counts, notes, money collections, and anything else you can imagine get you down. Even if you get upset about the interruptions, they will still occur and your students will sense your stress. If you can shrug your shoulders mentally, handle the important items instantly, and set the rest aside with a "Let's get on with it" attitude, your students will stay focused on the lesson. Seeing the lighter side of situations may keep you from over-reacting.

On the down side, making fun of a student or another teacher is not appropriate. Laughing at student mistakes is intolerable. Tasteless jokes fall in the same category.

If certain student behaviors seen distracting, stop and think about them before reacting. The behaviors exhibited at eight or ten years are part of that person's temperament and will probably be perfectly acceptable behaviors when the student is an adult. A student who always has one more idea to share, or the student who is slow and methodical, should not be perceived as a discipline problem. Your constant preoccupation with a habit could result in that child feeling inadequate or conspicuous. The child who picks up on *your* every little error might be the research scientist of the future. The dreamer may win the Nobel Prize for literature. A sense of humor will allow you to respect individual differences.

All teachers aren't funny and entertaining every minute of every day. It's too exhausting and often not appropriate to the curriculum. Besides, there are very few naturally funny teachers. If being funny and telling jokes or making puns about a situation does not come easily for you, don't do it. Be yourself. But don't he humorless.

Students once asked Gary, a high school humanities teacher, why he didn't laugh and tell jokes in class like a certain history teacher in school. He thought about it and then gave a straight, honest answer: He does not view himself as a funny teacher. He is serious and intense about what he teaches. Laughter and jokes do not fit his style. He explained to his students that they had to accept each of their teachers as individuals as we accept each of our students. But while Gary is not a *funny* teacher, he teaches with good *humor* and rolls with the punches in order to get the important things taught. Like Gary, you can teach with humor without being actively funny.

A good sense of humor also helps you deal with all the little oddities that go with teaching. You can be building up to the most important point in the whole lesson, pause to call on a flailing hand, expecting a thoughtful response, and get a "You have a big white string on the back of your jacket." You can respond in one of several ways.

1. You can get angry and frustrated because, obviously, the student is off task.
2. You can respond that you deliberately put the string there to bring the student's attention closer to your voice.
3. You can smile and say, "Thanks, I'll get it off later," and continue teaching. The last response is least stressful for everyone.
4. Often body language is an adequate response (a shrug, a cheerful flip of your hand, raised eyebrows, a wink, a smile), and you won't miss a beat in the lesson. Your body language can easily take the place of words and still show your sense of humor.

If a student points out an error you make while writing on the board, thank thhe student for being alert, and correct the error. A teacher writing on the board is doing at least three tasks simultaneously: thinking about the lesson, getting the concept on the board succinctly, and staying aware of what the 30 students in the classroom are doing. Students must see their instructors as human and fallible. You don't need to apologize for this; you just need to strive for improvement. Being open about your weaknesses can be a wonderful learning model for students. This attitude helps keep the learning process in perspective.

Teachers often put cartoons about test-taking on exams. This breaks the stress for students and gives the visual learners some variety in page design. Keep a file folder of school-related jokes and cartoons to add to tests, worksheets, and projects.

All these different expressions of humor can help prevent discipline problems.

Dealing with Student Humor

When you tell jokes in the classroom or something humorous is in the curriculum, your students will want to tell jokes in turn. Be prepared for the inappropriate stories. Sometimes junior high students don't know any other kind. Unfortunately, many kids honestly don't know what is appropriate or not.

The humor of elementary students is often hard to understand. A phrase that reduces them to giggling, tummy-clutching bodies rolling on the floor can sound like an ordinary sentence to you. Be prepared not to understand. Your students must feel the same way when they hear adult jokes.

Robert has a Gary Larson "The Far Side" cartoon in his classroom: the cave man is standing at a chalkboard writing, "I will not act primitive in class." One day Robert listened while one of his third-graders tried to explain to another why the cartoon was funny. Understanding humor and cartoons requires cognitive abilities and higher levels of thinking.

Yes, Miss H.
I am reading my book.

When a student wants to tell a joke, you could handle it in one of several ways.

1. Say, "Stop! Before you tell the joke, answer these questions: Does it contain offensive language? Does it relate to the lesson? Will it offend or embarrass any single person in this class?"
2. If at this point you still decide to let the student tell the joke, insist that if you find the joke objectionable for any reason, you will raise your hand and the student must stop mid-word and not continue.
3. Another way of handling the situation is to have the student write the joke down and hand it to you to read, or whisper it in your ear.
4. If this problem begins popping up frequently, a short unit on appropriate humor is in order and will probably be lots of fun to teach.
5. When classes perform oral presentations, use a rule of thumb that helps alleviate the potential problem of inappropriate jokes or behavior: Demand that students answer the question, "Can everyone's parents sit in this room and watch and listen without being offended?"

Sarcasm

When you're tired and overwhelmed, that next inane question or remark from a student can often solicit a sarcastic response from you. The student may well deserve every prick of your barbed remark, but don't say it. Bite your tongue. This is one of the hardest things you must do as a teacher. Sarcasm, condescending behavior, and rude remarks have no place in the classroom and may create discipline problems. You're trying to teach your students not to say hurtful things, so *you* should certainly know better than to say such things. Sarcasm just lowers you to the level of the student baiting you, so don't bother with it. Besides, insulting remarks hurt self-concepts, and one of our jobs is to build self-esteem so students can achieve their potential. If you treat your students with dignity, most will treat you with dignity in return.

Conclusion

Although each discipline problem is unique, common sense should dictate our actions. Steps to consider might include the following six: Use nonverbal messages to communicate your displeasure at the student's inappropriate behavior. If the behavior continues, issue a verbal warning. Next, talk with the student privately, the sooner the better. If the student still misbehaves, call the parents. Inform the counselor. Solicit your administrator's help.

Effective classroom management involves your willingness to state your expectations clearly from the beginning. Advise your students of the consequences and follow through. Following through is probably the most difficult part of disciplining, but it is crucial. A teacher who is fair, firm, and consistent is way ahead of the game. A touch of humor never hurts, either.

CHAPTER 3

The Classroom Setup

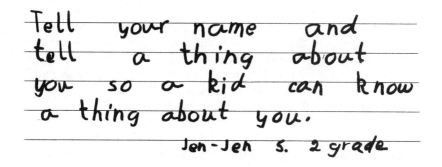

Tell your name and tell a thing about you so a kid can know a thing about you.

—Jen-Jen S. 2 grade

Before the First Day

To help set the tone for a successful year, organize your room before the students ever enter. "Decorate" the room and decide whether you wish to determine the class rules or allow your class to create them. Make sure your desk contains the supplies you'll need and that you have, to the best of your knowledge, the texts, reference books, and teaching materials you'll need to get started.

If you are a new teacher in a school, you've probably attended some orientation meetings already. It's a good idea to "scope out" your room as quickly as possible. The principal, department chair, or another teacher might help you find your room, obtain a key, and begin the organization of your classroom.

While you're in your building, acquaint yourself with the other facilities you'll probably be using. Locate the library, and ask about procedures for checking out books and periodicals. Find the counselors' offices. Locate the room where the audiovisual equipment is kept. Find out the procedure for checking out cassettes or film equipment. Your school will probably have a faculty lounge and a cafeteria. Where are they located? Find out where the restrooms are. The more you are organized and able to find your way around the first day, the better.

Daily Schedule

Scheduling is one area where elementary and secondary schools differ, since elementary teachers plan for a whole day with all different subjects. The middle school or secondary teacher plans for approximately hour-long slots with subjects that may be taught more than once during the day.

Usually before the first day of school you will have a general idea of what the daily schedule will look like. The meetings that occur during those first days advise you of times for beginning and ending the school day, tardy bells, breaks, lunch, and special classes students will attend. For elementary people, it is important to consider when specialists in physical education, music, computer science, reading, art, math, speech, and other areas will meet with your students. Using this information, you can draw up a rough outline of times (Charts 1 or 2). Using this outline, you can figure out where each subject or activity you are to teach will fit in. Then you can make a weekly schedule, noting special classes and time slots (Chart 3). Do this in pencil, because it will change. For now,

Chart 1

Example of Daily Schedule for Kindergarten—Outline

8:30 | 9:00	Opening Exercises -Attendance -Calendar -Songs -Read to Class	12:15 | 12:45
9:00 | 9:30	Free Choice Activities	12:45 | 1:15
9:30 | 10:10	Language Arts Activities Math Activities	1:15 | 1:55
10:10 | 10:30	Outside Play	1:55 | 2:15
10:30 | 11:00	Special Unit Activities	2:15 | 2:45
11:00 | 11:15	Closing - Stories or Songs	2:45 | 3:00

Chart 2

Example of Weekly Schedule for Elementary—Outline

	8:30–10:10		10:30–11:40		12:25–1:30		1:50–3:00
Monday	Opening <u>Jobs from</u> helper chart Sharing Read to class	Writers' workshop	Math		Spelling Journals Pleasure reading		Science Social studies Health
Tuesday		Centers	10:10–10:30	Math	11:40–12:25	Computer lab	1:30–1:50	Science Social studies Health 2:25–2:55 Music
Wednesday		Centers	AM Recess	Math	Lunch	Spelling Journals 12:55–1:25 Music	PM Recess	Science Social studies Health
Thursday		Math		Spelling Journals 11:00–11:30 P.E.		Writers' Workshop		Art
Friday		Writers' workshop		10:30–11:00 Library Spelling Journals		Centers		1:55–2:20 P.E. Small group games

Chart 3

Example of Weekly Schedule for Elementary

	Monday	Tuesday	Wednesday	Thursday	Friday
8:30–9:00	Opening Jobs from helper chart Sharing	Opening	Opening	Opening	Opening
9:00–10:10	Writers' workshop	Centers	Centers	Math	Writers' workshop
10:10–10:30	Recess	Recess	Recess	Recess	Recess
10:30–11:40	Math	Math	Math	Spelling Journals P.E. 11:00–11:30	Library 10:30–11:00 Spelling Journals
11:40–12:25	Lunch	Lunch	Lunch	Lunch	Lunch
12:25–1:30	Read to class Spelling Journals Pleasure reading	Read to class Spelling Journals Pleasure reading	Read to class Spelling Journals Computer lab	Read to class Writers' workshop	Read to class Centers
1:30–1:50	Recess	Recess	Recess	Recess	Recess
1:50–3:00	Social studies, Science, or Health	Social studies, Science, or Health	Social studies, Science, or Health	Art	P.E. 1:55–2:25 Games with small groups

however, your schedule will provide a general outline to work from.

This scheduling process is time-consuming but important. Planning and pacing are two of the most crucial elements for success in the classroom.

Try to set up several hypothetical schedules. During the first few weeks of school you should find which one works best.

Classroom Policies

The expectations you set for your students and your ability to be consistent about them are probably the most critical aspect of your teaching year. Although the cliché "don't smile until Christmas" sounds archaic and even inhumane, the idea of beginning the year with a serious, solid foundation is not.

As a beginning teacher, it is difficult to set standards when you're not even sure what they are. Through the years, you learn which rules to carve in stone and which ones to toss out. Refer to Chapter 2 for some lists of common expectations teachers have of students. Use your own personality to communicate the guidelines you choose to follow. You may wish to post them, incorporate them in an introductory handout, or state them verbally. Your introductory sheet might also state your teaching philosophy and include a course outline or syllabus. The first or second day of school, review the handout with your students. Seeing and hearing "the rules" should emphasize their importance. The most critical aspect of rule-setting is your ability to remain consistent and follow through. This point cannot be emphasized enough.

Class Procedure

The following are some topics and questions you will need to ponder before the first day of school. Some of these situations apply only to elementary and some are applicable to secondary as well.

Procedure for Entering Class

Where and how do you want your class to assemble before school and after breaks? If you have an outside door into your classroom, the students may be able to assemble just outside the door. If not, ask neighboring teachers what they do and if you have an assigned spot. The advantage of a line of students is that you can greet each child first thing in the morning, see each face after breaks, and give a calming word as each child enters the classroom. There is a direct connection between how students enter a room and how they conduct themselves while in that room. If they calm down before they enter the classroom, you save time and energy for more important tasks. Your goal is for students to enter enthusiastically and respectfully. They need to know that running, punching, pushing, yelling, grabbing, and whining are not tolerated.

Some schools do not allow students in the building before the first bell in the morning. Other schools allow students entry as soon as they arrive. If you find yourself in the latter situation, you will have an opportunity to spend a bit of relaxed time with your students before class. On the other hand, excluding students from the building before school gives teachers additional planning time and eliminates some supervisory duties. With this arrangement, you *must* greet your students soon after the bell signals the beginning of the school day.

Storing Personal Belongings

Where will students keep their coats, lunches, and personal belongings? Secondary students will almost certainly have lockers where they can store their things. In elementary situations you will most likely have a coat closet, "cubbies," or a set of coat hooks. If not, arrange for each student to have a place to keep his or her things. Large ice cream tubs, boxes, plastic crates, and homemade wooden cubicles form space to hold students' belongings. Classrooms are seldom large enough for students to keep all their possessions around them without someone tripping over a coat or a backpack. Some students would dearly love to surround themselves with their treasures and need to be reminded daily that this is a hazard. They enthusiastically bring things from home to share with the class (see below). Allowing and encouraging this shows that you value students as individuals and acknowledges that they have a life outside of school. However, require that these items be stored in a central place (a class museum) or in the student's backpack. This helps alleviate the distractions that "shares" can cause in class.

Bringing Personal Treasures to Class

What kinds of personal belongings will you encourage students to bring? Encouraging students to bring items or share thoughts about what you are currently studying makes the curriculum more meaningful and shows how it fits into daily life. You may have an established school policy regarding personal belongings; check. If not, think about what you and your class can tolerate while still accomplishing other tasks during the day.

Many disruptions are caused by students bringing personal belongings to school. No matter what the district, school, or class policy is regarding this, students bring "toys." Allowing elementary students to share stories, pets, or tales of adveenture at designated times may help to alleviate problems.

Middle, junior, and high school students bring portable stereo equipment, skateboards, leather jackets, and other valuable items to class rather than risk locker theft. Most schools remind students that school is not an appropriate place for expensive articles and have specific policies regarding this. However, if a student brings such an item to your class, have the student put the item in a place that will not be disruptive. Remind the student that you cannot be responsible for the article and that he or she should not bring it back. If the student persists in bringing "toys" that cause disruption, refer to Chapter 2 and disciplinary procedures.

Many students' most rewarding pieces of writing are about their pets. Bringing the pets to share makes them tangible for everyone. Yet some teachers will never feel comfortable with a rat or a snake in the room, no matter how gentle these animals are reputed to be. Request that students bring any "live share" in a cage. If the animal can't spend the day in confinement, it must be accompanied by an adult who can take it home after share time.

Collecting Notes and Money/
Taking Attendance and Lunch Count

How will you handle the daily tasks of lunch count, attendance, and note or money collection? For most situations a rotating helper schedule and chart takes care of daily routines. You may allow a student to fill out the attendance sheet if you double-check it and record who is absent or tardy in the grade book. Recording attendance and tardies should not be entirely a student responsibility. Another student may read the daily lunch menu and take a count of those needing lunch. Most of the note and money collection should be taken care of by you. You might require that all notes be placed on your desk. While your helpers take attendance and lunch count, you can look at and organize the daily messages from students. When you need a note from each student—for example, during parent-teacher conference time—record when each student has turned in a note, either in the grade book or on a separate sheet.

In the first few days of school you wiill be trying to keep track of numerous things students are required to bring: money for class magazines, school supplies, textbook rental, locks for lockers, and permission slips, for example. A quick way to monitor this information is to list names on a piece of graph paper. You could also make a copy of the first page of the grade book. (See the sample Class List on page 47.) Then laminate or cover the page with clear adhesive-backed paper or an acetate sheet. This makes a durable list you can reuse for other record-keeping. As students return notes or bring in money, simply record the information on the sheet. Having a reusable page saves time. Also, having several spaces to write makes it possible for you to note more than one thing at a time. If you laminate the sheet of paper before writing students' names, you could use it for more than one semester or year. To use a sheet for a whole year, laminate it and then write students' names with a permanent marker. Use water-based marker or crayon to record information. The water-based marker and crayon will wipe off with a tissue (the marker may need damp tissue), while the permanent marker will remain. You can completely clean off the chart using hair spray or duplicating fluid.

Heading Papers

How will you require that students head their papers? This sounds like a trivial matter, but if you are suddenly faced with 155 papers, it is much easier to sort and record them if students use some uniform type of heading. It is much easier for you and your students if you let them know what you want from the beginning. Make a small poster and place it so all the students can refer to it as needed. On the first day, explain how and why the papers need to be headed. Model what students' headings should look like for the first few times, or until most of the students have the general idea mastered.

In the primary grades, just getting students to remember to put their names on papers is a major task. Later you may want students to include subject, date, page number, number of problems, and class period.

Robert assigns each student a number corresponding to the line that student's name occupies in the grade book. As students turn in their work, Robert put the papers in numerical order. It is then easy for him to identify any missing assignments.

Class List

Room 206
Emerson Elementary School

	Field Trip $5.25	Field Trip Permission Slip 10/25	Lunch Money 10/10		Other
Wendy A.	✓	✓	✓		
Bobby B.	✓		✓		
Mindy B.			✓		
Alex D.		✓			Dentist- Wed 2pm
Beth D.	✓	✓	✓		
Alan K.	✓	✓			
Jennifer K.		✓			
Hailey K.		✓			
Micky L.	✓	✓	✓		mom-work 555-5852
Amy N.	✓	✓	✓		

Individuals Leaving the Classroom

How often and for what reason will you allow students to leave the classroom? Keeping interruptions to a minimum is important. Every student will occasionally need to go to the restroom, sharpen a pencil, get a drink, or check out a library book during class time. Check to see if your school has a policy concerning students leaving class. Strongly urge students to get drinks, go to the restroom, get supplies from lockers, buy lunch tickets, and sharpen pencils at the beginning of any break. A useful general rule is that only one person may be out of the room at any one time, as long as it's necessary and you are not giving directions to the whole group. To do this you might have one pass for out-of-class business, like a laminated piece of paper or an object. It is used for all temporary absences from class and insures that only one person is out of the room at a time. If the pass is available and you are not giving directions to the class, a student may, without disturbing anyone, take the pass and leave the room. If this privilege is abused, then the offender or whole class loses this right. Explain this all to the class ahead of time. It has a lasting impression.

Listing Student Supplies

How do you know what supplies the students need to bring? In most cases, if it is your first assignment, you will use what your predecessor asked students to bring. Keep a wish list in the back inside cover of your grade book of student and general classroom supplies you want to have the following year. The supplies you need will change as your individual teaching style and curriculum needs emerge. For example, next year you may want all your students to have a three-ring notebook and dividers to use as a writing folder. Other items on a student supply list might include pencils, pens, markers, crayons, paper, erasers, glue, paste, ruler, scissors, tissue, watercolor paints, lined paper, and folders.

Your list will vary from school to school, grade to grade, community to community. In some schools or districts, students pay a fee that covers all school materials and activities for the year.

Room Environment

Brian, a social studies teacher, has created a room that epitomizes an inviting classroom. An adept gardener, Brian has filled his window sills with begonias and geraniums, a fern or two, and even an azalea. Student mobiles dangle like wind chimes, and posters and projects wallpaper the room. Not that your classroom needs to look like an art gallery, zoo, or florist shop. But your classroom is an extension of you—it's your office and other home. Although some teachers don't wish their students to know one thing about them beyond the classroom,

other teachers feel differently. If you're an avid tennis player, backpacker, or musician, for example, you could hang a poster that portrays these activities. Your classroom should also be a place that reflects what your students are working on at the time. And whether it's stated in writing or suggested in photographs or paintings, your classroom should exhibit positive statements that encourage success and offer inspiration.

Katie teaches a junior high physical education class; she's a dedicated athlete and student of ballet. Her office and locker rooms display posters of gymnasts and dancers. A believer in wellness and self-discipline, Katie has created a working environment that models her philosophy and inspires her students.

Many teachers hang posters or photographs that suggest environmental awareness. You need, however, to practice sound judgment in what you display. Advertising certain values can be risky. Hanging a pro-life or pro-choice poster will probably result in a barrage of parental phone calls you don't need and a visit from an administrator you don't wish to solicit.

It's important that students feel comfortable and welcome in your classroom. Seeing their own work displayed provides them with a sense of pride and ownership. They also enjoy seeing pictures of themselves at work. For example, next to her posters, Katie hangs photographs of her volleyball players in action. Students get a charge out of seeing themselves stretching for that perfect spike.

It's critical, too, that *you* feel comfortable and that your room—your office—is a place you anticipate coming to each day.

When you enter your new classroom for the first time, it may look desolate and bare. Don't panic. It will take time to make the room your own. Robert inherited an elementary school classroom containing student desks and chairs in assorted sizes and conditions, a teacher's desk with no "big" chair to match, a pre–World War I world map, closets with some old and tired bulletin board decorations, a box of recycled computer paper, several editions of assorted textbooks, and loads of empty space. Over the years he had made and accumulated materials to fill the cupboards to be used for future units, but the walls and surroundings were still bare. Robert realized that the students could participate and suggested they help decorate their classroom. The students pitched in enthusiastically.

Make things look ready for school but not like the grand opening of the neighborhood stationery store. You do not need commercially produced materials to make your classroom inviting to students. Put up a few personal things, arrange your desk, set up learning centers, leave a blank name tag or sheet of paper on each desk, and prepare the walls for displaying student work. You may tell the students in your opening remarks that the room looks bare now, but you're glad they're there to help decorate it with their art and work. Students take great pride in the displays and general appearance of their classroom.

Some ideas for beginning-of-the-year bulletin boards include:

- a daily/weekly schedule
- a "Welcome to Students" sign or poster with class lists
- unit- or theme-oriented quotes, posters, or articles
- motivational posters or quotes
- seasonal decorations
- daily announcements, sports schedules, homeroom news, and pending school activities.

Many teachers, especially on the secondary level, share classrooms with other teachers. Talk with the others sharing your teaching space. Discuss how bookshelf space and file drawers will be shared. Find out which bulletin boards will be yours. If there are no stairs to negotiate and your subject requires a variety of materials and equipment, request a cart on wheels for your supplies. If you will be teaching on several floors, arrange for your own forms, pens, and pencils to be kept in drawers in each room. Make sure you've left the classroom at least as orderly as when you walked in. Is litter off the floor? Is everything you borrowed returned? Are books picked up? Are the desks cleaned of any marks? Are the boards erased? As petty as it sounds, many hostile relationships have ensued over messy roommates . . . just when you thought your college days were over.

For more information, see the Classroom Arrangment section in this chapter.

Your Desk

The contents of a teacher's desk are often instrumental in avoiding unnecessary trips from the classroom. Although teachers are no longer able to dispense aspirin, cough drops, or other medication, students sometimes have other needs. If most teachers had a nickel for all the tissues they'd donated, they could retire. Tissues are a must! Check to see if tissue is on your supply list.

If you teach in a junior high or high school, a bottle of clear fingernail polish isn't a bad idea for running nylons. Safety pins are in demand as well. A favorite educator who is now a junior high principal was well-known for her special supplies. As a counselor, she was popular with students, parents, and teachers, not just because she was a bright woman in her field, but also because she was caring and generous. Her office contained everything from thumbtacks to hair spray. She remedied ailments from static cling to shattered egos.

Keeping often-needed items available saves time, eliminates unnecessary trips to the restroom, and conveys the message to students that you care about them. Most students won't abuse these "freebies."

This is not to suggest that you become the building pharmacy and supplier, however. Especially if you're a beginning teacher, you'll have other financial priorities, and no one expects you to make these purchases.

Find out your school's purchasing system in order to take advantage of as many supplies as possible. Expect policies to vary among school systems.

When Marc, a math teacher, took his first assignment at a junior high, he was fortunate in obtaining an almost unlimited amount of supplies. When he needed liquid paper or a new stapler, he simply marched down to the supply room and took what he needed. Eight years later, he transferred to another school, naively expecting the same privileges. Wrong! The first day, when the old-timers were carting off their boxes of new supplies, Marc had none. He hadn't been there the previous spring to order. A few teachers did dig in and provide him with a spare pen or two and an extra roll of tape, but supply-wise it was a tight year and a lot of what went into Marc's classroom came from Marc's personal budget.

An inventory of many teachers' desks might include:

- file folders
- stick-on notes or note pads (great for separating papers and brief notes to students)
- cellophane and masking tape with dispensers
- thumbtacks
- stapler and as many boxes of staples as your budget can afford (start with two)
- triple-size or regular chalk and colored chalk for highlighting on the board (triple-size is easier for some people to write with)
- paper clips (all sizes)
- several calendars
- rulers
- compass and paper punch
- pens, pencils, and erasers
- rubber cement and glue
- felt-tip markers (water-based and permanent)
- scissors
- rubber bands
- staple remover.

In one drawer, keep a file containing schedules that have been distributed, memos concerning procedures or important dates, and forms pertaining to students (transfer, accident report). Retain this file from year to year, replacing schedules as they are updated. It is helpful to know the specialists' schedules if you deal with these people.

You'll also want to keep some personal-use items in your desk, like these:

- breath mints and a small mirror (If you have parsley on your teeth, most students won't tell you; they will, however, inform most of the student body.)
- thank-you notes
- lotion (chalk dust dries skin like desert sand)
- deodorant (for that busy morning when you forget)
- (for women) spare nylons and personal hygiene items.

Always be aware that any material that isn't cemented down can escape from the classroom. Even nails may not be sufficient to secure items in a classroom. Through the years Bill, a high school Spanish teacher, has "lost" books, coats, a wallet (with numerous credit cards), cassettes, pens, his favorite Albert Einstein poster, plants, tape dispensers, scissors, and even half-eaten candy bars. Do not bring rare books that your first lover gave you for Christmas, the orchid that you have been nurturing since 1981, or a poster from Earth Day unless you wish to donate them. Anything of value, and this includes tests and other materials you wish to keep from sticky fingers, should be left at home or locked in a file cabinet.

Regardless of what personal and professional items you choose to surround yourself with, your individual style will influence how your desk is organized. Gary has a desk that would make a drill sergeant smile, while the top of Marc's is usually cluttered with student papers, day-old passes, phone messages, a plant, and a snapshot from a summer vacation. Buried beneath the chaos is a desk-top calendar which Marc does manage to check daily. Both Gary and Marc have shelves within their grasps which house reference books, current textbooks, a dictionary, a thesaurus, a copy of *Writers INC* (a handy little manual which, regardless of your grade level or discipline, is a treasure—see Bibliography), curriculum guides, and other resource books and materials that aid in lesson planning.

Classroom Arrangement

Shared Equipment and Materials

Consider where to keep shared equipment and materials such as the yardstick, tape dispenser, and stapler. Set up an area for these items on the counter, shelf, or bookcase and clearly label where each tool is kept. Pictorial symbols as well as labels will help with quick location and replacement of items.

If possible, your room should contain a set of encyclopedias, dictionaries, thesauri, an atlas, and other texts or reading materials applicable to the curricula you're teaching. A screen, an overhead projector, and at least one file cabinet should be provided. If they are not, you need to communicate this to the administrator or person in charge of obtaining such supplies as soon as possible. If you plan to use an overhead, you'll need acetate sheets and water-based marking pens. Your inventory should include crayons, glue, scissors, scratch or construction paper, and old magazines so you can plan lessons that will appeal to a variety of learners.

Desks, Windows, Exits

If you have access to roster sheets prior to opening day, check the number of desks with expected bodies. Are there enough? Talk with the custodian and *respectfully* communicate your needs.

If your room has windows, check to see if there are shades or blinds to keep the sun from students' eyes and to allow you to darken the room for films. Cardboard or posters may work in a pinch. If there are no windows, is there a fan for adequate circulation? Check to see that outlets and lights work properly. Be certain that you've familiarized yourself with fire exits and the route you and your students will take during fire drills.

Desk Arrangement

The arrangement of student desks influences the classroom environment. When you're setting up your classroom, consider your goals and the types of activities you will be doing as you contemplate desk arrangement. Traditional rows are still standard in some rooms and serve some purposes well. When you want too foster small group discussion, cooperation, teamwork, or tutoring, arrange the desks in clusters. Ideal group sizes range from two to four students. When students need space for working independently or calming themselves, the desks can easily be moved apart. Chapter 4 provides more complete information on establishing and managing groups.

Time spent at the beginning of the year teaching students how to move their desks safely and efficiently will save you time and back problems later. Then, when the room needs to be rearranged, a quick sketch on the board or overhead lets students know where to move to. If the students can rearrange desks safely with a minimum of problems, do it as often as the need arises.

Let students know that they have the responsibility to choose what kind of environment they would like to work in. They should regard your permission to change positions in the room frequently as a privilege. If one or two students are unable to move desks without creating havoc, then they might lose this privilege.

When planning your room arrangement, you can save time by drawing a simple sketch of your room and doing some pre-planning on paper. Think about traffic flow and the types of activities you will be involved in. Use stick-on notes to represent desks and other stations in your classroom. You can easily move the notes around the diagram, yet they'll stay put once you've made your decisions.

Opening Day

Once your room is transformed into an environment that invites rather than intimidates, and your desk and supplies are in order, you can begin concentrating on the first day.

The opening of school bustles with eager as well as fearful faces. Old relationships are reestablished; students and staff anticipate another passage. Elementary, middle, and senior high schools all share the vitality that marks the first day of the school year.

Administrative Duties

Many schools do not meet for a full opening day. In middle, junior high, and high schools, the first time you'll meet with your students may vary from 10 to 30 minutes. Usually you'll have administrative duties to attend to. The first day might involve:

1. Writing your name and the title of the class on the board. This also encourages students to check the board.
2. Checking students in. This may involve initialing a computer print-out or a schedule sheet.
3. Creating a seating chart. You may decide to change this later, but it helps you in taking roll and learning students' names.
4. Assessing some information about your students: their hobbies and interests; what they learned last year; what their goals are for this year. You could use sheets like the Student Survey and/or Personal Information Sheet on pages 56 and 57 to gather student information.

Whether your school meets for a full day or a half day, the important thing is to set the tone immediately. Requiring that students have a pen, a pencil, and other materials helps establish a learning atmosphere from the beginning.

Students' First Impression of You

It is important to let students know immediately that you are the professional. This means looking, sounding, and acting the part. Until students know from experience that you are competent, fair, consistent, and caring, they will quickly assess you based on their first impression. You can convey confidence and a sense of self-pride through dress, voice, and body language.

STUDENT SURVEY

1. Your full name: _____

2. The name you'd like to be called in class: _____

3. Age: _____   4. Birthday: _____

5. Home phone: _____

6. What school did you attend last year? (Add the city
   and state if it was not Boise.) _____

7. Who was your English teacher last year? _____

8. What is your favorite subject? _____

9. What is your most disliked or worst subject? _____

10. What hobbies or activities do you enjoy? _____
    _____

11. What is something you do well? _____

12. What is your most treasured possession? _____

13. If you had an entire day to spend as you wished,
    what would you do? _____

14. If you could change one thing about yourself, what
    would you change? _____

15. What do you plan to do after high school? _____
    _____

16. How many people are in your family? _____

17. Do you have any pets? _____

18. What else would you like me to know about you?

PERSONAL INFORMATION SHEET

STUDENT'S NAME _____

PARENTS' NAME(S) _____

ADDRESS _____

HOME PHONE _____ WORK PHONE MOM _____
                                      DAD _____

DOES THE STUDENT WALK TO SCHOOL? _____ RIDE A BUS? _____

BUS # _____

GO TO A SITTER OR CARE CENTER
BEFORE/AFTER SCHOOL? _____

NAME _____

PHONE # OF CAREGIVER _____

PERSON TO CALL IN CASE OF EMERGENCY _____

PHONE _____

SPECIAL NOTES (health problems, food allergies, etc.) _____

_____

_____

_____

_____

Dress and Personal Appearance   As discussed in Chapter 1, dress is critical in communicating a message to students. Professional dress helps establish credibility. Even in physical education class, it is a good idea to dress "up" on nonactivity days. Since many art instructors wear smocks, they usually wear sports coats or jackets beneath the smock. Many school districts do not allow teachers to wear jeans.

If you are a young teacher or just beginning, it is all the more important to establish your role as teacher. Many young women have resorted to different hair styles to look more authoritative. Tami, a beautiful young science teacher, was having problems establishing herself as the teacher; she looked like her students. A friend in her department suggested that she try wearing her blonde mane on top of her head. The transformation really helped. Nick, a band instructor, was complaining of the same problem. "My students keep telling me how *young* I look," he'd say. "I know it's a compliment, but I think they would respect me more if I didn't appear so close to their ages." Nick grew a moustache and that, coupled with the other tips he received on effective discipline, appeared to help.

This doesn't mean that you need to emulate the stereotypical image of the ancient schoolmarm or schoolmaster. It simply suggests that dress and personal appearance are vital to establishing the tone that is so critical when meeting students.

Voice Control   Effective teachers articulate and enunciate. Could you become more effective by speaking more loudly and literally practicing voice control? Tape-record your voice from a distance and evaluate how you sound. Invite a colleague to sit in the back of your room and give input on your vocal projection.

Language Correctness   Correct grammar and usage are critical. Although many students may not realize the difference between an object pronoun and a subject pronoun, many others will. If you use poor English, your credibility is at risk, not just with those students but also with their parents, who will be quick to criticize. Quizzes, tests, progress reports, and any other written communication should be error-free.

If you squeaked by in college with shaky grammar, either review a text on usage or consult an English teacher in your building. It's done all the time: "Mary, I always get confused; is it correct to say 'with Jim and I or with Jim and me'?" Not only will you improve your speech, but also the teacher you asked will be glad you did. *Writers INC* is another excellent source for quick reference. The spell-check feature in word processing programs is designed to alleviate some problems. Be accurate. We reflect on each other.

Body Language   Effective teachers use body language. Move among your students. During group work, pull up a desk and talk with them. Walk up and down the aisles while lecturing. Check for understanding and students on task. Be aware of what's going on. If you actively rotate around your room, you'll be less likely to experience discipline problems. The most effective way to gauge your presentation is to videotape yourself during class. Then view and evaluate your use of body language.

No one likes to listen to someone drone on in monotone from behind a podium with no animation or enthusiasm. Most teachers will agree that they're performers. Some say teachers are salespeople with a product/subject to "sell" to "buyers."

Opening Assignment

Once you've established your expectations, it's important to create an atmosphere that conveys a climate that is academic yet also comfortable and nonthreatening. Many teachers begin the year with some sort of writing assignment that asks questions about the students' hobbies and interests. Mary, a secondary reading teacher, uses this technique. While her students are working, Mary moves between aisles, noting students' names and what they wish to be called in class.

Learning Students' Names

Learning students' names quickly enables you to deal with discipline problems immediately. Mike, a kindergarten teacher, shares a vivid memory of a first day of school not so long ago. He was reading *Miss Eva and the Red Balloon*, and most of the children were sitting around him, listening with rapt attention. He was entertaining them with his most expressive reading, making eye contact with many eager young faces, all while sitting on a 12-inch chair surrounded by 24 five- and six-year-olds. Fortunately, Mike had already learned the name of a boy whose attention was not on the story. Mike firmly stated the child's name and placed the boy within arm's reach, solving the problem. He continued his dramatic interpretation, and the classroom atmosphere remained intact. Mike had learned that young man's name almost immediately, as he had several of the other students, for various reasons. He had all 54 of his kindergartners' names learned by midweek.

Mike is skilled at putting names and faces together quickly. If you have a more difficult time, you can employ a variety of techniques to learn your students' names; name tags, desk tags, and seating charts are a few. If your students do not have assigned seating or move around frequently, the students may have to wear name tags until you and they become acquainted. Saying the student's name while looking at the face is an effective way to learn names. One resourceful teacher won the name game for himself and his substitute by creating a picture file for each class. During the first days of school, he grouped three to four students together at a time and took their pictures. He developed the film, cut apart the individual faces, and glued the pictures on a file folder in the same configuration as the seating in the classroom, labeling each picture with the student's name. The teacher keeps the file folders for each class on his podium so he can refer to them. He can remove or rearrange the photos as the need arises.

This same idea was adapted in a kindergarten class by placing the students' pictures by their names on a list posted in the classroom. It helped both teacher and students learn the names. It also made it possible for a substitute to address each student by name.

When students are working, look at your name list and make mental notes. Try associating some feature with the name. This may sound silly, but it works. If Tim has red hair and freckles, think of an association that will help you remember: A red-haired Tiny Tim with crutches, perhaps. A social studies teacher gave an example of a boy in class named Scott. She mentally placed a tartan cap on his head. Whatever it takes, the sooner you learn the students' names, the better.

The First Week: Study Teams

The first week of school is usually hectic. Even in the most "settled" of schools, some students will be trickling in all week. Many teachers pencil in absences, tardies, and even the first grades until they have a pretty good idea of just who will be in the class.

Establishing study teams is one method of getting acquainted with the class and conveying the expectation that the responsibility for learning rests with the students. When a student is absent, other study team members must collect notes, handouts, and assignments for their absent study team member.

Marc suggests establishing study teams in the following way: Assign three or four members to each group. Attempt to make your groups as heterogeneous as possible. Choose members with differing abilities, interests, and counselors. One purpose of the team is to help absent students; it's important that most group members not be involved in many of the same activities—if they are, they may be absent on the same day. Because you don't know your students well yet, you may base your decisions on where students sit. Students who know each other often sit together. Assign groups from varying parts of the room. Make sure that you're forming new student groups, not confirming already-established ones.

The first group activity may be to answer several questions on the board or overhead:

- What is your name?
- What are your hobbies/things you like to do?
- What is your favorite movie? book? song?
- Who is your favorite person?
- When is your birthday?
- What do you think we will be studying in class this year?

Tell the students to write the questions down and then meet for 15 to 20 minutes in their new groups. During that time, the students are to interview each other. Inform them that they will, ultimately, be introducing their group members to the rest of the class. These ice-breaking questions engage the group members in conversations that will introduce them to each other. Circulate among the groups, encouraging all members to interview and be interviewed.

When the discussion time has elapsed, bring the groups back together. Inform them that they are going to make a group collage. The collage must reflect words, phrases, and pictures that represent the groups' interests as well as the individuals'. Explain that by the end of the class period the next day, the group will introduce each other, using the collage as a visual aid. The collages will be hung in the room. Supply the group with old magazines, newspapers, glue, scissors, and a piece of poster board or construction paper. You may wish to assign a group grade based on the following criteria:

- Was it completed on time?
- Was it neat?
- Were all group members represented?

This activity not only provides the students with a study team but also allows the class to learn about its members and provides you with some valuable insight into the personalities of your group members.

Daily Interruptions

Among the most frustrating parts of teaching are the interruptions. They will start right away, and they will vary. They may be call slips from the office. Usually the office will notify you as to the urgency of the request. If the request is for "right away" or an "emergency," you will need simply to pass the slip on to the student. Otherwise, excuse the student at the appropriate time. Sometimes you will be interrupted for administrative business such as collection of picture money, maintenance calls, and other day-to-day occurrences that disrupt the momentum of teaching and learning. Maintain a sense of humor. Follow the suggestions in Chapter 5 for refocusing students after interruptions. If the interruptions become unreasonable, speak with the administration.

Most school districts do not allow interruptions by nonschool personnel. Find out the policy about such visits. Several years ago, a junior high teacher became an innocent victim caught between two parents who were fighting for the custody of their child. The parent who did not have legal custody came to school in an attempt to remove the student from class. The situation could, potentially, have become a legal nightmare. Do not release students unless you have written permission from the office or the legal guardian.

New Students

At the beginning of the year, you will often need to sign in a new student. In the middle of a class discussion, a new face will appear at the door, bearing a sign-in slip. This new student is probably more frustrated

A new student today

and embarrassed about interrupting your class than you can imagine. Smile, take a second to whisper quickly that the student may take a seat and you'll be with him or her in a moment. If possible, a vacant chair or desk near the door is excellent for these new students. Your file containing your introductory handouts should by handy; you can give these to the new student so he or she can peruse them while waiting for you. Then, when the class is reading, writing, or discussing on their own, you can take some time to sign the new student in. Assign her or him a study team and desk, and take a moment to find out where the student came from and perhaps what he or she had been working on in the past. If the student comes from another state, you may wish to ask about the move. Often, a student has been abruptly uprooted as the result of family changes. Many are upset about the alteration. A few kind words of welcome will help the student to believe that there may be a bright spot in the transfer.

Fire Drills

Fire drills may be announced or come as a complete surprise. The alarm will always startle you, but that is to be expected. Before the first day of school, you should become familiar with the route you and your class are to use in case of an emergency. Make a map and tape it up by your door so the class can become familiar with it as well. A substitute could also make a quick reference to the map if necessary. When the bell sounds, be sure to close the windows, turn off the lights, pick up your grade book, and close the door on your way out. You can assign students to some of these tasks.

As soon as you are out of the building and in your assigned spot, count your students and note anyone who is missing. Depending on your school's policy, you may need to send a runner to a designated area to let administrators know that everyone is accounted for. This may seem like a lot of needless routine. However, in case of a real emergency, the routine could prevent needless confusion.

Restroom Visits/The Nurse's Office/Illness

You will need to establish a policy for students visiting the nurse's office and restrooms when you discuss your expectations. You will also need to be consistent. Teachers often have a pass for the restroom, such as a key that states "restroom," a block of wood, or a laminated restroom card. Since writing a pass takes time away from other students and is an interruption, these preprepared passes seem to be the simplest solution. If a student is abusing the privilege, you may need to talk with him or her, explaining that passing periods or breaks are the time for restroom visits. Usually, if you offer to discuss a potential health problem with the school nurse or parent, the problem will cease. If students get the idea that you're on to them, they usually will save the request for legitimate emergencies.

If you have a student with bladder control problems, let the child know that he or she may make restroom trips whenever necessary. Discuss with the parents the need to have some dry clothes at school to help avoid embarrassment.

Allow students to leave immediately if they have a nosebleed or need to throw up. One day, Kathy was discussing a problem with a student. Meanwhile, an obedient but ill youngster was waving his hand in a violent attempt to let Kathy know he was about to be sick. Before the boy obtained Kathy's attention, he vomited all over himself and the girl in front of him, much to the chagrin of Kathy and her 28 sixth-graders.

Some students believe that the easiest way to escape responsibility is to "feel sick." Honor most of these requests. If time permits, talk to the student to better assess the situation. Often a "Why don't you wait until after the test?" or "The discussion we are having is very important" will encourage the student to hang in there. If the student begins to exhibit a pattern of becoming ill at certain times or being absent only on test days, see your school nurse immediately and inquire about the student. There may be a legitimate health problem; if so, a solution will need to be found. You don't wish to be cruel and deny help to an ill student. You just need to be aware that some young people will use illness as a convenient exit from your class. Don't allow this to become the case.

If any of your students have any serious health problems, note this fact on the permanent health record with a colored flag or marker. It only takes a little time to check quickly through your files. This will help you avoid any unpleasant or dangerous situations. Many times your school nurse will talk with you if a student has a serious health problem. School personnel will usually advise teachers of special cases, such as kidney problems, diabetes, asthma, epilepsy, and other conditions that require special attention. Encourage your nurse to provide you with this information, but remember that it's confidential.

The role of the school nurse is discussed in more detail in Chapter 9, "Ancillary Personnel."

The Suddenly Sick

Especially if you teach elementary school, you may witness and take care of things you never imagined possible when you deal with sick students. Make it a habit to reach for the trash can when a student grabs her or his stomach or complains. If the emergency is real, a student's face may suddenly flush and be excessively cool or warm to the touch. In this case, rush the student to the office or nurse's room. Depending on what you and your students are doing at the time, you may accompany the suddenly sick youngster or entrust that duty to another student. Advise a neighboring teacher whenever you need to leave the classroom for any reason. You may also have a call button next to the intercom system that you could use to summon help from the office.

You will also have the not-quite-so-sick and the not-sick-at-all students who claim to be suddenly ill. You will soon be able to recognize these categories. Sometimes complaints of aches and pains are signals of other problems, and simply giving some attention will help. Anxiety about not being prepared for class or other daytime dramas can cause a student to complain. You will need to determine what you are going to do in each situation. Some students will come to you and mention that they are not feeling too well when, in fact, they are on the verge of throwing up. Others will offer you a detailed description of their latest hangnail. Each student is different. A drink of water, a trip to the bathroom, or a quiet reading session in the corner may do the trick if the student's need was for attention. Be aware that this may be a ploy to avoid work! If any student persists with complaints and symptoms, a note or a call to parents may be necessary. Tell them that you are concerned. They may be able to help you figure out what is really bothering their child.

Emergency Illness

Ideally, as discussed in Chapter 2, you will want to handle your own classroom problems. Should, however, an emergency occur and you need assistance in a hurry, the following may help. You need to be prepared for emergencies from Day One on.

If a student has a seizure, fainting spell, or serious accident in class, quickly send a dependable student to the office. Tell the student to inform the administration about the problem and bring someone to the classroom immediately. Remain calm. Over the years, teachers have survived earthquakes, bomb threats, gas leaks, fights, loose animals, rabid dogs, fires, and other disasters.

If a student has a seizure, place a soft object under the student's head. Don't attempt to restrain. Move furniture away. Prevent other students from crowding the scene. When the seizure has passed, the student should be assisted to a comfortable place to lie down under a nurse's supervision. The remaining students may have questions. Explain what happened. They need to understand that it is possible for anyone to have a seizure and that the person is not someone to be feared.

Conclusion

Overall, the primary message in this chapter is to be prepared. Know your building and make sure you're organized in both your classroom and your expectations. As in building a house, the structure is as strong or as shaky as its foundation.

CHAPTER 4

Curriculum Decisions

My hint,
Andy:
3rd

I think it be fair
to let them have some
free choice like drawing, reading,
painting and other free choice.

Plan group activities that pull students together,
and work will each other.

Darcy
9th grade

An educator's enthusiasm, anchored in background knowledge, is vitally important in teaching because expertise and competence contribute immensely to student motivation. The effective teacher recognizes the varying abilities of students within a class. This teacher also knows that students learn in different ways; the challenge is to accommodate those differences.

If There Is a Scope and Sequence and/or District Curriculum

What to teach at a specific grade level might be dictated by your district's published scope and sequence or curriculum guide. The advantage of a school district having a clear scope and sequence is that you will know exactly what topics to cover during the year. You also can expect a specific skill level in students who have progressed through that curriculum. Another advantage is that when you need help and support teaching a unit, all the other teachers in that department or grade level are at approximately the same point and may have just used a lesson that will work well with your students. Then, if a student transfers from another teacher to your class during the year, that student will not be lost.

Although this is the ideal theory, it's not the reality. Not all students arrive in class with the same level of competency. Some transfer in from other schools, some were ill the week that skill was introduced, and some simply didn't care enough to learn.

Sometimes teachers are to blame for voids in the curriculum. Instead of adhering to the scope and sequence, they teach their "specialities." Some digress from the curriculum simply because they do not like being told what to teach. Others cannot meet the requirements due to lack of books, support materials, lab equipment, or specific physical facilities. One year Bill was "traveling" between the main building and portable classrooms every hour. He omitted many supplemental materials and lessons utilizing classroom-set-texts from his high school Spanish lessons simply because it was too awkward to move those materials from place to place. Poor weather conditions made moving even more difficult.

Occasionally, teachers encounter difficulties when they religiously stick to the curriculum, ignoring the personalities of their charges. They plod on, assuming everyone is the same. This approach is safe, but it removes the personal touch that often makes education meaningful. You must strive to reach a balance between the established scope and sequence, individual student differences, and your personal style.

Regardless of what the other teachers are teaching, you need to take some steps in a scope-and-sequence situation.

Written Copy of Scope and Sequence/Curriculum Find out if a scope and sequence—or at least a curriculum for the assigned class—exists and (sometimes the hard part) obtain one. Ask your department chair, principal, or curriculum coordinator for a copy. Regardless of the age, quality, or completeness of a curriculum, it can provide a path of continuity, especially during those first teaching years when you must be concerned with so many other bewildering details. Most likely, you will be held more accountable for teaching the contents of the curriculum than of the text.

Administration Expectations Find out what the administration expects. Are the teachers in your department required to be at a certain point by the end of each grading period? Does the administrator evaluate your use of the curriculum as a part of your performance?

Competency Tests Know if the students are required to take a subject competency test or state regents' test at the end of the year.

Intent of Curriculum Skim through the curriculum. Read through any introductory material to get a sense of the tone and intent of the curriculum writers. Is the curriculum written as a day-by-day plan, or is it a collection of possible units to teach stated skills? This longer compilation is probably constructed so that you can choose the best available sources for meeting the varied needs of students. Don't be afraid to implement your own creative ideas for lessons that will teach or reinforce the skills and information that you are to cover.

Materials for Each Unit Read through the first several units carefully. Are the necessary books, teaching tools, and space for materials and activities available? Look several units ahead to prevent surprises the fourth or fifth week of school. Ask where the materials are kept. Find out if they are within the building or have to be ordered from a resource center or other school. Another teacher, the principal, the head secretary, the custodian, or sometimes the most unlikely person knows the answers.

Discover if the needed—but unavailable—materials can be ordered *and arrive* in time for you to use them to teach the lesson. A rule of planning that sounds cynical but is true suggests that if ordered material is promised for Monday "without fail," don't plan to use that material until Wednesday. That way you can smoothly change plans and can laugh when the material finally arrives on Friday because it had first been delivered to the wrong school.

If needed material isn't available, plan an original lesson, or consult with an experienced teacher about how to teach that concept with existing materials.

Integrating Curriculum Parts   Consider integrating different parts of the curriculum. When you are teaching elementary school, it is effective and often appropriate to combine subjects. For example, after you've previewed different curriculum guides and texts, you may notice that in spelling, reading, and language the skill of recognizing and spelling homophones is introduced. Use the stories, word lists, worksheets, and other extending activities from all three texts and curriculum guides to teach that unit.

Another time to integrate the curriculum might be when you teach the skills of comparing, measuring, and estimating. These concepts are commonly covered in math and science texts. Look through both curricula and texts to determine the activities, vocabulary, and exercises that best support teaching these concepts. Reinforce what you are studying by using this vocabulary as the weekly spelling list, or read any stories from your basal that correspond to the theme of measuring, comparing, and estimating.

Ideally, an elementary curriculum would be totally integrated. You may be fortunate enough to have curriculum guides that cross-reference subject areas; if not, try to make up some yourself.

One way to accomplish this would be to make a master plan for integrating units you will be teaching during the year. To create a master list, get a large piece of butcher paper or poster board and divide it into nine or ten sections—one for each month of the school year. Next, go through your curriculum guides and begin penciling in concepts you are to cover. When you come across common elements in different subject areas, determine where they will best fit. Note all subjects, texts, and page numbers as you write in each unit. Do not introduce too many new concepts simultaneously.

If you find yourself in a situation where it is not possible to make a master list ahead of time, keep track of what you do and when you do it on the same type of list mentioned above. By spring, you will have a record of what you did cover and will be better equipped to begin rearranging for an integrated curriculum next year. There is no way you can do everything all at once. One of the advantages of teaching the same subject or grade for several years is having the opportunity to refine your units over the years.

If There Is No Curriculum

Mary has a friend whose daughter Janet, a talented artist, completed her subject area work and then her teaching credentials. The young woman's first job was to be *the* art teacher for a small district that had no art curriculum. In fact, developing and writing that curriculum was part of Janet's first-year assignment. She was excited. She envisioned wonderful art lessons evolving from her "free rein." Instead, she was overwhelmed with scheduling and traveling. In addition, she faced a lack of supplies. Since she was a pioneer in the new program, no one had ordered basic supplies the year before during the budget rotation. Finally, there was no other art teacher with whom to trade ideas, and Janet had to face the usual motivation and discipline problems alone.

Quality curriculum development is a mixture of a needs assessment (why do we need it?), "what works and what doesn't," teaching experience, background knowledge, and curriculum writing techniques usually learned in advanced-degree education work. Quality curriculum development occurs when there is time for discussion and contemplation; this seldom occurs in the whirlwind of the teaching year, even for experienced teachers. Neither Janet, the novice art teacher, nor her administration realized the sheer enormity of the task assigned to Janet that September. She did finish that school year, but, tragically, has not taught since.

If you are assigned to teach a semester or year-long course in your subject area for which no curriculum exists, here are some specific guidelines for survival.

Materials Available   Assess available books and equipment. Are there enough books for each student? Does the amount of equipment dictate work groups or individual practice of skills? If there is a huge amount of supplementary material and several texts, all of which look wonderful, begin mentally to choose only the very best so the students (and you) aren't overwhelmed with quantity and lose sight of the concepts being taught. Overteaching or belaboring a point can breed boredom or confusion.

Teacher's Texts   Consult any texts you may have. Teacher's editions usually contain scope and sequence charts for your level as well as the whole series. Use these as models.

Colleagues' Input/Brainstorming   Gather ideas and guidelines from other educators. Ask for curricula from friends in other districts (this can take some time). Contact your state department of education, which should be able to supply information about state guidelines.

   If others in your school are teaching the same subject, informally interview each to identify which concepts are important to that subject and grade level. If there are no other teachers to consult, brainstorm a list of content objectives. Keep in mind the grade level being taught, student needs, and the sociological nature of the community. A town in which everyone works at the local textile factory, or a small farming community, will likely require a different approach to curriculum than a large urban community or a university town in whiich many students are children of faculty. Keep your expectations high regardless of environment and be sure to challenge your students creatively and intellectually.

Arrangement of Curriculum   Rearrange the list you develop into a logical order. This sequence may be chronological, as in the case of history and some literature, or developmental, as in physical education, writing, mathematics, home economics, industrial arts, or a lab science. Another arrangement might be by large topics. You could arrange science by classification or the systems approach. Art units can build logically from black and white to color to three-dimensional projects. Literature is often taught by topic or theme.

   Choose an arrangement that suits the subject being taught as well as your personality. If it fits logically and accommodates your personal strengths, the first unit can go a long way in proving your ability and credibility to your classes. Also, give consideration to the units taught at the end of the year. Betty, a high school language arts teacher, saves a study of satire and humor for the last three weeks of the school year. She covers as much material in this as in preceding units, but it seems easier and more relaxed to her juniors because they are laughing. They end the class on a high note.

When your list is arranged, look it over again. Can you see logical divisions for grading periods and vacations? Carrying a unit over a testing period or vacation can be a real frustration for you and your students, so within each larger unit, think about how concepts might be rearranged. You might choose to teach a short, high-energy unit just before a vacation, saving that long, tough series of lessons on cell division or genetics for after vacation. You might teach a short novel between Thanksgiving and Christmas, completing the reading and analysis writing several days before vacation. Students then could use those last restless days for finishing projects or presenting skits based on the novel.

Once your list is arranged, make a copy to keep with your lesson plans. Glancing at it occasionally will show you that you are making progress and give you direction for the next unit. Remember that this list is revisable. During the year, if you think of a better time to teach a topic, make a note on your master list.

Section and Lesson Plans   Look carefully at your first unit. What specific concepts do you want your students to know at the end? Does this unit need to be divided into smaller sections with specific objectives for each section? How long do you expect each section to take? How will your text and other equipment support this objective? When you are planning a series of daily lessons to teach an objective for the first time, deliberately plan more than you expect you can finish. This way, if the students know more than you anticipated, or work more quickly than you estimated, they will still have a full period of work for practice and reinforcement. If the students are motivated and enthused about the unit and it stretches out a day longer than expected, the students will profit from the added practice.

Conversely, if you plan a one-hour lesson and the students finish quickly, you might have five or ten minutes of slack time at the end of the period. This slack time breeds discipline problems. It is not a time to get to know students personally through idle social chitchat. Few will quietly pick up a library book or rewrite an old essay. Fewer still will sit quietly and allow slower students a chance to catch up. Have a specific plan in mind for those moments at the end of the period. Planning ahead is the answer—the only answer. It is far easier to drop one or two activities when you can see time is running short than to do a ten-minute tap dance that doesn't relate to your main objective. Have related reading material available for students who finish early. Magazines and paperbacks work well. Other examples include supplemental activities like word searches, crossword puzzles, math games, or brain teasers. These are not for you to grade. They are simply for fun and enrichment.

Multiple Copies   If you need multiple copies, find out about your school's policy on duplicating. The school might require a 48-hour turnover time for duplication services or have facilities for self-service. Plan ahead, because copy machines frequently need service and are temporarily unavailable.

    If you duplicate a page out of a workbook that is copyrighted, be aware of the legal obligations involved with copyright. Be sure the publisher allows duplication, and note the source on each worksheet.

Supplementary Activities   Your planning time is precious. It may sound like a good idea to create a new review game and a new vocabulary worksheet for the next day. In reality, you have only so many hours in the day. You might make the game and worksheet eventually; just don't force yourself to complete the task all at once. Save some of these ideas for use in another unit. Meanwhile, many such activities for different subject areas are offered by educational publishers.

Evaluation Methods   As you plan your unit, plan your method of evaluation. It helps students to know how you will evaluate their work. If you plan an objective test, jot down possible questions under each objective of the unit. (You can make up the answer choices later.)

    Example: The three planets closest to the sun are . . .

            To support life, a planet must have . . .

    Be open about what kind of test you plan to give and mention possible questions as you teach. Writing down student questions and mentioning that the questions would make quality test items will give your students a feeling of control. Construct your tests to show what students *do* know rather than to catch them at what they *don't* know. (See the section on test-writing later in this chapter.)

Parallel Concepts   Tie the previous unit to the new one. Students learn better when they can see relationships between units. What might be an obvious connection to you is not to them. The less mature the students, the more difficult it is for them to see the connections. Find ways to help them discover the transitions. Point out the common elements in units. Charts can outline parallel concepts. When Betty finishes her unit on Emerson and Thoreau, she has students list all the beliefs of the transcendentalists on the board. Then she uses a different color of chalk to write the opposites, and introduces Herman Melville and the anti-transcendentalists.

Sometimes, when the connection between units is weak, or especially if two concepts in the two units are easily confused (meiosis and mitosis), you can deliberately *disconnect*. Tell the class that they have come to a new unit. Last week's material needs to be filed away in their notebooks and minds for later use, but for now you want them to start with a clean slate. Do a quick relaxation exercise. Change your voice tone momentarily or move to a different side of the room; use a clean board. A special poster or slide will focus interest. Sometimes a transition simply requires a statement that the agenda is changing.

Planning Lessons That Utilize Groups

All activities should move toward a goal. A variety of well-planned exercises may result in a noisy classroom, but this doesn't mean students aren't learning. Noisy students are usually involved and enthusiastic. We are a society that thrives on a variety of stimuli. Adults have limited attention spans; young students have even shorter ones. Attention spans shrink to milliseconds with the continual use of worksheets for drill and practice. Unless you are a natural speaker, avoid constant lecturing. Alter activities.

Working in groups should be a common practice in the classroom. Regardless of grade level or discipline, group work sets up situations where students are challenged to use higher levels of thinking and develop social skills. Businesses from banking to food service have indicated a need for individuals who can get along with others. Start with a few well-planned, short group activities until you feel comfortable with the process.

Group work allows students an opportunity to exchange ideas, listen to the opinions of others, collaborate on projects, and learn from one another. Students need specific guidelines for the task, their individual roles, how much time they have to complete the task, and how the group will be evaluated.

Enhancement of Social Skills

As you plan group activities, be aware that you need to teach or reinforce social skills. While we work toward making them second nature, listening, expressing opinions, and sharing materials are not innate.

When you set up groups, be sure you make them as heterogeneous as possible. You want to create groups that contain students of varied abilities. If a student has to explain something to another group member, he or she is synthesizing information. In addition, hearing others' ideas and opinions is stimulating. Everyone has unique strengths and weaknesses that can enhance group interaction. Consider personalities as you create your groups. Ideal group sizes range from two to four students. (Occasionally, you can allow students to choose whom they want to work with.)

After you have assigned students to their groups, think about necessary social skills. You could plan a brainstorming session for the first group activity. Have students discuss each social skill and describe what it will look like and sound like in your classroom if everyone is practicing that skill. For example, during group participation you might hear "I have an idea . . . " or "That is a good point." Desks would be in clusters around the room, and you will see people looking at each other and leaning forward as they talk.

Your role during group activities is to move around the room, meeting with the groups periodically, checking to make sure the students are on task, observing the students as they work, and answering questions. Watch for individuals who dominate the group or withdraw. Assigning roles helps to eliminate this problem. Question those who don't appear to be contributing. Offer encouragement to build self-confidence. Do not dominate the group yourself, but offer suggestions if students seem to be laboring too long over an issue. Often, a casual suggestion is all it takes to start the ball rolling. After the group has finished a task, have them evaluate how well they worked together. Ask them what went well and what they need to improve. This group processing will improve how the group functions on its next task.

Keys to Group Success

Keep in mind the following keys to group success.

- Tell the group how long they have to complete the task; also write this on the board or overhead. Assign one student as the timekeeper, whose responsibility is planning and utilizing time. Then, as you move around the room, consult with timekeepers about how the group is doing. This helps keep students on track when they've digressed from the topic.
- Assign one person as the scribe or secretary; this person's task is to write the information down or take notes on what the group discusses.
- Assign one person as the reporter. This person's task is to paraphrase or read the information to the rest of the class.
- Assign one student as the resource person. This individual's job is to gather the needed materials at the beginning of an activity, make sure the assignment is turned in, and supervise the cleanup at the end of the class period. The resource person doesn't have to do all the cleanup, just make sure the work space is clean. Another responsibility of the resource person is coming to you with questions after the group has exhausted their personal resources. Try to stress that your role is to answer questions only after everyone in the group has been consulted. Often one student in the group may have a question that another group member can answer. Students habitually consult only the teacher when they have questions. Help students learn from one another by encouraging them to consult each other.

Be sure to rotate the responsibilities during group sessions so each member has an opportunity to practice each role. The important thing is to insure individual participation and group achievement of the task.

Jerome Kagen and the team of Johnson and Johnson are among the many researchers involved in studying cooperative learning. Consult their publications for more information on forming groups, teaching social skills, and planning group activities (see Bibliography).

Students Teaching Students: A Large-Group Activity

There are some alternatives to the small-group techniques mentioned above. Here's an example of a large-group activity you might try when reviewing:

Divide the class into three equal groups, seating each group in its own large circle. Point out one student in each group to be called Number 1. Have the rest of the group number off consecutively until

Students Teaching Students Group Activity

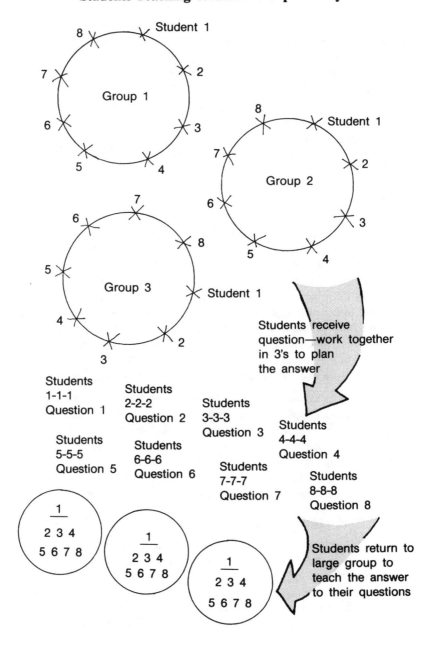

each student in the group has a different number. Then have the three Number 1's get together and figure out the answer to question 1 in their textbook on page 536, or whatever the task you've designed. The Number 2's answer question 2 on the same page, the Number 3's do 3 . . . . (You can create your own questions. Make sure the questions require some higher levels of thinking and more than a single-word answer.) Give the small groups a specific number of minutes (ten works effectively) to agree on the answer and take notes on what they want to say. The students then return to their large groups, and each one reads the assigned question and "teaches" the answer to the group. The rest take notes and ask questions for clarification.

As a teacher, your job is to establish the process, supervise it, and consult with small groups if they need extra help. Explain the whole process first and then walk the students through it step by step. It's fun circulating among the three groups and hearing echoes of the same information coming from three students simultaneously. This exercise creates high-intensity student involvement.

If you have one extra student, pair her or him with a classmate, or provide a separate question for that student to present to the whole class at the end of the group work. If you have two extra students, they can prepare a question together and decide which of them reports to the third group.

When planning group work, make sure that each member understands the assigned task and his or her individual role. Each member must participate in order for the group successfully to achieve the goal.

The Teachable Moment

That instant in time when students want to learn something significant related to the topic at hand can be the most exciting and rewarding. If you have the material they seek in your head or in a resource book in your room, you are lucky. Sometimes you are close enough to your media center with easy and flexible access that you can take your class right then and let them explore their own question. You can build future lessons on what your students found during their research.

Often, when students indicate an area they want to explore, the next day will still provide time to satisfy their curiosity. Betty's high school classes were viewing slides of American paintings. One student mentioned the price a Van Gogh had sold for the day before and asked why "that" was worth so much. It was a fair question. The class talked about art values, athletes' salaries, and Van Gogh. The students were fascinated by the man, so Betty brought in a short video on Van Gogh and his work. Since the focus of the class was American art and literature, she opened by emphasizing that Van Gogh was not American. The students urged Betty to start the film. Van Gogh surfaced in discussions until the last day of school. The students looked at and wrote about American artists with more interest and occasionally in comparison with Van Gogh.

Often you can inspire an unmotivated student if you adapt to include her or his personal interest. Help students locate information about these interests.

Robert had a youngster who wasn't enthused about what was going on in class. That same fall a number of spiders had entered the classroom after an early cold snap. The only thing that held Justin's attention was a spider floating from the ceiling toward an unsuspecting student. Seizing a teachable moment, Robert suggested that Justin check out a library book on spiders. Robert provided an opportunity for an unmotivated third-grader to become the class expert on spiders. Spiders made the study of math, science, and reading engaging while teaching a young student how to learn. Justin made up a multiplication game using spiders. He drew and measured webs, and he read stories, books, and articles about spiders. The teachable moment can brighten up a student's entire year!

Sometimes student interest can inspire you to present a short lecture, film, or discussion at the beginning of the next day's class period. You recognize a teachable moment and spend half the night using that idea to prepare for the next day. When you start the class with this material, however, don't be too surprised if the students take a "so what?" attitude. The teachable moment is gone. Sometimes it goes more quickly than that, even within minutes. Don't worry about it. If you can expand successfully on a teachable moment when it happens, enjoy the success. If you can't, stick with the original plan. Get that objective taught successfully and you will begin creating your own teachable moments.

Learning Styles

Knowledge about learning styles and how your charges learn helps you better plan lessons. You will learn to present lessons that appeal to a variety of learners so that you reach all your students, not just those who respond best to your teaching style. Telling students about how they learn gives them valuable control of their own learning plus a better understanding of those who assimilate differently. Students often aren't aware that they and their peers have a variety of learning styles. Check the Bibliography in this book for a list of some of the literature on learning styles. It is an intriguing topic with lots of day-to-day applications.

One year Barbara attended a seminar on learning styles. That year she had a large class of eighth-grade boys who babbled continuously. She tried separating them to the corners of the room; there were seven of them. She raised her voice; they didn't hear because they were talking. She tried moving them all to the back row where she wouldn't hearr them; they moved up front together and informed her they *had* to sit there.

One day, Barbara took time to tell the class about what she was reading about learning styles. She asked her students to fill out a short survey about what kinds of physical learning conditions they preferred. When she tabulated the results, Barbara found that the Babbling Seven preferred dim light. Sticking to her promise to pay attention to the surveys, she rearranged her seating chart to reflect bright/dim light and front/middle/back preferences. She had the janitor take out half of the fluorescent bulbs on the side of the room away from the windows and made him promise not to replace them. She placed the students in the new arrangement, with the Babbling Seven grouped together on the dim side of the room. Barbara made a point of mentioning that, since each student had personal seat preference, she expected positive student behavior as a result. Who had the most behavior improvement? Yes! All seven!

Several weeks later, Barbara divided the class into small groups for cooperative work and assigned each a section of the room. Suddenly the noise level rose, and Barbara's radar informed her that the loudest group was near the windows. She discovered that group had two of the Babbling Seven in it. Barbara movd the whole group to the dim side of the room, and work quietly resumed.

This story reflects only some of what's involved in learning styles.

Rita and Ken Dunn are among the researchers studying how students learn, and they have published some of their findings (see Bibliography).

Following are a few tips for helping students learn better.

Seating Position   Some youngsters need to sit in the front row so they can concentrate on you and not be distracted by watching others.

Some pupils need to sit in the back because it makes them feel safe when they see other students working on the same task.

Tactile Learning   Some students are very tactile. They need to manipulate something to help them remember. These youngsters will take volumes of notes, chew pencils, hair, or jewelry, scribble in margins, or draw. There is a fine line between doodling-and-listening and doodling-when-tuned-out. Asking the student to summarize the current topic will keep him or her focused on the lecture.

Continual Talking   Barbara had another student who talked continually. Everyone else thought this student was an airhead. That label made Barbara angry, so she started listening carefully. The talk almost always verbalized what was happening in class. Barbara moved the young girl into the front corner of the room where she could snag the student's attention when she needed it, surrounded the student with others who didn't mind extra noise, and let her talk. The young student's grades and self-confidence increased.

Physical Movement   Some youngsters need lots of movement. This movement can be in the form of stray trips to the pencil sharpener, wastebasket, or writing files. Be tolerant of this movement, but, at the same time, teach students that there are times when it is *not* appropriate to budge: during a lecture, student presentation, film, or assignment directive. On days you know students will be restless (Homecoming, Halloween, the days before vacations, assemblies), plan movement even if it involves just moving in and out of small groups. You might schedule a 30-second wiggle-and-stretch every so often. Have students stand, reach for the stars, touch their toes, and shake out their arms.

Time of Day   Students are affected by the time of day. One reason kids-at-risk sometimes fail at day school is that they are at their best in the evening and might be more successful in night school. Since most students have little choice about when they meet a class, you might teach them coping techniques:

- Consciously take more notes in frustrating classes and work with a study-buddy.
- Make an appointment for a few moments of tutoring with the teacher during a better learning time.
- Identify ideal learning times (people usually have to discover their ideal times through their own experience).
- Study for the hardest classes at the best learning time.
- Study in half-hour segments.

A class taken during a student's weaker learning time is *not* an excuse for failing. It should be viewed as a situation for using other learning techniques to overcome this weakness. When a student is aware of her or his learning strengths, this knowledge can make the difference.

Room Temperature   Room temperature will affect some students and not others. Move students who prefer warmth away from windows, doors, and fans. If a student is consistently cold, encourage him or her to store a sweater in the room. A consistently hot student usually sits between the door and windows or near a fan. Encourrage students to dress appropriately for their individual preferences. You can also ask students not to complain because there is often very little control you can exert over the climate of your room. They have more control by altering their dress.

Eating and Drinking   Some students learn better when they eat as they work. You may agree with the concept in theory but still not want students eating or drinking in your classroom. You might find it distracting and, inevitably, you will end up with half-filled soda cans, wrappers, and unattended gum. Your school may or may not have a rule about eating in the classroom. If there is no school rule, your personal desires prevail. The noise and distractions of sharing food detract from the learning. Brian has the rule in his classroom that if a student needs to eat, she or he must be discreet and not leave garbage behind. If Brian can't see or hear the food, it doesn't bother him.

Classroom Arrangement   How you arrange your classroom can reflect your teaching style as well as your students' learning styles. Sometimes the subject matter dictates the arrangement, but if not, you might arrange the desks in rows, a large circle, or groups. Room arrangements reflect the type of lesson to be taught. Keep in mind that walking into a rearranged room will distress some students. If you want to startle students and capture their attention with the novelty, don't tell them before you rearrange. If you don't want them distracted by the new arrangement, warn them the day before.

Auditory vs. Visual Learning   When Betty was a third-grader, she had a teacher who would give her class an oral math problem every day (3 + 2 x 7 – 4 . . .). The student who got the answer first went to lunch before anyone else. Betty never went to lunch first that year, but she did get the message that she was not good at math. In high school, Betty could never figure out why she scored so high on the math sections of standardized tests, since she believed she was weak in that area. She knows now that she is capable in math; she is just not a strong auditory learner—she doesn't learn well when she only listens. She needs to repeat, take notes, or read along as she listens.

You will have similar learners in your classes. Help them learn material you present orally by writing important points, short questions, or problems on the board as you speak. Or distribute handouts containing the oral problems or material so your poor auditory learners can read along as you speak.

Other students remember everything they hear, but have problems comprehending what they read. These students might need to take notes as they read or underline in books they own. These students will ask you what you mean by a certain question on a test. All you do is read the question aloud without explanation, and they will say, "Oh, yeah, I get it now." Read test directions aloud as students read them silently and explain that this technique supports both auditory and visual learners.

Global vs. Analytic Learning   Learning-style researchers also study brain dominance or brain preference. Here's a quick inventory to do with your students to find out if they are global or analytic learners:

"I'm going to describe two approaches to the same situation. When I finish, I'm going to ask which approach is more like you and then tell you what that says about you as a learner.

"When we are hiking in Yellowstone, my husband will suddenly point and say, 'Look at that owl in the tree.' I look in that direction and see the forest, the sky, and the meadow in front. Then, slowly, I will be able to pick out the brown bird deep in the branches of one of the trees.

My husband sees the owl first. Then he will notice the trees, the sky, and the meadow.

"Now what kind of learner are you? Do you see the forest first, then the details? Or do you first see the detail and then notice everything else?"

Explain that those "forest-seers" are global learners and like overviews and large concepts. Those "detail folks" are more analytic and want the facts in the proper order and don't really care about the big picture. Emphasize that both are equally acceptable approaches to learning and then structure lessons that give assignment choices so that both global and analytic learners will feel comfortable doing the work.

Cindy Ulrich of Seattle, Washington, has published a very readable, usable book on this topic of global and analytical learners called *No Sweat!*

Assignment/Response Balance   Some students work and learn best in groups where they can talk, share ideas, plan together, and present group projects. Others abhor these experiences and become stressed; you might allow these students to work by themselves on some assignments. If the objective of the assignment, however, is to improve group skills, present the leesson and explain that all have to participate to get credit for the assignment. Make the next assignment an "alone" project to balance.

This balance among types of assignments is also applicable to student responses. To give variety to your classes and give students with different styles and talents a chance to shine, responses could alternately be written, presented orally, illustrated, or student-planned.

Overall Balance   Another researcher in the learning-styles field worth noting is Bernice McCarthy, who developed the 4MAT system. The theory is that, in the course of a unit or lesson, every major learning style should be utilized, therefore appealing to every student in the class. McCarthy's books are helpful in planning lessons. This is a system you might want to look at if you have gained some teaching experience and are ready to begin reading about learning styles.

Alter the presentation of your lessons so students have a variety of stimuli. Provide visuals or manipulatives where appropriate. Encourage note-taking and allow time for students to assimilate information covered. One technique that allows this review is to stop the lesson at intervals during a lecture, video, or reading assignment. Then have each student, with a partner, verbally summarize what has just been covered,

How Do You Learn Best?

Put an *X* on the continuum that best represents you.

	Sound	
lots	doesn't matter	silence

	Light	
bright	doesn't matter	dim

	Front/Back	
front	doesn't matter	back

	Food	
yes	doesn't matter	no

	Time of Day	
early	middle of the morning	afternoon

—Ronda Konst
Hillside Jr. High
Boise, Idaho

draw a diagram of the material, make a list of important points, or brainstorm a list of key vocabulary.

Variety in the Day's Lesson

We hope, as you read through specific suggestions in this book, you have noticed that we always try to offer a variety of ideas to appeal to all types of learners and teachers. Rule Number 1 in choosing teaching ideas is that if you feel awkward or uncomfortable doing an activity that has worked for someone else, don't do it. One year, Barbara shared a room with a male teacher also new to that grade level. He would prep at his desk in the back of the room while Barbara taught. Then, the next period, he would teach the same lesson (which was fine with Barbara), but he couldn't figure out why Barbara's jokes and explanations didn't work when he repeated them. Their styles just weren't compatible.

Here are some ideas for structuring a class period using a variety of teaching strategies.

Start with a short activity to focus on the lesson. This activity should engage every student. It could be a five-point quiz, a cartoon or phrase on the board to discuss, an open-ended question to which each student must prepare a response, or a brainstorm of current knowledge about a subject. Have each student write the response in a journal or notebook. As soon as you finish roll, you could walk around the room and record points or a check for every written response. This keeps the students accountable and gives you a starting point for the day's discussion. Brian frequently walks into his government class, newspaper in hand, and asks, "How many of you read the story this morning about . . . ?" Soon a majority of the students are skimming the newspaper before arriving in order to have a contribution to this opening conversation.

After stimulating interest, present the day's lesson. This might involve note-taking, the first explanation of the essay, or the introduction of the new concept. Take time to give students concrete examples of what you expect them to do with this new knowledge. This is an opportunity for you to demonstrate your own expertise in your subject area. Language arts teachers read their original writing sample. Music teachers play the proper rhythm pattern. Math teachers work through a difficult problem on the board while explaining orally how they are solving the problem. Physical education teachers exhibit proper form for setting a volleyball into play. Plan small group activities or work time that provides reinforcement of the concept, and allow students to demonstrate their understanding of the concept. In the last minutes of the class, call students back into a whole group. Have students review what they accomplished that day, mentioning assignments and upcoming due dates. Comment on good work habits or an especially creative project that the whole class will see the next day.

Within each day and within each unit, try to plan for something to strain the brain, something to smile over, an excuse to move, and a reason for one student to talk to another about school. Plan an exacting assignment for your analytical students and a creative assignment to appeal to your right-brained, global students. Try to vary activities at 20-minute intervals.

One thing many teachers feel they never have enough of in their lessons is *think time*. "Take two minutes to think quietly about the bizarre relationships among characters in 'The Fall of the House of Usher.'" After these two minutes, students may record their thoughts in journals. These thoughts could provide a focus activity for the next day's lesson. Teachers often get so busy occupying every minute of class that students do not get time to ponder what they are learning. Of course, there's a Catch-22 to "think time": Is the student really thinking about Roderick Usher's relationship with Madeline, or is he musing on last week's dance? Making the student accountable usually keeps him or her on task.

Thoughts on Journals

The use of student journals, while widespread, is often a perplexing topic. Student journals/logs can range from a few pages stapled together, to spiral notebooks of varying sizes, to cloth-bound blank books purchased at the local bookstore. The following suggestions are made for this learning tool.

The journal of a kindergarten student might be a wallpaper-covered book with pages that the student fills with symbolic representations of thoughts and feelings. These might include pictures of houses, family members, or drawings of classroom plants in various stages of growth.

As children become more competent readers and writers, the symbols begin to take on the appearance of conventional writing. Primary students use their journals to respond to daily occurrences in and out of the classroom. If students have just returned from a field trip, the teacher might ask them to write and draw their observations. The next day the journal may be used to respond to a different topic or question. The teacher may write comments in each child's journal or direct students to exchange with classmates for reading and responding.

From upper elementary grades through high school, students begin using separate journals for each subject. These notebooks may be called thinking, reading, or observation logs, and they are instrumental in developing critical thinking skills and writing fluency.

Regardless of the subject, journals/logs may be used in the following ways:

- Beginning or ending a class period. A phrase, problem, or question relating to the day's objective may be written on the overhead or board. Writing on this topic serves to focus every student. Students may be asked to share responses occasionally or the teacher may collect them at intervals. Students earn a completion grade, mark, or points for this writing. Asking students to write a summary-response to the day's lesson allows them to collect and review their thoughts about the material.

- During a lesson. Logs may be used for note taking, problem solving, idea summarizing, or reflecting on a topic. Ideas may be generated for essays, poems, or future assignments. Student writers might predict an outcome of a science experiment or the next chapter. Student journals/logs provide an opportunity for students to think and respond at their various levels.

Occasionally calling for journals holds students accountable and dignifies each individual's thoughts without judgement. *Inside Out* offers helpful insights about setting up and using student journals. Books that would be helpful for elementary teachers include *Transitions* and *Assessment and Evaluation in Whole Language Programs*.

No matter how a journal is used, teachers must always respect student privacy. No journal entry should be shared with anyone without a student's permission. However, when teachers first introduce journal writing to the class, they must explain that instructors are bound by law to report illegal occurrences or life-threatening situations. See Chapter 7 for more on legal considerations.

Planning Lessons

Studies suggest that experienced and novice teachers spend about the same amount of time planning for lessons, but experienced teachers do a great deal of that planning in their heads and write little, while novice

LESSON PLANS   WEEK OF March 4-8   TEACHER Betty H.

		Senior Lit 1st 2nd 3rd	Junior English 4th & 6th	SUBJ OR CLASS
MON		Urban folk tales – why? society implications Other myths Intro to Homer & The Iliad	(Faulkner) Discuss "a Rose for Emily" Break into small groups – ½ to prepare a reader's theatre ½ groups prepare a visual	MONDAY
Tues	Faculty meeting 7 am Library	Oral reading and discussion Writing style Plot in epic poetry drawing – setting	Present group products reinforce vocabulary prewriting / brainstorm for essay How does Faulkner demonstrate regionalism through his characters?	TUESDAY
Wed		Small group work – each has a different question or task – work time	Library research time on Faulkner – Librarian to show how to use <u>Short Story Index</u> Assign reading "The Hound"	WEDNESDAY
Thurs	Parent Conference after school 3:15 Counselor's Bring Billy's wtg folder	– Present to class Discussion Asking why… + what if… questions	Discuss – "Hound." – info from Library – progress on essays reinforce vocabulary	THURSDAY
Fri	Curriculum planning 4 pm – usual place	finish questions Speculate about what comes next Quiet reading time	Essays due Due monday vocab quiz Small group → on How are Faulkner, O'Connor, Steinbeck & Anderson related – present findings	FRIDAY

teachers write volumes. Teaching from either type of lesson plan is equally effective, so don't let the sketchy or voluminous lesson plan books of colleagues intimidate you. Find out what works for you.

Most schools provide some sort of lesson plan book for the teacher. You might decide that the space provided in each block is not enough for your needs. An alternative might be a spiral notebook or looseleaf binder to keep track of daily lessons. Plan to keep this record for next year. Your old lesson plans will save you hours of new planning time, plus provide a pacing guide through the year's units.

Write your lesson plans in pencil. Don't consider any plan cast in stone or you will drive yourself crazy long before your retirement party. Be willing to change plans based on student needs, your instincts about the learning process, and outside distractions.

Here's a step-by-step approach that can help you plan lessons:

1. Think over the whole unit and estimate how many days the unit will take. Pencil this information into your lesson plans.
2. Think about major assignments within the unit and the evaluation at the end. How many different assignments will you give? Will the culminating activity be a test, an essay, or a group project? What will be graded?
3. Next, consider how first to capture students' attention and focus it on the topic and how to get students to become aware of what they already know about the topic.
4. Finally, decide what you are going to do day by day, writing your decisions in pencil. Try to formulate fairly comprehensive plans a week in advance. This advance planning makes sure the materials you need are at hand. If you work closely with special-services teachers, you can send them an overview of your upcoming lessons so they can help their at-risk students in your classes meet assignment deadlines.
5. By Wednesday, there will probably be arrows in your plan book, indicating a part of a lesson that got moved to another day because of time restrictions or because students were not ready for that activity. Just because you have the week planned doesn't mean things will always go that way. Be flexible and allow for modifications.

When you are writing the plans for the individual days of your unit, it helps to write what you expect your students to be able to do at the top of each lesson. This will keep you focused on the task of working through the unit's concepts in a logical order. On the day you teach that lesson, tell the students your learning goal at the beginning of the session.

If you have a wonderful activity in mind, but it does not fit any specific learning objective for that unit, save the activity for another lesson. Decide what you want to teach, how to pace that material in steps the students are capable of accomplishing, and what specific activities will teach and then reinforce those concepts.

Lesson planning might include the specific dialogue and details you want to cover in your introduction. If you think about all the things you want to say, then actually write them down, you need only to refer to your notes for quick cues and your introduction will appear rehearsed and polished, thus adding to your credibility. Many teachers also include a long list of questions to help lead discussions on assigned reading material. Using Bloom's taxonomy or another schema showiing levels of cognitive thinking from recall to evaluation, write out three or more questions on the material at each thinking level. As the discussion progresses, encourage students to formulate their own questions. Even if you don't then use every one, the original questions in your lesson plans can be invaluable in making sure the discussion covers all the concepts in your learning objective. Use these planned questions adroitly. Address all levels of questions to all students.

Creative Assignments—Beyond the Text

Many new textbooks include sections suggesting creative responses to the units or chapters. Skits, science experiments, genre changes, art projects, interviews, and role-playing are just some of the methods that assess learning and offer alternatives to written assignments or tests. Although students need first to be able to understand the material being presented, these creative enrichment assignments often help students relate the material to their own lives, and that increases retention.

Especially in your first few years of teaching, you may feel safer avoiding assignments that are loud, messy, or less structured. Many of these activities occur in groups; having guidelines will help provide a sense of structure. If these projects still make you feel uncomfortable, integrate them gradually into your plans, beginning with smaller blocks of time and smaller projects. Although you should not execute an assignment you're uncomfortable with ("All the other teachers are doing it" is not reason enough to present an assignment), you will need to choose a variety of activities to accommodate learning differences.

Less traditional activities can be highly rewarding for you and your students. Start by doing one creative project in conjunction with a unit

Fairy Tales "à la Poe"

Name	Poe-like Vocabulary	Interest	Similarity to Original Tale	Original-ity	Poe-like tone, Feeling	Total

you feel comfortable teaching. Try an assignment a colleague has used successfully. He or she can give you exact directions, warnings about pitfalls, and examples of finished products. This person can also give you hints about grading and involving students in the evaluation process. If you notice something creative happening in another classroom, don't hesitate to ask that teacher about the assignment. "I really like what your class is doing. How do you think it would work in my class?" Your colleague will be complimented.

Student-Evaluated Creative Assignments

A creative language-arts assignment might follow a study of the stories of Edgar Allan Poe, always a student favorite. Talk to students about "voice" in writing—what word choice and word patterns make a story obviously Poe's? This is a difficult concept for students. When they do understand, they will be able to demonstrate it by writing fairy tales in the voice of Poe. Students will be eager to hear other versions of familiar tales, so you might invest a whole class period reading the results. At the same time, create a situation where every student must actively listen to each tale. As each reads, remaining students list the reader's name on a score sheet and then award 1 to 5 points in various categories. In the right column, students total points as each reader finishes, circling any score above 20. Students then turn in these score sheets, and class choices receive special recognition from peers. Your score (usually close to their average) determines the grade. See the example on page 93.

The same student scoring procedure could be used for a social studies assignment to write a poem reflecting the feelings of women or children left behind in wartime. In science, such a class evaluation could be applied to skits about a scientist's life or speculation about the role of science in the future. You need only to make the assignment, model a possible response to help students understand the assignment, and decide what categories will be scored. This scoring system, with criteria changed to suit the assignment, can hold every student accountable during student oral presentations.

A science class might also engage in a project that utilizes student evaluation. When discussing genetic engineering, the future, and pre-dicted food shortages, you might assign either individuals or groups the task of planning how they could modify bacteria to break down cellulose into a usable food source. The rest of the students could then evaluate

Special Award

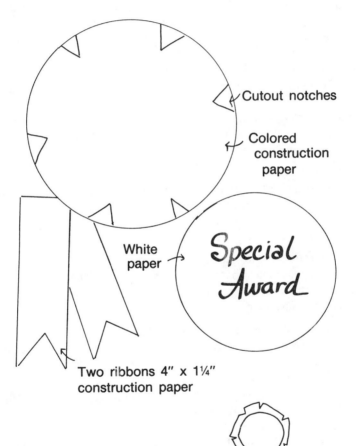

Cutout notches

Colored construction paper

White paper

Special Award

Two ribbons 4" x 1¼" construction paper

each plan according to plausibility, creativity, efficiency, scientific accuracy, and commercial possibility.

Interpretive Posters

These creative approaches to assignments often help students make personal meaning out of a difficult concept. American History students often struggle with the colloquial language of the Declaration of Independence. You might ask students to choose one sentence or phrase from the document that has personal meaning for them. Hand each student a 12 x 18 sheet of drawing paper and haul out the scissors, glue, crayons, and box of discarded magazines. Each student writes the phrase on the paper and interprets feelings in a magazine-clip-art collage. Hang these in your classroom. Take time after the posters are hung to point out each poster to the class while repeating the phrase, stating the poster-maker's name and something you like or noticed about the collage.

Grades on these posters might be based on:

- being in on time;
- following directions (phrase on front, name and period on back); and
- interpretation of the chosen phrase.

Award Ribbons

A creative way to recognize or reward students' endeavors is with handmade construction-paper ribbons. You can use the sample on page 95 and the following directions to make construction-paper awards in any color combination.

1. Cut a five-inch circle out of construction paper. A collection of plastic lids from coffee cans, jars, and oatmeal boxes is convenient for drawing circles and safer than compasses. Cut five or six half-inch-deep v-notches around the edge of the paper circle.
2. Cut a three-inch circle of white paper. On this circle you can print award names, student names, and/or dates. Use a calligraphy pen to add a flair to the printing.
3. You might also cut a four-inch circle of aluminum foil or wrapping paper to put between the background color and the white circle. A glitter stick could add the same accent.
4. Cut two rectangles of colored paper, each four inches long and one to one and a quarter inches wide. Deeply notch one end of each.
5. Layer and glue the circles on top of one another. Glue the ribbon-rectangles so they hang from the bottom.

Any age group likes these simple recognition awards. You will see them still carefully preserved in lockers or writing folders at the end of the year.

Borrowing from Other Teachers

Using other teachers' lesson plans, project ideas, and worksheets can be a real time-saver if you use these materials judiciously. First, these borrowed items must suit your content objectives, your teaching needs, and your teaching style. You'll probably borrow a basic idea and modify it to match your classes. Write the name of the source person on any handouts or notes that you keep in your file. This way, if you want more background information about the assignment, you know whom to consult.

Sharing lesson Ideas

Giving public credit to the originator also pleases that person, who will then probably be more likely to share other tidbits of information with you. Writing the author's name on any reproduced material acknowledges copyright. Borrowing is using bits and pieces from others to create a lesson that reflects your personality and teaching style.

Borrowing also implies giving something back. Keep ideas that worked successfully in class tucked away in your mind to share with others. "I used this film and activity today, but the film does not have to be returned until Wednesday. Do you want to use it?" More experienced teachers do not know it all and welcome fresh ideas from new teachers to add spark to traditional topics. New teachers haven't had time to accumulate an inventory of successful activities and are pleased when veteran colleagues share their tried-and-true ideas with them. Some departments/grade levels hold occasional noon hour sandwich meetings where each teacher brings along the description of one assignment that worked well. Everyone leaves feeling rejuvenated with several fresh approaches to tempt their students. If no such group exists, start one. An interdepartmental or multigrade group might prove especially stimulating.

Sub Folder

Every teacher should maintain a substitute-teacher folder and keep it in a prominent place for emergencies. Usually you will know when you are too sick to teach another day or that you have professional leave the next day. In these cases, leave detailed lesson plans for your sub that reinforce the current unit.

Sub folders are for emergencies when you don't have a way of getting that day's assignment onto your desk before the sub arrives. You might lack the energy to call even your best friend at 6 A.M. and dictate an assignment in a dripping, raspy voice. You'll need an alternative plan.

Many schools print a two-pocket folder with school rules, a spot for a schedule, and a few advertisements on it. This makes an ideal sub folder. Add a bright red label on the front with the designation "SUB FOLDER," your name, and your room number.

Inside include a map of the school, a fire evacuation route map, your class or daily schedule, a list of students who attend special classes, your classroom rules, discipline referral forms, a notation about the hall pass policy, the location of your school policy manual, and current seating charts. (When you make out a new seating chart, make a copy and put it into your sub folder.) Also, include a form that helps the substitute teacher detail what happened in class that day. If your school does not provide such a sheet, you may wish to prepare and include your own. Next, include a brief directory, telling the names of neighboring teachers and the location of the restrooms, the vice-principals' offices, and the cafeteria.

If the sub is unable to carry out your original plans, include details for an alternative lesson. This should be a one-day unit, general enough to be appropriate at any time, but relevant to your subject or grade. The sub need only announce that your absence was an unplanned emergency and that she or he is presenting a one-day unit. The sub should tell the students that there will be a quiz on the material the following day. This holds students accountable and reduces discipline problems for the substitute. When you do return, act quickly to address discipline problems or acknowledge good behavior. Try to make time once each grading quarter to change this emergency assignment to match more closely the curriculum you are studying.

A Note from the Sub

TODAY WE WERE ABLE TO ACCOMPLISH ————————

————————————————————————————

————————————————————————————

I THOUGHT THESE THINGS WENT WELL ————————

————————————————————————————

I THOUGHT THE PLANS WERE ————————————

————————————————————————————

THESE THINGS NEED YOUR ATTENTION ————————

————————————————————————————

COMMENTS ————————————————————

————————————————————————————

SIGNED ——————————————————————

Substitute Teacher

Class Summary

Name _____

Date _____

Return to Office at End of Day

Class Period	Absences	Tardies	Cooperative Students

1. Place all papers, assignments, and notices in the regular teacher's mailbox.
2. Sign the "Claim for Substitute" form in the main office *before leaving the building*.

Lesson Plans Adequate _____
Lesson Plans Inadequate _____
Substitute Folder Complete _____
Substitute Folder Incomplete _____

Uncooperative Students	Lesson Plan carried out as Follows	Specific comments and/or Suggestions

3. Please return to main office at the end of the day. Thank you for your cooperation.

Substitute Teacher Resource Note

Welcome to our classroom. I appreciate having you fill in for me while I am gone, and I hope this information will help you.

If you have any questions, don't hesitate to ask our

principal, _____, or the secretary, _____ .

_____ in room _____ would also be happy to help.

YOU WILL FIND:
LESSON PLANS _____

SUBSTITUTE FOLDER _____

CLASS SCHEDULE _____

SEATING CHART _____

DISCIPLINE PLAN _____

TEACHER'S MANUALS _____

EMERGENCY EVACUATION ROUTE _____

ANY SPECIAL INSTRUCTIONS _____

_____

Thank you again for your help.

_____
Classroom teacher

Writing Tests

Contrary to what students believe, teachers do not create tests to use up time or seek vengeance. Content testing is an important part of the total curriculum. Test results provide measures of progress for the student, the teacher, and the parent. Tests also provide information about concepts mastered or those that require review, and they close out a unit.

Test writing should be viewed as a continuous process. No test is perfect; there is always room for revision from year to year.

The best time to begin your test is when you plan the unit. As you list your objectives and decide how to teach the material, consider what kind of test you intend to administer.

If you are teaching a lab science, a lab test is more valid than one requiring a pen or pencil. A music class evaluation could include performance or listening, and a writing class is best judged by a writing assignment rather than a mechanics worksheet.

Once you have listed the major concepts you wish to test, and have decided on the test form, begin listing possible questions; don't worry about the answers at this time. For each concept, list five to ten questions. The number of questions should be directly proportionate to the time spent on the concept. All of your test items should address the areas you have emphasized in class. If you produce more questions than you need for the test, save the extras for make-up exams or file them for next year's test revision.

When you begin typing your exam, head the test clearly, and provide a name space if students are to write on the test paper. Make sure the directions are specific. If necessary, write statements about the use of dictionaries, notes, or study cards. Let students know how much each question or section is worth. Type the test so it is easy for students to read. Your test should appear professional and businesslike. Word processors make test writing easier because of quick-indent keys, spell checks, and storage ability. Rewriting tests, creating make-up tests, and creating alternate versions of a test are made easier by the computer's memory and blocking functions.

Group similar questions together (true-false; short answer; multiple choice; essay; matching).

A source for unit and chapter tests might be publisher-prepared tests available with your textbook. Use these with discretion. Look them over carefully. Often the questions violate the basic test-writing techniques mentioned below. Students will be able to pick out the correct answer from the design. Take the test yourself and make sure that the test covers each important item or concept. It is usually most appropriate to use some of these prepared questions on your exam and mix them with original questions of your own that reflect what you emphasized in class.

Multiple Choice   When typing multiple-choice questions, be sure the questions are grammatically correct and the answer choices parallel.

Here is an example of a poorly written multiple-choice test question:

The three planets closest to the sun are:

A. Mars Mercury and Pluto [Needs punctuation.]
B. Saturn but not Mercury. [Items are not grammatically parallel.]
C. Mercury, Venus, and Earth. [This correct answer supports use of the mnemonic device *My Very Efficient Mother* that science teachers often employ to help students remember these facts.]
D. not able to sustain life. [Not parallel to the other answer possibilities in content.]

A better version of this test example is:
The three planets closest to the sun are:

A. Mars, Mercury, and Pluto.
B. Saturn, Mercury, and Venus.
C. Mercury, Venus, and Earth.
D. Mars, Mercury, and Venus.

Your next question could then address the concept of which planets support life.

Be aware of common multiple-choice test-writing pitfalls that give the answer away to test-smart students whether they know the content or not.

1. If one distractor is noticeably longer than the others, it is often the answer.
2. The correct answer is frequently in the fourth or third position.
3. If you use a fifth distractor only occasionally, and it is "all of the above," it is often the answer.
4. If you use one silly, nonsense distractor because you can't think of four legitimate distractors, you give your students a 25 percent gift. A legitimate purpose for this might be to relieve test stress.
5. If you include material not covered in class as an answer possibility, students will know it is not the answer.

Some multiple-choice test sections start by listing all of the possible answers. Directions instruct students to use these answers in responding to all the questions in the section. For example:

Use the following 5 answers to respond to the first 20 questions on your Chapter 2 chemistry test:

A. hydrogen sulfide
B. sulphur dioxide
C. ammonia
D. hydrogen peroxide
E. iron oxide

Students find it frustrating to have to refer back constantly from each question to the list of answers, so we advise you to avoid this type of multiple-choice test construction. It is especially difficult for slower students. If you do choose to use this format, be sure to write directions clearly and state that answers can be used more than once. If this section of the test goes beyond one page, relist the five responses at the top of each new page.

True-False   Certain factors affect the best guessing odds on true-false test sections.

1. Teachers traditionally include more true than false items, so guessing true gives the student better than 50 percent odds for a correct answer.
2. Words like *always, never,* and *only* mark false questions.
3. Words like *something, usually,* and *mostly* mark true statements.

True-false tests can be frustrating for students when:

1. the test writer makes all the items true or all the items false. Patterns like these are easier for students to figure out and allow them to get points without displaying knowledge.
2. a minor detail, name, or reversed date is inserted to make the item false. This technique tests visual discrimination rather than knowledge.
3. typographical errors or poorly constructed sentences cause confusion.
4. students are asked to mark true statements with anything other than the word *true* (+, x) or *false* (–, o). Instead of accepting symbols, require that the students write out the words *true* and *false.* This forestalls the clever youngster who uses the tr-alse (⨍), a letter than can serve as *T* or *F*

as needed. If you find the letters quicker to check than the word, you might prefer that students write only a *T* or *F*. If so, make it very clear to students that you will need to distinguish easily between the two letters, and if you can't, that the answer will be marked incorrect.

Matching   When you are constructing matching sections, it's best if each column contains no more than ten items. If you have more items than ten to put into a matching format, create two or more sections. Each section could focus on a different type of information: vocabulary, terminology, or dates, for example. In the directions, tell students whether every answer can be used only once or if it can be used more often.

Fill-in-the-Blank   These items are difficult for students and especially frustrating for those susceptible to test jitters. Fill-in-the-blank items may test memorization more than knowledge. Decide what you are actually testing. If you are testing memorization ability, give the students practice working with these kinds of items before they experience their first graded test.

Essay annd Short-Answer Questions   These require different types of student responses. Short-answer items test student recall and are similar to fill-in-the-blank. Clearly state how many responses will earn credit: "Give 3 examples . . . ". Directions should state whether complete sentences are required or not and how many points will be awarded for the content and how many points will be deducted for mechanical/ spelling errors. Before you assign an essay question on a test, write out an answer to your own question. By definition, an essay question requires a response in a sentence, a paragraph, or paragraphs. If you have a hard time producing an answer yourself that you are satisfied with, rewrite the question.

Essay questions test three skills simultaneously: knowledge, organization, and writing skills. If you do not wish to evaluate spelling/ mechanical/writing skills, ask for the information in the form of a diagram, drawing, list, or outline. If you want your students to write strong essay responses, you have to write clear, thought-provoking questions and teach students how to write the essay.

During a review session, or in a separate lesson on how to write essay responses, show students what you expect to see in a full-point answer. List verbs normally used in essay questions in your content area and discuss what each verb means. For example:

illustrate—give examples or actually draw the response.

define—without using the original word, write an extended description.

tell—use a conversational, narrative style.

explain—give three or more examples.

trace—arrange the response in chronological order.

list—give information in a column.

outline—use formal outlining techniques.

conclude—give arguments and lead up to the final statement.

summarize—give a broad overview of the main points.

compare—tell the similarities.

contrast—discuss the differences.

identify—give characteristics that make the concepts different or related.

Have students practice writing topic sentences in response to the various verbs.

To teach organizational skills, you might give students a scrambled list including broad topics and supporting details that are related. Students then organize these phrases, identifying broad topics and details in preparation for writing. Page 109 shows a sample of this type of exercise, with suggested answers filled in.

You might teach students to do "thumbnail outlines." After they read the essay question, they should scribble ideas in a small box that they draw to the side of the writing area. Next, they go back through that list and number the ideas in the order of importance. Now they are ready to begin the writing of the essay response. If students are faced with several essay questions and little writing time, creating these small "thumbnail outlines" can show a teacher that the ideas were there, but the student did not have time to complete the response. This alone might earn some points, where a completely blank space will earn none.

If you want to give a mid-term or semester test that includes essay responses, but there is little time between the testing time and when grades are due, you could:

1. administer the essay portion of the exam a week early so you have ample grading time. Give the objective portion during the formal testing period. Administering the essay portion early might be incentive for students to study seriously for the objective test.

(continued on page 111)

Organizing Data

Junk Food: What is good about it and what is bad?

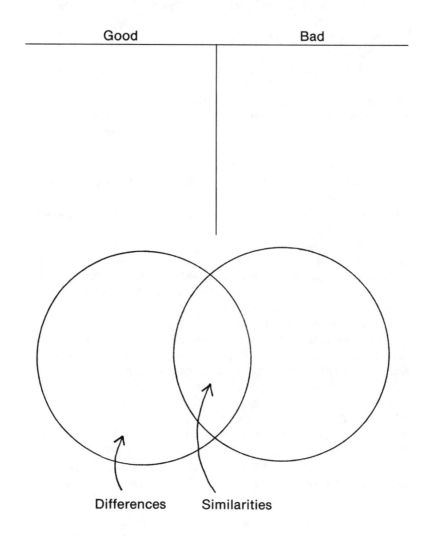

Good	Bad

Differences   Similarities

How are grasshoppers and crayfish alike and different?

Essay Practice

This exercise demonstrates how to organize your ideas in preparation for writing an essay answer. Mixed in the two columns below are a main heading, three subtopics, and a variety of details that relate to those subtopics. Two pieces of information do not fit at all.

Identify the main topic of this list. Write it down. Next identify the three subtopics and list them as A, B, and C, with spaces in between, below the main topic. Then go through the lists again and put each detail under its correct subtopic heading. Remember that two do not fit at all.

Can't write an essay answer
Fear of dogs
Bad traffic
Anxious about grades
Parents worry about their
 children
Health problems
Classical music
Anxious about a new job
Did not study enough
Afraid of losing love
Will children be successful
 as adults?
Will the child be popular?
Afraid of tests

Parents are afraid for chil-
 dren's safety
Lack of preparation for a
 test
Stress happens to everyone
Marriage and divorce
Afraid of meeting new
 people
Don't know how to take
 tests
Pizza with mushrooms
Catch the panic bug from
 other students
Whom does stress affect
 and how?

(continued)

Main topic: *Whom does stress affect and how?*

    A. *Stress happens to everyone*
        Health problems
        Anxious about a new job
        Afraid of losing love
        Marriage and divorce
        Afraid of meeting new people
    B. *Parents worry about their children*
        Parents are afraid for children's safety
            Fear of dogs
            Bad traffic
        Will children be successful as adults?
        Will the child be popular?
    C. *Afraid of tests*
        Can't write an essay answer
        Anxious about grades
        Did not study enough
        Lack of preparation for a test
        Don't know how to take tests
        Catch the panic bug from other students

    After you have your outline set up, you are ready to build each section into a paragraph and each detail into a sentence. Don't forget to add your introduction and concluding sentence.

2. require that responses be in the form of lists, drawings, outlines, or maps rather than paragraphs.
3. have students write in paragraph form, but circle the main idea and underline supporting details.

Creating Test Versions

Essay tests are not especially conducive to cheating, but objective tests are. Giving two versions of the test curtails this problem. You will want both versions to test the same concepts, yet you do not want to spend hours of time creating two entirely different instruments. Here are some quick ways to produce second versions.

1. If you begin with a matching section followed by a multiple-choice section, put the multiple-choice section first in the second version.
2. If you have more than one matching section, reverse their placement in the test.
3. Reverse the test, question for question, and renumber.
4. Keep the questions in the same order, but change the order of the answer possibilities.
5. Many teachers are beginning to include small illustrations or jokes on their tests. This relieves the stress and breaks up the visual impression of the test for your more visual learners. Putting different cartoons at the top of different versions shows students that there are two tests so they won't waste their time trying to cheat or straining their eyeballs.
6. Numbering your test versions in two different colors and telling students there are two versions discourage cheating and help you make sure no tests leave the room. If you are using answer sheets, make sure students put their test number on the answer sheet, too.

Make-up Tests

If you have not yet returned the test to the rest of the class, you can probably use the same test on the day the student returns to class. If you stored your test on a computer disk, you can construct a third version of the test by rearranging the sections and changing the essay questions. Some teachers save the company-prepared tests for make-up, while other teachers trade tests on the same units and use a colleague's test for make-up. Neither of these two solutions is ideal because neither truly reflects what has occurred in your class.

Certain students will "cut" consistently on test days. If this avoidance reaction is due to test anxiety, a conference with a counselor might help the student deal with the stress. If the cut is to get test information from other students, a tough make-up test cures this habit quickly. A multiple-choice test can be quickly converted into a fill-in-the-blank test. It will test the same information but severely tax the lazy student.

Grading Tests

When you are grading your tests, watch for items that most of the students get wrong. If you are using computer or electronic grading aides, the machine can analyze the responses and indicate those that most students missed or that everyone got correct. You can collect this same data if you score the tests yourself. If you have an item that did not work, throw it out; do not count it as part of the grade for any student. If you tell students that you discarded a question and tell them the response you did want, you still achieve your purpose; you are making students award of important information. You are also demonstrating to students that you are fair.

Curving grades can spark hours-long philosophical discussions in the teachers' lounge. You might curve a test that was obviously beyond your students' abilities. You might curve to bring the point value of a test to 100%. You might choose not to curve at all. If several students get more than 90% correct, your test is probably constructed for the class learning level. You don't want to get a reputation with students as a teacher who will curve the test to passing grades no matter how poorly students do. That will take away their incentive for studying. Conversely, don't make tests so difficult that no one can pass or do well.

Handing tests back and reviewing them can be a chance to reteach, reinforce concepts, and boost student self-esteem. If you asked for essay or short-answer responses on your test, keep track as you are grading of which students wrote the best responses. Then, as the class reviews the test, call on several students to read their answers aloud. This is extra praise for the student and lets others hear ways to answer questions. It also gives you a chance to call on shy or slower students who wrote good responses. You might ask the students to rename the main points of the unit based on the questions on the test. This provides reinforcement for the central concepts before you go on to the next unit.

Returning tests, however, can also turn into a nightmare. Students can make a game—or even an art form—out of complaining and whining about test answers. They can become hostile, insulting, and shrewish if they think they can intimidate you into giving back points. They then are no longer interested in the right answers or the main concepts; they are in a power struggle with you. Bill asked one whining class why they thought that tone of voice would work on him. They named several other teachers who routinely gave back points. "We thought we'd try it on you."

If one student is angry about a test score, announce that you will not discuss an individual test in front of peers. Tell the student to calm down, make an appointment to see you outside of class time, and bring along the test, text, and notes. Say that it is certainly possible that you misjudged or misinterpreted an answer, but that you will not deal with individual problems in front of class. Do not even debate the point. Change the subject.

If a student thinks a question was graded wrong, have that studdent circle the item on the test and mark on the front page "recheck questions 13, 16." You can go over these problems when it is quiet. Everyone is fallible. You will make mistakes when grading or figuring scores.

If a class is debating a test item, ask the students to get their notes and texts out and find the citation to prove their point. They might be right, or they might prove themselves wrong, but they've done their own research.

When he was a high school student himself, Bill found that a teacher had missed marking eight points wrong on a test. Bill pointed that fact out to the teacher. The teacher agreed and promptly dropped Bill's grade from an A to a B. Bill never again pointed out such errors to a teacher, but as a teacher himself has urged students to point out such mistakes, knowing he will never deduct points. He sends the message to his students that testing is a learning situation for all involved. If students notice such errors, they are learning the right answers in the process.

Bill also does a brief presentation before he returns the first test of the year. He points out that a calm, questioning student gets more consideration on test score changes than do whining, aggressive students. He tells them how to make appointments to see a teacher outside of class and reminds them to bring along textbooks and class notcs. Not only is he returning tests and reinforcing unit concepts, but also he is teaching valuable human-relations skills.

Conclusion

You make curriculum decisions to meet learning objectives for the day, the unit, the semester, and the school year. Those decisions must be creative and allow for the learning styles of individual pupils. They must reflect your personal teaching style and meet the requirements of the district. You set up daily and unit lessons, plus a substitute folder, based on these concepts. You round out your curriculum with well-prepared and -evaluated tests. Every curriculum decision you make, whether it concerns a daily activity or a unit test, affects how students learn.

CHAPTER 5

Curriculum-Based Problems

Explain why you do what you do concerning both teaching and discipline, however, don't be lengthy or too professional.

Listen to 'under-the-breath questions. They are sometimes asked by the timid students most in need.

April R. 12th

Barbara recalls several years ago when she was sermonizing to a group of yawning 9th graders about the importance of placing commas around appositives. Barbara and her class were stewing in the first stages of spring fever. The students had just gotten back their latest essays, and their papers bled with comments. But even low mechanics grades were not motivation enough for rapt attention.

Barbara watched for signs of eager learners: faces turned upward, nodding; pens gripped, writing furiously; a wave of raised hands. One blond in the back row jerked her frizz-permed head in an effort to stay awake; her eyes rolled in pre-REM stages. The boy in the seat by the window counted on his fingers. His total matched the number of times the custodian emptied his grass-catcher bag. Another young man watched, fascinated, as a spider rappeled from his tennis shoe.

Barbara slapped her chalk on the front desk, jolting the young man who occupied it back to earth. An expletive escaped his mouth. She eyed the room wearily. "I swear, I could stand up here on my head naked and I still don't think you'd pay attention." Giggles and titters. One boy who aspired to be a casino dealer in Las Vegas spoke up. "Yeah, we would," he drawled, "for maybe five minutes."

Like Barbara, you will have days when the struggle to engage your students' interest is monumental. You'll also have days, especially if you are a new teacher, that seem to be consumed with classroom management and discipline. The best way to avoid or eliminate these problems of restlessness, inattentiveness, and misbehavior is through effective curriculum presentation. Your aim is to develop teaching practices that engage every student. Then, when you face a situation like Barbara's, you'll be prepared to switch strategies in midstream and respark your students' interest.

Brain research continues while educators, psychologists, and other gurus continue to interpret the overwhelming variety of learning theories. Space does not permit us to survey all these theories, and we've vowed not to pack these pages with statistics. So we're limiting our comments on this topic to what our experience in the classroom has taught us about solving curriculum-based problems.

Clear Directions

Students can be auditory, visual, or tactile learners. Most students seem to comprehend better if they both hear and see the information presented. It's for this reason that students should see directions on an overhead, handout, chalkboard, poster, or chart or in the text while you explain the directions orally. This way, students both hear and see the material and therefore make stronger connections. Any writing students do while taking notes, copying assignments, or drafting responses reinforces learning for tactile learners. During group projects and presentations, you might require that students incorporate visuals to help the rest of the pupils better understand the presentation.

An ideal way to reinforce directions is to model or demonstrate the process or show samples of possible products. For example, math teachers solve sample problems on the board before students begin working independently. English teachers use early drafts of essays to show students the process of revision. Volleyball coaches demonstrate proper spikes and sets.

Although it's important for students to understand what's expected of them, showing models does have its drawbacks. The model may inhibit divergent thinking. Students may perceive that the model you show represents exactly what you require. For this reason, give the more creative assignments without a model.

Your directions must be clear. You'll grow exhausted repeating yourself. The most frustrating questions you'll hear are those that follow an explanation you believe is concise. It's a good idea to check periodically for student comprehension. As you make specific points, giving directions or demonstrations, ask the students to tell you what's going on.

- "Tell the class in your own words what each of you must accomplish at home tonight so we can do the science experiment tomorrow, Jamie."
- "On this slip of paper, I want you to write down the topic of your essay and three arguments you will use to prove your thesis."
- "As you begin your silent reading, I will walk past each desk and check to make sure you understand the assignment."
- "Will you tell the class what pages to read tonight, Kelly? . . . Is she right, Andy?"

Questioning Students

Teachers commit numerous errors when asking questions. One common mistake is to state a student's name before the question: "Sally, what's the answer to question 7?" The problem with this technique is that

Sally is put on the spot while the other 25 students are immediately off the hook. "Why think when I don't have to?" is the silent response of many students. Ask a question, pause, and allow time for 26 minds to search for an answer—then call on Sally to respond. You might also call on one or two others to validate Sally's answer: then ask the rest of the class to nod or raise their hands if they agree. You can use these techniques even if you have asked a question requiring a single, specific response.

Many curriculum topics allow for questions that might elicit a variety of answers rather than one correct answer. You might like multiple responses because several students are involved instead of just one. Tell students to think about the question you are about to ask without raising hands or speaking. This allows everyone to focus. Ask the question. Then ask several students to share their thoughts. If a student pauses at the end of a statement, don't assume he or she is finished. Wait a few seconds before calling on someone else. Often the first student has more to add and is pausing to organize thoughts. During discussions you might ask a student to record individual responses on the board. After six or seven answers, call on one student to summarize. If you like quiet and order, require raised hands, but wait before you call on the first student. The objective is to provide enough time for everyone to *think* of a response. Mentally count to five to make sure you allow that time.

If a student gives an inaccurate answer, you might ask another question to clarify: "Do you mean 1990 instead of 1890?"

Another strategy is to provide the question that correlates with the student's incorrect answer. While Robert was reviewing directions for a math assignment, he asked, "What kind of problems require a quotient for an answer?" A student answered, "Multiplication problems." Robert dignified the response. "Products are the answers to multiplication problems. We're still dealing with sets. What kind of problems yield quotients?" In this statement, Robert linked the student response with the correct question, then tried a new prompt to get the desired answer.

If a student has no response, say you will come back to her or him. This holds the student accountable for listening more carefully to other responses. You might ask a student to paraphrase or summarize previous answers.

The way you acknowledge a response is critical. **Never** humiliate a student. While sarcasm for some seems appropriate, such negative reactions may come back to haunt you. For most correct answers, a simple "Good" or "Great" may be adequate. Nonverbal acknowledgments such as a nod or wink serve the same purpose. If the answer is a winner, an "Excellent, Johnn" may be appropriate. If the answer is not complete, respond by saying something like, "You're on the right track; can anyone take Ryan's idea further?"

Clowns and Ringmasters

Occasionally you'll be blessed with a clown who believes that you and your class live for his or her witty comments. Sometimes a dose of nonthreatening humor will silence the offender. A smile at the student

The Class Clown

and a short "Not today" may do the trick. Often, ignoring the remark and concentrating on the responses from the rest of the class will solve the problem. Usually the primary goal of this student is attention, and the sooner you can deal with the behavior, the better. If ignoring or making light of the situation doesn't work and the comedian continues the act, you could move toward the student, use a stern tone saying, "Sean, that's enough!" and proceed. If the offender still persists, you're probably ready to look at the student, state "I'll see you after class," and proceed with the steps discussed in Chapter 2.

Especially when you are a new teacher, you may encounter the youngster who wants to be viewed as "The Authority." This individual likes to flaunt self-proclaimed brilliance. To catch you unprepared or without an answer is the goal. If this student begins to dominate the discussion, you could acknowledge the student's obvious interest in the topic and make this person the "research authority." The student's job is to listen quietly and serve as backup authority. The student gets attention, yet others have opportunities to respond. Be sure to use your "authority" to double-check answers or summarize from time to time.

Sometimes students ask questions with the best of intentions, and you honestly don't know the answer. Admit you don't know and suggest an investigation. Either name a source for the information requested or attempt to find it yourself. Often the student doesn't require an explanation as detailed as the one you will provide, but she or he and the rest of the class will see that you want to learn with them.

If you are well prepared, the attempts to trip you up will fail and
students won't wish to expend the energy pointlessly challenging you.
Don't discourage challenges, though. Show students that intellectual
curiosity and questioning are part of the lively learning climate you like
in your classes.

Relevance

Much of what teachers present in the classroom does not seem to
students to have immediate relevance to their lives. It is your task to
assist students in making connections, even if the connection is as simple
as "Yesterday, when we finished reading *Sarah, Plain and Tall*, I
understood why Sarah felt lonely. Have you ever felt lonely? Today
we're going to discuss and write about what to do when we feel alone."

As an effective teacher, you must demonstrate the *why* of learning.
Some subjects and lessons lend themselves to this. It's not difficult for the
aspiring engineer to see the relevance of math, the futuure attorney the
benefits of debate, or the contractor the importance of drafting. For the
classes or lessons that don't appeal to students, for one reason or another,
it's critical that you demonstrate relevance and personal enthusiasm.

One afternoon, Betty was introducing Edgar Allan Poe in a Junior
American Lit class. From the back of the room, a red-haired girl who
was prone to gum-popping whined, "Why do we hafta learn this? I'm
gonna be a bag lady." She grinned at the boy next to her. Betty informed
her that Poe was a master of the macabre, wrote excessively on themes
of premature burial, insanity, and revenge. She could sense that she had
related to a few in the room. Betty continued, explaining the connections
between Poe and Stephen King, which sparked a few comments like
"Yeah, like the Usher House and the Overlook in *The Shining*." Betty
continued, smiling at the young lady, "Poe haunted the streets often
himself. He was found unconscious in an alley, and three days later, he
died." The redhead quit chewing her gum.

Flexibility and Pacing

You need to consider critical thinking, cooperative learning, and
problem-solving in classroom planning. Allowing for individual work
time is equally important. Some students work best if they're left alone;
others need interaction—if not for boosting their own wavering self-

esteem, then for the simple release of energy. You are not an evil teacher if you allow students to read a poem aloud in pairs, look up answers as a team, or use a colored crayon instead of a pen or pencil. Effective classroom management requires variety. Ideally, activities should change every 15 to 25 minutes, depending on the age and maturity of the students. Here are some suggestions to infuse your class time with variety.

- If students have been reading for 20 minutes, focus the class's attention back to you, and have the students discuss or write about what they've been reading.
- If you've been lecturing for 25 minutes, stop and give students time to peruse their notes and exchange ideas with a classmate.
- If students have been playing math games in small groups, call them together so they can all view the chalkboard. Lead a total group activity, focusing on the concept used to play the games. This could be a demonstration, board work, or role-play. After you've assessed student comprehension, give directions for the day's independent practice. Allow the remaining 20 minutes for quiet, uninterrupted work time.

There are, of course, exceptions. When you're deadlining on a film or the teacher down the hall is pleading for the room set of books you're currently using, every minute is critical. If you explain this dilemma to students, they are usually cooperative about a change in scheduling.

Flexibility is also critical in giving assignments—both in creating them and in interpreting them. If you know your objectives, you should, in many cases, offer a variety of options to your students for achieving these objectives. Students participate better when they're allowed choices, like these:

- In a science class, consider several methods to achieve the same goal. For example, in a cooperative team, one student might take the flower apart while the second draws. The third student might talk about what they are seeing, while the fourth records it in a field journal.
- In math class, offer a variety of problems and allow the students to choose among them, or have pairs act out story problems.
- Use task cards, with the students choosing among different activities in a category.
- List as many as ten writing options. The students complete one or two.
- On the essay portion of a test, list several questions that test the same skill. Let students choose which to answer.

Obviously, options are not always appropriate but whenever possible, incorporate them. Assignment choices can stretch student minds beyond simple recall into sophisticated thinking.

Dealing with Distressing Events

The need for flexibility in the classroom surfaces in another way: as a response to current events. When the space shuttle *Challenger* met with its violent end, students could talk of little else. The San Francisco earthquake had a similar effect, as did the Persian Gulf war. Students need to communicate about such events, and brushing aside a national disaster or war without some comment seems to contradict the whole point of relevance that teachers strive to achieve.

If a death of a classmate occurs or several students are involved in a traffic fatality, those moments of human experience contain a lesson. Betty had an experience with a student whose friend had committed suicide over spring break. The student announced that fact to the class, but would say no more. It was obvious that he was deeply affected and in agony. After class, Betty talked with him about his loss. She asked the school social worker to talk with him. At the time he was angry with her for interfering, but two days later apologized with a shaking voice and thanked her for her caring.

A second-grade girl in Robert's class was the victim of a fatal car accident. Thursday she'd occupied a desk; Friday she was dead. The administrators called the parents of the other children in Robert's class, informing them of the little girl's death. They encouraged parents to talk with their children before school the next day. The class united in their displays of sympathy. They donated money for flowers and made cards for the family. The school nurse was available for individual conferences. This became an important lesson to these second-graders about learning to deal with the death of a friend.

Whether your students are faced with a personal tragedy or a natural disaster, be flexible and compassionate. Shift the curriculum a bit and discuss earthquakes a month earlier, or just spend a few minutes listening to students. The class will see you as a human being with concerns like theirs, as opposed to some robot that self-destructs each day at 4:00.

When students are upset, you might have them begin an impromptu journal-write on the topic distressing them. You could do a write-it-and-tear-it-up activity to purge students' feelings of anger or fear or frustration. You might talk about appropriate and inappropriate ways people handle emotions.

You could talk about TV programs or books on similar themes. You might suggest a past piece of literaature that included the same theme. After being given this opportunity to express and share their concerns, your students should begin to calm down and refocus on the current lesson.

After the crisis, talk with colleagues about what happened. They will relate stories of similar experiences, and you can store their solutions in your mind for future use.

Refocusing After Interruptions

Besides the usual interruptions of messages, call slips, and announcements over the intercom, discussed in Chapter 3, your classroom routine will also be disrupted by assemblies for student government, upcoming games, health education, and cultural enrichment. Several-day, schoolwide testing schedules will also surface to break the flow of your lessons. And short, unexpected interruptions will sabotage your best-planned learning experiences.

These interruptions will happen, so don't let them upset you; just learn to adjust with good humor. Early warning helps, of course, which you'll get in the case of most assemblies and test days. As soon as your administration announces these events, write them into your lesson plan book even if the dates are months ahead.

Assemblies

Sometimes assemblies occur on short notice. Creative teachers learn ways to adjust. Once again, getting upset only hurts you. If students are to report to class for roll call before moving to the auditorium, you could use that opportunity to announce before they leave: "Since we will not work together today, I need you to read the following material at home tonight." If you want to be sure students follow through, you could add, "There will be a quiz on that reading when you walk in the door tomorrow." Also, you could take the few minutes when you have the class's attention before the assembly to remind the students of proper assembly manners, school pride, and maturity. They can never hear that material too often.

When your students resume class, you might spend some time discussing what happened in the assembly (good or bad) and why schools have assemblies. This is an opportunity to talk about large-group behavior. Ask students how assembly etiquette might apply to other situations in their lives. Ask how school assemblies are the same or different from professional ball games, rock concerts, and parades. Write down related questions before class. Your discussion will run most smoothly from the security of written response-leads that you've thought through. It's best not to wing it.

Sometimes part of a class or several classes are affected by assemblies or other interruptions and others aren't. If you want to get your classes back in synch, assign drawing, writing, or reading activities related to what you've been working on in class. This will allow you to do something different in the classes that you do meet, and you won't have to play "catch up" later on. On the other hand, different classes will have different levels of interest in the same topic, so being at different places in the curriculum in different classes is perfectly appropriate if you prefer that approach.

Testing Days

In the spring, many districts administer achievement tests at specific grade levels for four or five days. Last year, Betty taught her juniors the first two periods, tested 30 juniors (not all her usual students) for 110 minutes, the equivalent of two periods, for five consecutive days, had lunch, and taught her last two periods. These tests are hard on the kids and hard on you. Here are some specific things to keep in mind (rather than losing it) when doing several-day testing:

1. The students will be emotionally tired in the classes where tests are not being administered. Do not give unit exams or have major assignments due at this time.
2. Plan activities in class that change frequently and involve student movement, small group work, planned group responses, and a bit of fun. You can still cover the concepts, but you need to plan for students' active (physical and mental) participation to distract them from their testing fatigue.
3. You might plan a half-day lesson on test-taking strategies. Include relaxation techniques. Talk about how you handled tense testing

situations in college. Tell your students about taking the National Teachers Exam. Let them talk about test anxiety and discuss strategies for dealing with that cold fist gripping your insides and freezing your brain.

4. Plan alternative methods for teaching. Betty taught a short story unit lasting the duration of the testing days in the classes she did meet and culminated with a film of the short story the day she had all her classes back. The students involved in testing saw the film their first day back. This caught them up with the other classes and gave them a rewarding visual break while helping them mentally get ready to return to regular class routine.

5. *Don't schedule "free" time.* This quickly disintegrates into a free-for-all and a management nightmare.

Unexpected Events/Student Removal

Sometimes classroom lightning strikes not once but several times in a period and the lesson stalls: The projector breaks and there is no replacement. The film shreds. The film is 50 minutes long and you have just been informed that an emergency assembly will begin in 30 minutes. How do you refocus student attention?

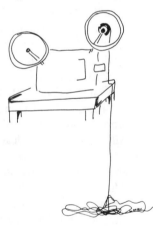

You might say, after distraction number 379, "I've lost my train of thought. Help me. What were we talking about? What do you have last in your notes? Let's go to page 156 in your text and pick up the concept this film would have taught if the hungry projector hadn't eaten it." These questions and statements can help refocus your students and you.

One type of interruption is certain to crumble students' attention to the lesson: At times, police or administrators might remove a student from your class without warning. Having a student pulled out of class is disturbing for you and the other students. If your goal is to establish a trusting, safe environment, these abrupt actions ruin that safe feeling. Try to convince administrators to deal with student problems *after* class, or before class begins. If a student *is* pulled out of class, ask the authorities on the scene to deal with the student down the hall, out of sight and earshot of your classroom. If your students are particularly disturbed by what's happening to their classmate, follow some of the suggestions in the "Dealing With Distressing Events" section above before resuming the day's lesson.

Creative Lesson Planning Ideas

Begin building a file of ideas for activities that reinforce the concepts you are teaching and that end with the bell. You might use these same exercises in the beginning of the period to help students actively review the previous day's lesson or focus their attention on the new lesson.

You can continually glean ideas from listening to other teachers, attending share fairs, or reading professional magazines. Here are some ideas for activities in specific curriculum areas.

Language Arts

- Hand the students a sheet of unlined 8 x 11 paper and have them draw the house or a favorite character in the story you are studying, draw the path of a character's movement through the story, or illustrate the symbols or theme in the story. Have students share their work and base evaluation on amount of detail and symbolism rather than artistic talent.
- Have the students write a scene that is *not* in the story. For example, in "The Devil and Tom Walker" by Washington Irving, the conversation between the devil and Mrs. Tom Walker is not included. You will seldom get identical responses to this assignment.
- In small groups, have students plan and present a very short skit about what happens after the story ends.
- After students read E.B. White's *Stuart Little*, have them write or tell the ending to the story.
- Have students illustrate their vocabulary words.
- Have students jot down three "Why . . . " or "What if . . . " questions about the story and then ask classmates their questions. These questions elicit multiple responses, so every student answer can be correct.

Math

- Have each student create, on a fresh sheet of paper, three new problems that illustrate that day's concept. Students then pass the

paper two classmates to the right for computation, one classmate
forward for checking, then back to the originator for scoring. Talk
about what makes a good example and what does not.

- Use cooperative groups to begin homework.
- Hand each small group a different brain teaser. Each must solve the
  problem and then explain how they did this to the rest of the class.
- Have students measure the classroom and use these statistics to create
  original math problems, using the concepts being currently taught.

Science

- To review lab procedures the day before doing a lab exercise, put the
  students into small groups and hand each a written description of a
  student performing a lab exercise. Have each group report to the rest
  of the class about what was done correctly and what should have
  been done differently to ensure an accurate, safe lab experience.
- Share a short essay. You might begin collecting a file of essays on
  science. James Thurber wrote several. Current authors who appeal to
  students include Barry Lopez, David Quammen, and John McPhee.
- Show a science-oriented cartoon. Ask what makes it funny and why.
- Have students write out "How come . . . " questions on the current
  topic and take turns asking class members for answers.
- Build a collection of current science magazines in your classroom.
  Students can browse through these periodicals, locate an article of
  interest, read it, and complete a short written or oral report about it.
  Just looking through current science magazines demonstrates to
  students that science is an ongoing field in which fresh discoveries are
  continually being made—a perspective students might otherwise lose
  sight of.

Social Studies

- Have small groups prepare short skits of famous events from another
  viewpoint: V-E Day from the perspective of a German private, an old
  villager, or Eisenhower's assistant . . . (a different person for each
  group).
- Have students think and jot down ideas and be ready to share: What
  person in history would you like to meet, and what would you talk
  about? You could limit this topic to one era, one incident, or one
  specific group of people. Having students write down what they are
  going to talk about keeps each student responsible for participating.

These ideas could be the foundation for a creative writing assignment.

- Have small groups write a specific number of questions and answers on the front and back of notecards. Then discuss and collect the cards to use at the end of the unit or the semester for a Jeopardy-like review game.
- Have small groups look for links or similarities between historical events and daily national, local, and school news events. You could cut paper into strips and have students write their responses on these shapes and hang them in the room in a chain.
- Speculate about what a teenager's life might have been like in the era you're studying. What would life have been like then?

Manual Arts

Manual arts classes include art, home economics, industrial arts, wood shop, and vocational classes.

- Hands-on classes seldom seem to have enough time for work and cleanup. If you also need focus time, showing a student's project in progress and discussing the process could benefit other students working on similar tasks.

Music

- Keep rehearsing; let students direct.
- Have students illustrate their impressions of musical selections as they listen.
- Have students compare and contrast contemporary music with music from another period.

Physical Education

- Have small groups of students plan drills to practice specific skills safely.

When Lesson Plans Don't Work Out . . .

Sometimes a lesson will fall flat. Before the next class begins, ask yourself these questions:

1. Could the material be better learned cooperatively rather than individually?
2. Would your students understand the material better if you assigned

small groups two questions to answer before whole-group study and discussion?

3. Would the activity be more effective after the film rather than before?

4. Would an explanation work better if you role-played? Could students stand in the configuration of the molecule, walk through the battle, or represent the parts of the story problem?

5. Can you adjust the topic to relate it more closely to the students' interest? Would a discourse on Thoreau's "Civil Disobedience" explore the same ideas if students wrote about civil disobedience today? Could the same topic be related to war protests?

What can you do when you give a wonderful lecture, complete it with a dramatic sweep of your hand, and notice blank paper and blank student faces? Try this approach: Tell your students, "Now you've heard the material. Using that information, let me show you how I would put it in my notes if I were sitting at one of your desks hearing this same lecture." Then proceed to review by writing a skeleton outline on the board or overhead projector, drawing an idea-tree, or listing the steps of the procedure. Ask questions as you work: "What was the next point I made? Is this a new support point or an example for the previous one? Should I put a drawing here? Would that help my notes?" Besides providing a review, this process can show students *how* to take notes. After all, study skills are not genetically passed from generation to generation. As an alternative, you could put the main points of a lecture on the board or overhead before class or with students during class. This has the added advantage of helping students to see the transitions.

If you have presented information and helped your students take notes, but the confusion remains, try this: Ask, "What is the one main idea of today's material? On a fresh sheet of paper, write that topic in the center. With your notes covered, write down everything you can remember about that topic." Then ask students to look over their papers and circle the three most important ideas. They might trade with a neighbor and add at least one more detail before trading back. Ask various students to read aloud one of their circled ideas. Some may be repeated, but that only reinforces importance. (This is an ideal time to call on less-able students so they can give a correct response in front of peers.) Ask why the student felt the mentioned point was important. Responses reflect higher levels of thinking. This review process can also work as a focus the next day to start the lesson.

When your students just don't seem to grasp an assignment, try giving different examples and more guided practice on that concept. Ask your students if they can explain why they are having trouble with the assignment, and discuss learning techniques they could use successfully. Use the lesson to reinforce study techniques even if you have to work through the assignment step by step. Then go back and look for the central concept together.

Cooperative work can help get your students through an assignment that is difficult for them. "I can see we are all suffering. Instead of finishing these at home, be sure your name is on the paper and turn in what you have done so far. I'll score that. Tomorrow we'll review the concept and give some more examples, and you can work with two classmates to complete the activity. I'll score this revision." Sharing answers and working together can be a positive technique. You can structure work sessions that begin with individual effort and later move to group reinforcement.

If students are struggling with a tough reading assignment, pair them up and have them read aloud to each other. At the bottom of each page, the pair should stop, talk abbout what they read, summarize the main ideas, and write them in their notes. This is a noisy activity, but everyone is involved in seeking meaning. During the last ten minutes of class, call students to order and have them share their notes. Then, based on their notes and listening, have them summarize the main ideas.

You might want to have a short worksheet, essay, or quiz as an alternative if disaster strikes and the lesson simply doesn't work no matter what you do. You may prepare this extra lesson segment and not need to use it. However, file it away for future use.

You can minimize lesson flops by always staying focused on the unit or concept you are teaching and planning everything you do in your classroom to relate to the teaching and reinforcement of that concept.

If you know you are usually an effective teacher, don't take an occasional disappointing lesson too much to heart. Students are much caught up in their own world, and it can be hard to get them to share in your enthusiasm or concern. Lessons will bomb now and again: that's a given. Never let fear of a "disaster" keep you from trying new, creative strategies.

Dealing with a Too-Difficult Text/Too-Easy Text

If you are a beginning teacher or one new to a district, you probably won't have much time or opportunity to choose the textbook(s) you'll be using. Most likely, your school will be using district-adopted texts. If you must make a choice early on, consider using the text your colleagues are using. This will make it easier to share ideas and teaching problems.

If you do find yourself teaching with a textbook that is too easy or too difficult, keep in close contact with fellow teachers for teaching ideas. Utilize the teacher resource center, if you have access to one, through your district or a nearby college. Read professional magazines in your field. Try some of the coping suggestions below.

The best way to alleviate textbook problems is to become involved in textbook adoption. Check with your department chair or building administrator to learn how to join these committees.

A Too-Difficult Text

If you've met your students and it becomes apparent that the text is too difficult for them, you might try some of the following techniques.

Shorter, Modified Reading Assignments   Plan shorter reading assignments. Students need not read every word of a difficult text. Instead, they might read a few passages to get the general idea. Use other ways to present the material: You could view a video, bring in a guest speaker, create a trivia-style game, or enlist another class to help tutor. When using difficult textbooks, other students or adult volunteers could read the material aloud or onto cassette tapes as the students follow in their books. Often you can locate modified versions of "classic pieces." Check with your department chair or librarian.

Discussion Buddies   Have students work with a discussion buddy, reading aloud or silently, then take notes after each section or paragraph.

Vocabulary Games   Make a game out of vocabulary learning. Introduce the vocabulary before reading, act out the meanings, then review and test the students later. Computer programs are available to build crossword puzzles. Students might create their own learning games. You could award points for using the word correctly in the lab report or essay. Students could also illustrate vocabulary words.

Prereading Skills and Techniques   Teach prereading and preview skills. If possible, ask the reading specialist to come in and teach while you watch. Then repeat and reinforce these skills for *every* reading assignment. You might practice these skills on easier material first.

Teach your students to use the summary at the end of the chapter and the review questions as a prereading device. Don't just tell the students to read these parts on their own; read them together in class and discuss what students might learn in the chapter. Model the techniques you want the students to use.

Tell your students what they are going to read about before they begin. Pique student interest by referring to the mysteries in the story: the main character's unknown past; the conflict that triggers irreversible decisions; the clues that lead to the surprising climax. However, *never* tell the ending. Tell your students, instead, that you took a vow when you became a teacher *never* to reveal conclusions.

Character Identification   Write the characters' names on the board with an identifying phrase for each. Have students copy and keep the list for quick reference during the unit.

Study Guides   Create a study guide that focuses on the important concepts in the reading. Add "Why . . . " or "What if . . . " questions for every fourth or fifth item that can only be answered after reflection.

No Oral Reading by Students   Do not conduct round-robin reading sessions. They do not make good use of learning time. This method puts inappropriate stress on the poor oral reader, lets those not reading off the hook, and bores the faster readers to tears.

Whole-Class Reading   When introducing a novel, you might read the first chapter aloud and have the class work through the first study questions together. When students begin to get interested in the book, let them continue silently at their own best pace. Every few days at the beginning of the period, have students identify which page they are reading. This assures the slower students that they are not alone and gives everyone incentive to manage remaining reading time. It also helps you plan for the next part of the presentation.

If you are starting students on a science or social studies chapter, model being the student yourself. Read the first paragraph or section aloud and then pose questions to yourself about what will come next in the chapter. Ask your students these questions. Then let the students read on to find the answers. You might break the entire chapter up into small chunks and lead the students through one section at a time.

Note-Taking Assistance   Encourage your students to outline, take notes, and interpret the text on their own, but help them through the process. Merely handing out a summary will not help the students use the book independently. Prepare an outline and then delete occasional headings, lists of details, or vocabulary words. Students can then fill in the missing information as they read.

Support Materials   Teacher's guides often indicate how to modify lessons for various abilities. These modifications may include shortened word lists, altered math assignments, or guidelines for creating appropriate essay questions. Other support materials that may accompany texts are transparencies, computer software, audio and video cassettes, posters for discussion, math manipulatives, and suggestions for enrichment activities that reinforce the central concepts of the text. Ask colleagues in your school or department if these materials are available. Be sure to check in your school media center. They may be stored there or in another central area. Sometimes a phone call to your publisher's local representative is all it takes to obtain some of these items.

Acknowledge   Begin the unit by assessing your students' existing knowledge. Have the students read sections of the text that support and expand correct concepts and realign misconceptions.

Challenge   You might also discover that slower classes are able to use the same text as your average students. You will need to express your feeling that the class is capable of handling the curriculum. Tell students that if they faithfully try every task you ask of them, you will prepare the assignments to suit their learning strengths. Students need and want to be challenged beyond their learning levels and will succeed according to the teacher's expectations.

A Too-Easy Text

If the text is too easy for your students, you might use it only as introductory, background material. Challenge your students with activities and supplementary materials at their learning level. You might find more challenging texts, even if you only have one of each.

Copying essays and articles for the class might be a solution, but be aware of copyright law. Before you make wholesale use of the copy machine (and make the rest of the faculty hate you), talk to your principal or department chair about investing in a classroom set of appropriate published material. Talk to other teachers. One might have a classroom set of supplementary material gathering dust in a long-forgotten corner that you can use.

If your science book is too easy, be cautious about replacing or supplementing it with an old text. The field of science is changing so rapidly that texts are out of date the day they are published. It would be better to use an easy, but accurate, text and build on that base with exploratory lab experiences, supervised library research and reports, and student-supplied related magazine articles. Fortunately for science teachers, educational television features many hours of intriguing science material for supplementary enrichment. This is true of other subjects as well.

Inappropriate/Too-Heavy Teaching Assignment

When you sign a contract, you usually have a clear idea about what subjects you will teach. However, difficulties can arise when, in the course of the teaching year, your work load seems to extend beyond what even a computer can handle.

This is most likely to happen to you during your first year of teaching or your first year in a new assignment or building. The first assignment in any setting can be overwhelming to anyone. Five years ago, Marc accepted a position that he knew would include slow-learning seniors. He taught five classes of 32 to 36 slow or lazy learners who had convinced the counselors they needed an "easy" class. These classes had no texts and no specific curriculum, and there were no other math teachers on Marc's floor. The students in one class frequently bragged to Marc how many teachers they had caused to quit.

When the burden of a tough teaching assignment begins to weigh upon you, try a few of these strategies.

Changing One Thing at a Time   Make a list of what is going well and what is most overwhelming. Identify the first thing you'd like to change. If discipline needs to improve, plan highly structured daily lessons. Start each lesson with a journal-write, quiz, or story problem. This will give you time to take accurate roll and focus the students on the lesson. When your students realize you are there to teach, most will go along with the plan. For those who do not comply, it is critical that you begin to implement a discipline plan. See Chapter 2 for ideas.

Consulting with Colleagues   Seek out colleagues. Experienced teachers can give you advice and suggestions for coping with your workload. If you are a beginning teacher, get to know the other new teachers. You might form a mutual support group and, in the process, find out you all are doing better than you thought.

Coping with Written Assignments   Assigning written work is one way to hold your students accountable for what you are teaching. However, you must be able to cope with all the papers they produce. To do so, try some of these ideas:

1. Have students exchange papers and score them. This is a valid way to reinforce correct answers.
2. Have students answer 5 questions each day on a 20-question worksheet and hand the paper in at the end of the hour. You need only to put a check mark in the margin where they finished and return the paper the next day. Grade it on the fourth day.
3. Grade daily work on the plus, check, minus system: + = assignment done exceptionally well; $\checkmark$ = assignment done, full credit; – = assignment turned in, not completed. You can group students' papers into these three general categories without reading each item word for word. You might record all plus/check/minus grades on one sheet and then assign one overall homework grade to students' daily papers at the end of the grading period.
4. After determining grading criteria, peruse each student paper without marking individual errors and assign a grade. Evaluate the next assignment with comments so students can learn from their work.
5. A real dilemma is grading for mechanics and spelling errors. One quick way to accomplish this is to place a check mark in the margin of the line in which the error occurs. This alerts the student to check the line for a spelling or mechanics problem and requires students to be responsible for their own learning.
6. Skim for key phrases and stack the papers in pilles, depending on how each paper compares with others in quality and completeness.
7. Have students trade essay responses. You need to identify on the

overhead or chalkboard what students are to check for in their peers' work, for example underlining main ideas, circling spelling errors, and checking where punctuation is needed. This will serve as a prereading aid for you.

8. Have your students outline some essay answers rather than write prose. Take time to review the outlining rules; don't expect the students to remember the skill from previous years.

9. Have students trade papers and, with a colored pencil, underline the main ideas or supporting details.

10. As the students work, walk past each desk, making helpful suggestions or pointing out answers you especially like. Then put a check mark on the paper and in your grade book as a record of having seen that assignment. At the end of the period, students need only to file these papers in their notebooks. Encourage students to keep these quick-grade assignments by allowing them to use such papers when taking quizzes.

In the beginning of the year, your paper load tends to be heavier. There are reasons for this. You need to see student work to assess abilities, spot students in need of special help, and learn if each student is understanding what you are trying to teach. You might also gain information about the amount of background your students have in your subject area. As you and your class begin functioning as a team, you will find ways of lessening this load. You will also find you do not need to collect work from each student every day to keep the students on task.

Coping with Background Reading If you feel your teaching assignment is overwhelming because of the amount of background reading required to prepare each lesson, consider using several cooperative learning techniques. Place students in learning groups, providing the material or helping them find it in the media center. Give specific tasks for each group to accomplish. Each group then presents what they've learned about the topic, giving you breathing time. Your job is still to present the introductory material and the main concepts of the units, but students can contribute the supplementary information. You then correct misconceptions and reinforce main concepts. When the groups are presenting their material, keep the rest of the class responsible for what they hear by taking notes yourself and including the material on your next test.

This process can also model good note-taking for your students, so let them see the notes you take. In the margin jot down possible test questions, key phrases, and vocabulary. You can also take notes on the chalkboard or overhead. Discuss both the material and your note-taking techniques with students.

Dealing with One Main Area at a Time   When you teach, you are functioning on at least three levels simultaneously: classroom management, content, and method of presentation. If you feel you're about to explode if you have to deal with one more detail, consider dealing with only one of these three main areas at a time. Teach a topic that's easier for you so you can concentrate on the discipline. Fall back on what's familiar to you. Cut back on paperwork by utilizing peer-scoring techniques for some assignments or requesting oral responses. Read Chapter 11 on wellness.

Difficult Teaching Situations

Whether you are a new or established teacher, your schedule is likely to include one or more slow-learning classes. Working with these students can be both challenging and rewarding. The key is attitude. Although the following suggestions are aimed at helping you deal with these difficult teaching situations, you'll find you can apply the ideas to any class.

High Expectations   All students can learn a lot more than we think they can. Ideally, classrooms should be a heterogeneous mix of abilities and learning styles. All levels of students should be provided the same learning opportunities. In reality, many schools are structured in homogeneous tracks, based on a variety of criteria. The learning process for "slow learners" may take longer, but these students often make original connections and arrive at creative conclusions that others, conditioned to following rules and putting their minds in neutral, miss.

Personal Background   It is easier to be objective when you don't know a lot about students' lives. Try to send the message that outside problems do not have to get in the way of classroom success. Make your classroom a safe place to be. Tell students that your classroom is a place to experience success. Knowing a student's background may make your approach toward that student more compassionate, but your expectations must remain the same; your students need and deserve that stability.

Phone Calls Home   Try to make many positive phone calls to the parents of these students. Unfortunately, that technique sometimes back-fires. You might introduce yourself and relate a positive occurrence. Then you might get a long pause . . . and, "So what did Sam do now?"

Barbara remembers calling a father about his son's improvement, hoping the father would mention the improvement to Sam. The father was pleasant. Three days later she made a comment to Sam that she was surprised he hadn't mentioned the call to her. The student was mystified: His father had never told him that Barbara had called.

Tell a student that you are going to call and what you will talk about. Use this moment to double-check the phone number, an appropriate time to call, and the parent's name. Not knowing a name change from a remarriage can get a call off to an awkward start.

Trust-Building   Spend time building trust. Use activities from *Building a Positive Self-Concept* and explain why is is important to work together as a group, that cooperation is a valuable life skill.

Learning Techniques   Tell your students how and why you are teaching each unit. Teach them how they learn and show them how they can use that information to gain control over their learning in other classes. Separate technique from content. Technique is often more interesting to these students, perhaps because it makes their schooling more applicable to their lives.

Small Information Units   Teach small units of information; go back and do activities that link that information. Give quizzes regularly to hold students accountable and help them assimilate smaller amounts of information.

Variety   Try to appeal to each learning style in each lesson. Plan for movement, writing, drawing, talking, and student-directed sections. Allow times for students to consult and contribute.

Frequent Evaluation   Take a no-surprises approach to these students' grades. Frequently advise the students of their progress and any missing assignments. Many schools sent out mid-term progress reports to parents. Consider having your students write comments on their progress reports. Then add your own comment before sending the reports home. This straightforward approach can be time-consuming, but it builds trust in your classroom.

Support From Colleagues Don't allow teachers who are bitter and angry about their situation to influence you. Spend time with thhose who are working to make school successful for the students.

Students' Moods Be flexible and sensitive to students' moods. Right before Christmas your students will be restless with joyful or unhappy anticipation of the holidays. Preholiday students often welcome a chance to work quietly at short-term assignments, listening to a story you read aloud or collecting and classifying ideas. They do not do well when confronted with nonrelated videos or group work this week.

The Personal Touch One year Allen, a junior high math teacher, recognized class birthdays with a note on the board or a verbal greeting. In September, it took lots of organization time and a large calendar to accomplish this, but students appreciated the attention. Those with summer birthdays got six-month half-birthdays.

By actively looking for the positives of teaching you will notice the rewards. Students appreciate someone who cares enough to set tough parameters and high expectations.

Cheating on Tests

Cheating is one of those subjects like abortion: people are rarely neutral about it. You may hear some heated debates in faculty rooms over methods of dealing with cheaters. Your school may have a written policy to cover cheating incidents.

In a world where students hear parents openly discussing ways to beat the IRS or lie to get little Susie or Grandpa into the movies at a reduced price, it's no wonder that students find devious and creative ways to cheat. Cheating techniques have ranged from the wandering eye to the microsheet rolled in the fountain pen to the full-fledged copying of acquired tests and selling them for profit. Teachers often comment that if students spent as much time studying for a test as they did preparing the cheat sheets, they'd all ace the tests. No one advocates or condones cheating. However, when students do cheat, it seems to be the teacher's blood pressure that skyrockets. It is the teacher's day that is ruined. When confronted with their cheating, most students don't feel guilty about material not learned. Nine times out of ten the student is more upset that he or she has been caught.

The key is to set students up for success right from the beginning so they're less likely to cheat. Encourage them to use notes on quizzes, but change quiz questions each period. If they know what you expect, there's less anxiety. Students say they cheat because they are unsure of the material and don't want to risk a low grade because of home or academic pressures. Robert encourages his younger students by telling them they will do better than they think. He tells them to write down what they know.

Unfortunately, some teachers at all levels set students up to fail. These teachers use trick questions or require impossibly detailed diagrams. Tell your studennts what you expect them to know, why they need to know it, and how they can learn it. It's amazing what they're capable of.

Sometimes, for a test, you might give each student a 5 x 8 index card to make into a review tool. Each student compares information with a partner and writes important information down on the card. Seeing, writing, and discussing information all reinforce the material. As archaic as it sounds, one of the major aspects of learning is repetition. The more students see the material, write it, talk it, and read it, the more likely they are to remember it. And that, of course, is the goal.

Teach test-taking skills. Show students old tests or give them a practice exam before they take your first graded test.

Some teachers pause at certain points in a test, let students confer for two minutes, and then instruct them to go back to test-taking. Unorthodox? Perhaps. But if our ultimate goal is for students to learn the material, what better way than from each other? In many subjects memorization is an appropriate, testable skill. Whatever your philosophy in administering tests, do not lose sight of your curriculum goals.

However, even though you try to prevent it, cheating is a fact of life and students will continue to do it. If a cheating situation occurs in one of your classes, you have several options. Schools vary in their policies dealing with cheating. Check with your administration. Interview other teachers. For most classes, it's an automatic F or zero on the test. Discuss the incident with the student privately. Remind him or her of the consequences for cheating. Call the parents and relate the situation to them exactly as it occurred.

Recently, a student teacher discovered a young woman who'd been absent and was taking a make-up test by copying from another student's test. Obviously, some good samaritan had absconded with a copy of the exam and provided it to the making-up student. The student teacher was horrified that a copy had escaped. In a later conference, the student teacher and her cooperating teacher discussed how she could prevent this type of cheating in the future. You can follow the guidelines these two teachers worked out:

When passing out tests or other materials you do not wish to leave the room, make sure you have counted carefully. Number your tests or handouts so you know what hasn't been returned.

Finally, you can use some simple classroom-management techniques to minimize cheating. Distribute two versions of the test. Circulate around the classroom when administering the tests.

Ultimately, the best way to keep cheating out of your classroom is to set up your students for success in the first place.

Copied Assignments/Plagiarism

Sometimes a student will turn in an assignment that is practically identical to another. Invite the two students to comment on the similarities. Usually, one of the sttudents will admit that he or she has copied the work. They realize, somehow, that you weren't born yesterday and that some coincidences are just too amazing. Depending on the task, you may wish to let the copier redo the assignment for a late grade, or you may assign a different project that no one else has done. Your plan of action depends on the standards you have set from the beginning.

When Brian discovers two identical assignments, he divides the grade between the two students. He also confers with the students and advises parents of the situation.

On the elementary level, Kathy states that when her students cheat, she expects them to do a different, additional assignment that emphasizes the same skills. Students must do this new work during free time: recess, lunch break, before or after school.

Plagiarism in assignments is something to watch for. When a

student, for example, turns in a report on snowboarding copied from the latest kids' sports magazine in lieu of an original story, you must deal with the issue. Many schools have a written policy on plagiarism. Define plagiarism for your students. Explain why it is illegal and inappropriate. Teach your students how to give the author credit for copied material. Kathy says, "This author must be given credit for his/her work. You are still responsible for the original assiignment. You will need to write your own story."

One way to check for plagiarism is to compare a student's writing style on a prepared-at-home paper with one written in class. If you have suspicions, create an in-class writing assignment. This, along with earlier samples of the suspected plagiarist's work, will give you something to bring to a student conference: comparisons of sentence structure, usage, general sophistication or style of expression, vocabulary, etc. Plagiarism is a difficult matter, but it can be dealt with.

At the secondary level, plagiarism is definitely a problem—especially in research projects or book reports. As with elementary students, discuss the gravity of plagiarism. Make sure students know how to cite sources, and give practice in writing bibliographies. Requiring that students turn in a rough draft along with the final copy also helps. Sometimes you may sense that a piece is plagiarized, but you can't find the original source. When this occurs, question the student and be honest about your doubts. If the student is adamant that the work is original, but your doubts are still strong, you could ask the student to sit in the classroom and write another version of the same material without other resources. Students must understand that the learning of the material is the goal, and that plagiarism undermines that goal.

Missing Assignments

A retired teacher friend of Barbara's has a favorite saying: "He who deceives me once is a fool; he who deceives me twice is a wise man." Apply this to your students. If a student offers what appears to be a legitimate excuse for not having an assignment, be reasonable. Acknowledge the problem, discuss a fair compromise, and perhaps agree to an extra day to complete the assignment. (See the section on Late Assignments below.) Remind the student of the consequences should the incident occur again. Remember, you've already informed the students of the consequences in your opening day rules. Rarely do students hold you in contempt if you are fair, consistent, and firm. Facing up to consequences is a lesson in responsibility.

Late Assignments/Make-Up Work

Kathy found herself at the end of each week with a two-inch stack of make-up work in addition to her regular assignments. Her policy had been to allow students to turn in missed or "re-do" assignments any time before the last two weeks of any grading period. Her intent was to help ensure success for her students. What she was inadvertently accomplishing instead was overworking herself and enabling her students to put things off or turn in sloppy assignments the first time. During the second semester, Kathy finally realized this policy was burying her in paper. She knew that change was impossible at this point in the year, but she began to revamp her policy for the following year.

A late/make-up policy that might work for you could include these three elements:

1. If a student is in school, the assigned work is due. Have students hand it in at the *beginning* of class so they will not use your class time to complete the previous day's assignments while you are presenting today's lesson.
2. Make-up work is typically due two days after a student returns from an absence. In special cases, a counselor or other administrator may help you set up a contract or independent study for make-up work. Extended absences will be handled according to the circumstances.
3. If you allow students to redo assignments, you may want to establish a strict "work due within the week" policy. This means that an assignment from Tuesday needs to be redone and turned in by Friday.

One of the major annoyances for many teachers is the late assignment. You've already handed out an expectation sheet the first day of class which clearly states how much a student's grade will be reduced based on the number of days an assignment is late. A B grade, for example, would become a C. Stress to your students, from the beginning, the importance of meeting deadlines. When you enforce deadlines, you help build students' competence. You can always allow some redoing and revising of daily work *after* deadlines are met.

Some teachers feel that a student who eventually does an assignment, albeit late, is learning more than the student who does nothing. To encourage students who have missed a deadline to do the assignment anyway, help them to recognize that a late grade is better than no grade.

Absences

Chapter 3 discusses the formation of study groups. These groups can provide members with information presented in class that a member missed because of absence. This is helpful to you because it alleviates questions that teachers hear at the most inappropriate times: "What did I miss while I was gone?"

To help absent students get back up to date when they return to class, you could keep a large calendar in the room listing what you did in class each day. This calendar can also note pending due dates. Absent students can check the calendar to find out what they missed.

You might post a make-up date two days after a quiz or test. Allow students a make-up time before or after school. Post a time that is agreeable to you and possible for students to attend. Do not feel that you must skip lunch and remain in your room every minute for students.

A question that is sure to grate on your nerves like a fork scraped across the chalkboard frequently comes from parents after absences due to illness or before or after extended vacations: "Jenny didn't miss anything, did she?" Using your best social skills and most diplomatic manner, let the parent know that yes, indeed, Jenny missed some things, because every class period is a valuable and some ways unique educational experience. Go on to explain, however, that while Jenny won't be able to duplicate the learning experiences she missed, you will give her some suitable make-up assignments to help her cover the missed material.

When you know that a student will be absent for several days or weeks, you can give that student some standard assignments to complete during the absence. Here are some suggestions.

1. Keep up with any assigned reading done in class.
2. Spend a minimum of 15 minutes reading self-selected materials.
3. Complete any daily assignments that can be easily understood. (You shouldn't assign new concepts unless you have talked with the parents and they understand that they are introducing the concept to the student. This will work in some families and cause tension in others. Be sensitive to the situation. If the absence is for an extended period of time, make an annotated report of this on the students' permanent record and report card.)

4. A student going to Mexico on a two-week vacation will have experiences that cannot be duplicated in class. You might ask these traveling students to:
   A. keep a daily journal of activities on the trip.
   B. select a subject pertaining to the destination and prepare a report to be presented to the rest of the class.
A second-grader spent the week after Christmas break in Hawaii and kept a daily journal detailing daily activities. She took photographs, drew pictures, read books on volcanoes, and gave a presentation to the class about the volcanoes on her return. The whole class benefited from that trip.

Help yourself by creating a form to keep track of assignments for ill or traveling students. You or study partners may fill in this form, depending on the age of the student and the type of activities.

It's difficult when a parent asks for assignments for two weeks in advance. It is perfectly reasonable for you to explain that it is impossible for you to give advance assignments without several days' warning. Then use this opportunity to plan ahead and sketch out your lesson plans for the whole class.

Homework Problems

At all grade levels, homework is becoming a major issue. Your district may already have policies regarding homework, or it may not. In any event, you almost certainly assign your students some homework. On the other hand, students today have after-school commitments ranging from gymnastics to piano lessons, or they are cared for away from the home until the evening meal. Furthermore, in a recent survey of 85 high school juniors, almost 80 percent had jobs during the school year.

At a recent meeting of educators and businesspeople, this topic of homework vs. outside commitments—specifically, employment—surfaced. Several teachers at the meeting suggested to the businesspeople that students should not be closing businesses or otherwise working late on school nights. The businesspeople, especially those in the restaurant field, argued that, although they sympathized, their labor needs were best met by willing high school students. A lengthy discussion followed with no solutions.

These same teachers then addressed groups of parents at a Back-to-School night, sharing concerns about the rapidly growing number of students who dash from the classroom to the job. Many parents agreed that the priority should be academics and that if their Tim or Nancy were slacking off, the job would have to go. In reality, though, the grades continued to slip and the student remained gainfully employed.

This is not to suggest that students shouldn't work or participate in after-school activities. Life does extend beyond the school day. However, the growing trend of students with many after-school commitments is creating a whole new perspective on homework. Many parents and educators argue that homework, if it is required, should assume top priority; the job or extra-curricular activities are secondary. Others don't agree and react to undone homework with a shrug and an "Oh, well." We have found it fascinating and disturbing over the years to witness this evolution.

A colleague tells of a recent conversation with a student:
"So why do you work?"
"I have to work to have money for gas and insurance for my car."
"So why do you need a car?"
"So I can get to my job."
This ludicrous logic made perfect sense to the student. No wonder he had no time for homework!

In the past, students would fabricate hundreds of excuses, be absent, or negotiate for an extra day when an assignment was due. Now, many students will tell you what Greg, a tall, quiet, droopy-lidded young man, told Betty when she asked him why he didn't have his assignment: "Sorry, Mrs. N, I worked all weekend loading cargo and didn't get my homework done." He yawned. "I need more time." What he needed was sleep.

However, even if students aren't rushing off to work or soccer, they may face many evenings without support or encouragement. From kindergarten through high school, teachers have heard students say, often tearfully, that they didn't understand the assignment and no one was home to help. It's difficult to reprimand students for something beyond their control.

The homework issue for you boils down to this: either the work is turned in, or it isn't. When the work isn't turned in, you might give the student a zero, but that doesn't meet the learning objective. The real problem is that the student without completed homework is not ready for the next day's assignment. If you are an elementary teacher, you could require that the student complete the missing work at school that day. On the secondary level, you could allow more out-of-class work time with a grade reduction, but make it clear to the student that the homework was given to achieve a learning goal and is not busy work, to be done whenever (and if) the student chooses. At any grade level, you might give homework a completion check in your grade book so that the assignment is acknowledged, but you aren't overburdened with grading.

You can use several techniques to ensure that your students understand the homework assignment before they leave the classroom. Students might write down the assignment and share what they wrote with others in their study group. You could also check assignment understanding as a way to close each lesson. As Robert stands at the door to say goodbye to his grade-schoolers, he asks each child to tell him what homework she or he is going to remember to do that evening. In a middle or high school, you might use the last minute or two before the bell to ask, "What's your assignment for tonight?" You could direct this question to the class at large or to individual students.

To hold students accountable for homework involving reading, you may wish to administer a short quiz that tests strictly recall. The responses may simply be a word or phrase so the quizzes are easy for you to grade. If you teach in a secondary school, alter the questions from period to period to alleviate information exchanges between classes.

One of your toughest homework-related calls is that well-meaning parent who does the homework for the child. If a student who normally hands in an assignment that squeaks past failing suddenly turns in work that resembles a doctoral dissertation, you have cause for concern. If the student insists, after a conference, that he or she did do the work, you might verify this with a parent. If the parent also insists that the student did the work—and parents occasionally will—the in-class work should tell the tale. Whatever your decision in such a case, make sure that the method you choose to deal with the student is legal. In other words, the procedure is the same: You acknowledge the work that was done and then you make time during the day for the student to do additional work that demonstrates knowledge of the concept. The student and his or her parents might have done a book report together. During the next day the student might give you an oral report that exhibits an understanding of the book.

Extra Credit

You will also need to be prepared to answer questions regarding extra credit. Thinking through these points first should help you formulate answers to students' questions:

1. Are you going to allow extra-credit activities to replace required assignments that the student chose not to turn in? Many teachers adopt the philosophy that extra credit is enrichment and should be done only after all required assignments have been turned in.
2. Does the extra-credit assignment meet a specific educational goal?
3. Can you make the directions clear enough so the student can complete the assignment independently?
4. Are you willing to invest the time to evaluate these extra-credit projects?

If you are a beginning teacher, you're already overwhelmed with daily planning and grading. You probably don't have the additional time required to plan and evaluate extra-credit projects. The more experience you've gained as a teacher, the more likely you are to have developed a file of easily evaluated, educationally valid extra-credit activities.

If you choose not to offer extra credit, your comment to students might be, "I do not accept extra credit, because I'm more interested in having you do the best job you can on required work." The final decision regarding extra credit remains your individual choice. The four points above should help you make that decision.

Conclusion

No matter how students are grouped in classes, their needs will vary. Some may be "at risk" or diagnosed as having a learning difficulty. Others bounce from parent to parent like a tennis ball and may not know where they're going to be sleeping that night. In that same class, you'll find motivated and gifted students. So in arranging your curriculum, creativity and flexibility are critical. Flexibility is also required as you refocus students' attention after classroom interruptions.

All students need a clear perception of the concepts you covered in class. You can accomplish this by:

● clearly stating the objectives.
● explaining the material's relevance.
● reviewing how and when the learning will be measured.
● leading the students through the material in a series of steps.

Your students will be learning and you will have drastically reduced your curriculum-based problems.

Finally, you have to set a fair, consistent policy to deal with cheating, copied or plagiarized work, late or missing assignments, make-up and extra-credit work, and homework.

CHAPTER 6

Record-Keeping

The school principal came to Robert needing information on a student's attendance. A local judge had asked how many days the student had been enrolled in the district. The authorities needed the date of entrance, absences, number of tardies, and the date the student checked out. All of this information was in the computer in the office, but the secretary had been sent to the district office with the school's attendance disk, leaving the principal temporarily unable to access this information. Robert's records were the only readily available source. Robert and his principal were able to piece the student's attendance history together within minutes because all the information they needed was in Robert's grade book.

As you face a new class for the first time, keeping accurate records may be the furthest thing from your mind. There are so many other things to consider. However, you need to establish a plan for keeping track of who attends your class, grades, lessons you've taught, student behavior, and personal records. Your grade book, faculty handbook, and master contract are all legal documents. With a system of record-keeping and filing documents that suits your personality and teaching style, you can handle the necessity of keeping records efficiently and leave more time for the other aspects of teaching.

You may come across some wonderful-sounding and elaborate plans for keeping track of daily attendance and grades, but if they don't fit your personality and teaching style, you won't follow through. To help you work out your own system, this chapter outlines what kinds of records you will most likely be expected to keep and offers some examples of ways you can accomplish this record-keeping.

Attendance

Keeping track of who attends your class and when each student arrives is a daily or hourly chore that you must deal with quickly. Your school will have an established procedure for reporting attendance and tardies. Your grade book is the legal record of this information. Whether it's to provide information to an administrator, confer with a parent, fill out a tardy notification, or complete report cards, you need to have easy access to accurate documentation. You'll want to take attendance quickly in the first minutes of class. Having the forms available and your grade book set up are two ways you can simplify and expedite this process.

Robert allows a student to fill out the attendance form that must be sent in to his elementary school's office every morning. This job is handled by all the students on a rotating basis. Absences, tardies, and the lunch count are noted, and the slip is then hung on the door to be picked up by an office aide. Robert quickly checks around the room to be sure the report is accurate and then personally marks any absences or tardies in his grade book. Robert uses a system of A for absent, T for tardy, and 1/2 for half days absent. In an elementary classroom, the teacher is responsible for recording attendance only once a day, and Robert's system is not too hard to handle. If a student arrives after being marked absent (A), Robert erases the A and replaces it with a T. Additionally, if a student leaves during the day, Robert notes it with a 1/2 in the grade book.

Gerry, a high school music teacher, also allows a student to take roll. She feels pushed for rehearsal time and wants to begin class as soon as the bell rings. She assigns a reliable student as secretary to complete the attendance task for her. The student completes the school's attendance form and marks an attendance sheet which is kept separate from Gerry's record of student grades. Later, Gerry transfers the attendance information to her own grade book. Although Gerry starts class as soon as the bell rings and leaves roll-taking to a student, she makes mental notes of students who stagger in late or are missing. She is responsible for the accuracy of the records she keeps, and she wants to be on top of the situation; she double-checks the student assistant's record. If you want to try this, get to know your students a little so you can determine who would be able to handle this task. You could also confer with an experienced teacher in your building about which students would be reliable helpers.

Many administrators, however, do not condone students having roll-taking responsibilities. Betty greets her students as they enter the room and gets them started on the day's assignment, already written on the board. As the students are working, she checks over her seating chart and notes missing or tardy students in her grade book. Betty has six classes each day and sees 160 students. She has devised a system of symbols to denote absences and tardies, as shown on her sample grade-book sheet on page 152. Finally, Betty marks those same students absent or tardy on the computerized report sheet that goes to the office.

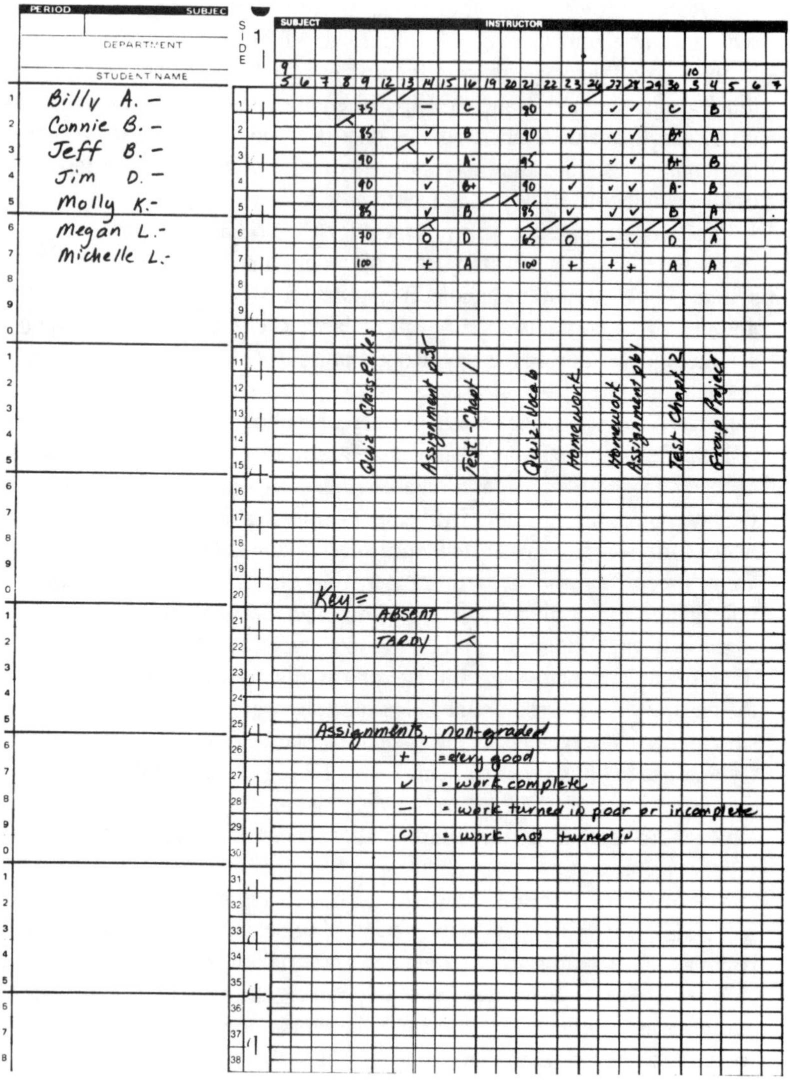

PERIOD	SUBJEC	SIDE 1	SUBJECT								INSTRUCTOR										
DEPARTMENT			9																	10		
STUDENT NAME			5	6	7	8	9	12	13	14	15	16	19	20	21	22	23	24	27	28	29	30	3	4	5	6	7
1 Billy A. –	1					75		–			C		70	0	✓	✓		C	B	
2 Connie B. –	2					85	✓		B			90	✓	✓	✓		B+	A	
3 Jeff B. –	3					90		✓		A-		95	✓		✓	✓	B+	B	
4 Jim D. –	4					90		✓		B+		90	✓		✓	✓	A-	B	
5 Molly K. –	5					85		✓		B		85	✓		✓	✓	B	A	
6 Megan L. –	6					70		0		D		65	0		–	✓	D	A	
7 Michelle L. –	7					100		+		A		100	+		+	+	A	A	
8	8	
9	9	
0	10	

Column headers (handwritten, vertical):
Quiz – Class Rules / Assignment p.3 / Test – Chap 1 / Quiz – Vocab / Homework / Homework / Assignment p.6 / Test Chap. 2 / Group Project

Key = ABSENT ╱
        TARDY   ◁

Assignments, non-graded

    + = very good
    ✓ = work complete
    – = work turned in poor or incomplete
    ○ = work not turned in

Grades

Planning relevant and creative lessons is the heart of your curriculum, yet monitoring student progress is the blood of this process. You need to allow students plenty of opportunities to display how they are assimilating the content, and you must keep accurate records of student progress.

Kathy was conferencing with a parent who was having some trouble accepting the grade his child had earned in math. Kathy tried to explain to the parent that, while she was not denying the student could be grasping the concepts covered, the student was not displaying that knowledge. The student's daily work scores were average, many assignments were missing, and test scores were barely passing. Finally, in desperation, Kathy reached for her grade book and said to the parent, "Perhaps we need to look at the grades again. I may have made a mistake." Kathy had recorded daily assignment and test scores, made tally marks noting participation, and kept track of the completion of in-class and homework assignments. By looking at the grade book, the parent began to understand why the child had earned that grade.

Recording observations, assignment and test scores, and class participation can be a time-consuming job. Try to find ways of streamlining this tedious task. Numerous computer grade-book programs are readily available. These programs will weigh (value) special assignments and test scores, average grades, and allow you to print out a weekly or mid-term grade report. It will take you extra time to become familiar with a computer program and to enter all your students' names into the computer at the beginning of the year or each new term. However, in the long run, using a computer grade book can save you time.

Brian enters all of his grades into a computer. He records scores on a daily basis in his grade book—this serves as a backup hard copy. Then, at least once a week, he sits down and updates the computer file. He is surprised at how little time it actually takes to do this. At mid-term, Brian prints out class averages, and within minutes he is able to fill out progress reports or provide this information to students, counselors, or parents. Additionally, any time during the year when he has a parent conference, Brian can print out an individual's grades.

This system works well for Brian because he's a computer buff. Betty, on the other hand, uses her personal computer for word processing but can't be bothered by the extra time needed to enter students' names and scores into the computer. She keeps track of everything in her grade book and uses a calculator to average grades when needed. Neither Brian nor Betty permits students to record grades in the grade book.

Again, the method you choose needs to fit your personality while also promoting correct results. The key to record-keeping is accuracy.

The most efficient way to set up your grade book is to enter students' names in alphabetical order. Elementary teachers set up separate pages for attendance and each subject taught. Middle school, junior high, and high school teachers have one page for each class period. You could keep attendance on this same sheet or have an extra page for attendance.

As you create assignments, determine how many points a student will receive for completing the task or if you will assign a completion grade. Then, when you grade the assignments, you could record the total points possible at the top of each column and enter each student's score in that column. Noting the assignment at the top or bottom of the column helps you quickly identify needed make-up work or missing assignments. (See the example of Betty's grade-book sheet.)

Robert uses a system of +, /, and – to record completion grades. He does this for homework assignments and daily work completed in class. This not only saves him time correcting work but also makes it easy for him to keep track of students' progress. Then, when it is necessary to average grades, a + is worth three points, a / is worth two points, a – is worth one point, and a zero denotes a missing assignment.

Robert also encourages students to share what they know during in-class discussions. While most school districts discourage teachers from giving grades based on attitude, you can reward students for positive in-class behavior by keeping qualitative participation grades. Betty makes a tally mark by a student's name as each contributes to class discussions. This not only allows Betty to observe and keep track of students who contribute but also allows Betty to note if one student is being given more response opportunities than another. She looks over the log to see if anyone is dominating the conversations while another is being left out. Betty determines how many times she would expect each person to respond. This would indicate the total number of possible participation points and serves as the standard when she averages grades.

Lesson Plans

Chapter 4 details how to write lesson plans. We mention them here again because they serve as a record of what you have covered in class. If a student, administrator, or parent inquires about content taught during a specific week, paging back in the lesson plan book can provide information your brain cannot remember at that instant. Robert refers to his lesson plan books from previous years to determine if he is pacing himself and will have time to accomplish his learning objectives. He also reads over these plans to review how he taught specific concepts or units of study. Your lesson plan book will serve as the log or journal of your teaching year.

Sometimes you will need to reserve material or equipment in advance. If you've kept a record of when you used materials previously, you can plan your order ahead. Brian has to fill out his film requests in March for the following year. During his first few years of teaching, he was unsure of what was available and how to judge when to order that material. While he doesn't stick to a strict schedule year after year, he does go over last year's plans to get a general idea of when he and his students will be exploring topics. He then orders films to enhance the curriculum.

Mike keeps loads of detailed information in his kindergarten plan book along with lesson plans. This information ranges from his favorite play dough recipe to the name and phone number of the woman from the Poison Control Center who gave the great presentation last year. He refers to last year's plan book to see how many parent helpers he needs to contact for the field trip to the science museum. Mike's plan book is a log not just of his learning objectives but also of what his class was able to accomplish, what equipment he'll need for a successful project, and changes he wants to make in the unit the next time he teaches it. He has a record of the sequence of instruction, length of time required, and notes about what went well or flopped.

Student Files

As you fill out referrals for admission into special programs, receive notes from parents, file a discipline report, or complete a report card, you need to keep a copy. Elementary teachers can set up a separate file for each student. The file then holds all the paperwork and correspondence pertaining to that student. Junior high, middle, and high school teachers cannot logistically set up a file for each student. Betty solves this problem by having one folder for each type of form. She maintains another folder for correspondence. Within each folder, the forms are kept in alphabetical order by student name.

It is essential that you keep track of discipline referrals and attendance. If you ever have a serious problem with a student, your only successful course of action lies within the documentation you've kept. Chapter 2 on discipline outlines, in detail, how and what you need to keep track of to ensure due process.

Student files are also the place to record amusing anecdotes and positive things that happen in class. For example, being able to share a student's insight about the difference between engineering and inventing establishes a lasting link between you and a parent. Mike uses a three-ring binder that holds a personal information sheet, previously completed by a parent, on each student. This is followed by a blank sheet on which Mike records classroom observations. He writes down at least one of the positive things that has happened in class that week to each of his kindergarten students. Mike also notes any problems he is having with students. These observations are nonjudgmental and simply record what has happened. Mike carries the notebook home when he has to make calls to parents in the evening. He then has access to phone numbers and parents' names.

Years ago a colleague of Betty's noted a student's behavior with a derogatory comment next to the student's name in the grade book. The grade book mysteriously disappeared. A short time later, the teacher was confronted by the administration. The thief had made sure the contents of the grade book became public knowledge. The parents, angry with the derogatory comment, stormed into the principal's office. This story illustrates why you need to keep your records objective, nonjudgmental, and secure.

One last note about student files. They are confidential records. Observations, referral forms, attendance notices, and personal information are not to be shared with others and should be kept in a locked file. If you are careless with this type of information, you could be exposing yourself to legal action, and you are betraying the trust you have tried so hard to establish with your students.

Personal Files

Master contracts, faculty handbooks, insurance policies, and faculty bulletins are all legal documents and contain information that you are responsible for adhering to. While you are expected to follow all the rules, regulations, and suggestions, no one can expect you to remember all of this. Save yourself time and frustration by setting up a file for all this information. Whenever you have a question about what you should be doing, you can refer to the handbook or the appropriate faculty bulletin. Brian recently read in his weekly "Notes for Notice," his school's faculty bulletin, that the principal was reminding teachers to stand in the hallway between classes in order to insure correct behavior and reduce littering. Brian was confused. Based on information in the teachers' handbook, Brian thought he was supposed to be inside his classroom as students entered. By standing in or near his doorway, Brian discovered he could help reinforce correct hallway decorum as directed yet still greet incoming students and keep track of what was happening inside the room. In this case, the faculty bulletin is considered a legal written document, and Brian needs to observe it as well as directives in the teacher's handbook.

For financial reasons, you'll benefit by keeping records of your personal absences. Tami received her paycheck one month and the amount was less than what she expected. She didn't know why she had been docked. When she called the district office to inquire, she found out that the record showed she had been gone for two days that were not allowable sick leave. Since Tami keeps track of when she signs leave reports, she was able to check with her building secretary the next day and clear up the matter quickly. If Tami hadn't had these records, it would have been difficult to resolve this matter.

You may want to add these items to this file of personal papers: a copy of your signed contract, letters of your assignment, observations and evaluation reports, paycheck stubs, and other communication concerning your employment.

Conclusion

Keeping accurate records is one of your duties. It may not be your favorite thing to do, but it is essential. Set up a system that is easy for you to maintain—one you know you are likely to follow. Don't think that just because something works for someone else it is going to work for you. As long as you can locate information and you are accurate, your bases are covered. Things you'll need to keep track of include attendance, grades, what's happened in class, and personal information.

CHAPTER 7

Legal Considerations

Don't have a nervous break down if students don't seem to like you.

Toby #10

Never become
discouraged !

grade 6
Todd

Jeff is a science teacher and a coach. Enthusiastic, sympathetic, and kind, Jeff is a hero to students. Fellow teachers don't see Jeff much, as he's usually in his room, chatting with a group of kids. The students, eager to have finally found an adult who relates to and understands them, will tell you he's their favorite teacher.

Jeff began to receive notes. Unsigned, they were harmless enough, mostly thanking Jeff for being such a caring teacher and for being "so cool" and easy to talk with. Since Jeff spoke with so many students and the notes were complimentary, Jeff shrugged it off and forgot about them.

The notes continued, and finally a quiet blond girl began to seek Jeff out between classes, at lunch, and after school. A caring teacher, Jeff listened as she relayed problems of drug and sexual abuse, divorced parents who shipped her from state to state, and other horror stories. Jeff listened and assisted the girl in obtaining help from counselors, nurses, and school psychologists.

One rainy fall night, Jeff was curled up in front of his fireplace with a bowl of popcorn, enjoying a rare moment of watching football instead of coaching it. His doorbell rang. He answered it. There, drenched and intoxicated, stood his young blond student. Since students had visited the house before, Jeff instinctively opened the door and assisted the now-sick young woman to his bathroom, where she promptly threw up and passed out. Jeff cleaned her up, drove her home, and left her in the care of an older sister, the girl's "guardian." Several weeks passed before a distraught principal and district supervisor informed Jeff that they were all about to be sued. For the second time in his life Jeff would be going to court: The first had been for a minor traffic infraction; the second would be to face charges of sexual molestation.

Two years later Jeff will tell you that the "stupidest thing" he did was open the door that night. He'll tell you that although he still cares about adolescents, he doesn't listen to them the way he did before or meet with them alone or at his house; he'll tell you that he doesn't offer them rides when it's snowing outside or touch them even if it's just a pat on the back. He'll tell you that nothing was more frightening than the year of anticipation before the case ever went to court. Waking up in the morning to the headlines and facing his students, colleagues, and family were a living hell. Knowing he was innocent but having to live with an accusation of sexual molestation had never occurred to Jeff. He'd cared about kids; he was a teacher.

Never before have teachers been so vulnerable to lawsuits. With increasing emphasis on child abuse, professionals who deal with young people are continually in the public eye.

This chapter doesn't cite cases or provide a detailed description of educational law—space does not permit it, and that's not the purpose of this book. Laws pertaining to education are numerous and vary from state to state. Laws exist about issues from student dress to search and seizure. One of the most valuable yet unfamiliar classes offered to teachers is a course on educational law. When you have the time, you may wish to take such a course. For now, here are some suggestions that may help prevent potential problems.

Because most educators are caring individuals, they often don't stop and analyze possible consequences before they act. The elementary teacher who hugs a crying third-grader or the physical education teacher who offers a ride home to the boy in her second-period class doesn't often think that a possible lawsuit may result from a fabricated or exaggerated report submmitted by an angry student or a parent on a witch hunt. Jeff certainly didn't. Most liability problems could be prevented if educators were aware of their extreme vulnerability and used common sense.

Even though you will probably not have time during the first weeks with a new class or in a new school to read them, there are several legal sources you need to keep with your records and refer to. You will probably have access to a policy manual for your school district, a master contract from your teachers' association, and bulletins from your school administrator informing you of policies and requirements within the building. These are critical, as they represent written "law." If a controversy arises, this written information may be what determines guilt or innocence. Keep in mind that if you choose not to follow the policies, you may have to accept consequences that will be anything but pleasant. Adhering to the policies will definitely help you to avoid conflict.

Physical Contact

It is a sad comment on our society that we can no longer touch people without a tinge of fear. It's especially tragic that with so many children in need of affection and attention, we feel powerless to fulfill that need. Although it sounds heartless, be careful about touching kids. Find out what your building or district policy is on physical contact. If it is a "no-touching" policy, adhere to it rigorously, making no exceptions.

To do otherwise might risk your career. If there is no policy, or if you can use your own discretion, read on.

If you are a "distance" person, a no-touching or limited-touching policy probably won't be a problem. But if you're one of those types who can't have a conversation without a hug, tap, or pat, be careful. It's best not to initiate physical contact. Sometimes, especially in elementary grades, students will rush up to embrace you in a moment of grief or joy. Avoid frontal hugs. Robert gives such a child a quick, soft shoulder squeeze, being careful to maintain distance. He also tousles hair and pats backs if he has students who need extra attention.

Adolescents are less likely to initiate physical contact; however, you will encounter teenage students who crave affection and will rush at you when you least expect it. Be aware that others may not perceive these adolescent displays the same way they would in the elementary grades. Maintain your distance. Rely on a sympathetic ear, a kind voice, and a sense of humor to show your students that you care.

Physical contact is not always positive. *Never* touch students if you are angry. For many adults, a common response to anger is to grab a youngster's arm or shoulder. Instead, if a conflict arises, distance yourself from the student until you both have cooled down. Having the student wait just outside the door allows both of you time to think. You can deal with the student after class.

Chapter 2 discusses what to do about fights. While following the Chapter 2 guidelines, keep the liability problem of touching in mind.

Students in Your Home

If a student visits your home, you must exercise extreme caution. Lack of awareness about this almost destroyed Jeff. Seriously consider the responsibilities involved in having students visit your home.

Kathy has a spring picnic for her 6th-graders at her residence. The students get signed permission slips from their parents allowing them to attend. Many parents help plan the function, which they also attend, assisting Kathy in the supervision. Parents and students have anticipated this event since Kathy first initiated it.

Marc invites his high school wrestling team to his home for a barbecue at the end of the season. Other teachers and coaches attend and, in Marc's school, the event has become a traditional closure to the season.

As positive and well-supervised as these activities are, risks are still involved. Here are some tips regarding students visiting your home, to minimize those risks:

- Never admit a student into your home if you are alone. If the student is ill or intoxicated, have him or her wait outside. Provide a coat or blanket if necessary. Contact the parent, your building administrator, or 911.
- If a student appears on your doorstep "to talk," set up an appointment to see the student the following day at school. If the student claims that she or he has been abused, proceed as above. If the student claims that the parent was the instigator of the abuse, contact your building administrator or school nurse.
- If the student needs to talk to you right away, set up a meeting in a public place such as a restaurant that does *not* have a liquor license. Meet the student there.

Your decisions about students and home visits depend on your community, your relationship with the parents, and your school's policy. Just be aware of the risks involved.

Corporal Punishment

As a teacher, corporal punishment is not your responsibility. Neither should you promote it in your school or district. Corporal punishment is nearly always destructive and demeaning. Its damage is often far more serious than the physical pain it inflicts.

Although "swats" still occur, they are ineffective; many students consider them a badge of honor. If a school official chooses to administer "swats," this type of punishment should *never* occur without a witness.

Being Where You're Supposed to Be

You may be found negligent if something happens to a student when you're not in the room or where you are supposed to be at a given time. The "being where you're supposed to be" expectation might seem unrealistic or even impossible sometimes, but is is an important fact of life in most teaching situations. Teachers can be held legally responsible for what happens in their absence.

If you must leave your room for any reason—to use the restroom, to make an emergency phone call, because your bra strap breaks or your fly refuses to close—ask a dependable colleague across the corridor to watch your class until you return. Even then, you run a risk. It's always better to stay with your class until you get to an authorized break period. If you're supposed to monitor hallway behavior between classes or during passing periods, stand in your doorway so you can also keep your eye on the kids in your classroom.

Permission Slips

This is more of an issue in elementary school, for field trips, but as older students become more mobile because of trips to competitions and enrichment opportunities, you will have to obtain permission from parents or legal guardians for these students as well. Do not assume you can herd a busload of youngsters off to the local cheese factory or statehouse whenever it fits your schedule. First, you'll have to find out what you need to do about obtaining permission in writing for each student.

Evaluation

You cannot give "attitude grades" and expect administrative support. Chapter 6 discusses participation grades. Often there is a strong correlation between a student's attitude and participation in class.

Since the grade book is often the legal record, it is critical not only that you keep thorough, accurate records but also that you are able to justify the grades you assign your students. Grade as objectively as possible. You'll often have to explain grades, especially after report cards are sent home. Make sure that you could tell an angry parent why Susie received a B instead of an A.

Legal Obligations About What Students Tell You

Students can provide you with unexpected information. To build trust, tell students from the beginning that anything they write is between you and them unless the audience is otherwise specified. Usually you should not share an essay with a class, an administrator, or a parent without that student's knowledge. However, make it clear to students that if they write about illegal occurrences or life-threatening instances, you are bound by law to report such things, as a way of protecting them from harm.

While meeting with a student about an essay topic, Mary heard him talk excitedly about a beer party that might take place that weekend. Calmly, she counseled him not to attend and not to participate in underage drinking. She was also careful to explain that if she were to *know* that a party was taking place, and when and where, she would have to report its existence to the appropriate authorities.

Another time Mary was shuffling through a mountain of papers that had had names removed during peer evaluations. (Code numbers were helping her put names back on papers.) A paper and a poem surfaced, heavy with black images of death and suicide. Even students who responded to the anonymous writer sensed something wrong and suggested that the writer seek help. Mary sought immediate help. Counselors had the student out of class in ten minutes. As it turned out, his home life was very stable and he was only experimenting with the power of words. He was successful. Mary didn't get angry with him. She explained the procedure she follows when a student appears to cry for help and that she reports such information because she cares. The student became interested in all the support services he had suddenly discovered and he felt good that they were there. Mary asked him for an autographed copy of his first thriller when it made the best-seller list.

Teachers must report any knowledge they have of illegal activities or possession, abuse, suicide, or neglect. Students don't always want help or intervention, but your responsibility to them and yourself, and under the law, is to report what you know to a counselor, school resource officer, school nurse, vice-principal, or principal.

Due Process

Chapter 2 discussed steps in dealing with discipline problems. If you follow the outlined steps, you are allowing your students due process—the right to be made aware of consequences and the right to be heard. Making arbitrary decisions backs you into a corner, and no one is happy with the results. If your student has not received due process, it is unlikely that you will receive administrative support of your action.

Statements to students like "Either do this or get out of class" accomplish nothing. You set up a power struggle. If the student does not cooperate and you follow through with your threat of removing him or her from class, you also remove the student's responsibility to complete the assignment. If you back down from your threat, you lose credibility with everyone. To avoid these types of confrontation, set up clear expectations and consequences in the beginning.

Time Spent with Students

Although conferences with students should be held privately and are not for all to hear, it is important that you hold these meetings with  doors open, especially if the student is a member of the opposite sex. This is as important in elementary grades as it is in secondary. As child abuse becomes more of a focus, it's paramount to use common sense in time you spend with children. Keep doors open and avoid suspicion.

You will likely be asked to chaperone dances. This can be an enjoyable way to get to know your students in a different setting. They appreciate your interest and even find your presence amusing. They may ask you to dance. Although most teachers will good-naturedly shake a leg or two, avoid slow dancing with students. High school girls, more often than boys, are quick to approach favorite male teachers in hopes of a sultry clinch. You can save face and decline without hurt feelings if you summon your sense of humor: "I'd like to, Sally, but that fast one wore me out," or, "I promised my wife all the slow ones," should do the trick. Saying no to a beautiful 17-year-old who thinks you're incredible may save you from a lawsuit and possibly losing your job.

Most districts have specific "chauffeur policies" regarding school personnel who drive students to activities. Coaches and other teachers often drive vans or busloads of students to and from school. If you are required to chauffeur students, check with your school's policy on insurance and liability. You are at risk if you drive students home. Even with others in the car, you're still liable if the student is under age and the parents decide for any reason to press charges. If you're involved in an accident, the results could be disastrous; if not, you could still run a risk of being accused of battery or sexual or physical abuse. You may be surprised how many people believe the child and not the adult in these cases.

Dress

Years ago, students could be asked to leave class for wearing blue jeans or if their skirts were too short. Depending on your school, you may not have any latitude in determining what students wear in your classroom. The key to decision-making about student attire breaks down to this: Does the attire interfere with the teaching/learning process? With the emphasis on antidrug and alcohol programs, some schools and districts have adopted policies forbidding clothing or jewelry that pertains to drugs or alcohol. In many urban schools, clothing and accessories associated with gang colors, names, and symbols are strictly forbidden. Check with your administration and adhere to its policy. It is not your job to monitor students' clothing. However, enforce your school policy concerning student dress.

Contraband

If you suspect students are harboring contraband (weapons, alcohol, narcotics, or explosives), report your suspicions to the administrator or resource officer promptly. Provisions involving search and seizure are too numerous to cover in this chapter. Refer your suspicions to qualified personnel and let them handle the matter.

Enforced Patriotism

If a child refuses to stand during a flag ceremony or sing the national anthem, do not force participation. Chances are he or she will explain the reasons and either choose to stand or sit quietly. If this sort of behavior is unacceptable in your community, it is preferable for you to allow a school official to initiate dealing with the student.

Special Education

Special education teachers operate under the guidelines of a whole different set of rules. In addition to your district and school procedures, you also have to deal with federal and state regulations about special ed. If you are a special ed teacher, you've probably become acquainted with these in your training. If not, and you have "special" students in your class, check with your building administrator or special education facilitator. Due to the nature of the many forms and documents required in this area, accurate record-keeping is mandatory. It's also essential from a liability standpoint.

Coaching

You may very well, at one time or another, be asked to coach. Coaching offers rewards in that it allows you to see a whole different side to kids; often the ones who do poorly in academics shine when placed on a volleyball court, balance beam, or football field.

In many cases, coaching solicits a high degree of loyalty and, consequently, influence. Don't abuse this power. Your primary goal should involve the kids' welfare. Often, in the frenzy of competition, coaches forget this and let victory supersede what's good for the individual.

You may be asked to coach a sport you've never played or have only engaged in once or twice. Learn the rules. Your school may have an athletic facilitator or director. Ask questions. Attend meetings. The rules of coaching are much like the rules of teaching. Consistency and fairness are the keys. Abide by what policy states.

The very nature of sports implies more risk than in the classroom, so it's especially important when coaching to be where you are supposed to be. If students are training with weights and you're not in the weight room, you could be liable in case of accident or injury.

As a coach, you may have to treat injuries; sprained ankles, broken collarbones, and eye injuries are some of the most common. Most personnel who work in situations where injuries are likely are required to attend seminars or courses in first aid. This is an area where you are extremely vulnerable. Do not guess about treating injuries. Be sure you have been properly trained before you administer treatment. Do not hesitate to send an injured student to the school nurse or, after regular school hours, to the hospital emergency room. You will probably have to file an accident report immediately. Be certain to check your school's policy regarding the treatment of injuries and what you are expected to do in the event that they occur.

Classroom Equipment

The weight room, science lab, home ec kitchen, industrial arts shop, theater, auto mechanics bay, or classroom all offer potential horseplay dangers. A circular saw in the hands of a 16-year-old could make Vincent Price shudder. Train students in equipment use and safety. Monitoring and guiding practice is critical. Most importantly, remain in the room with the students and the equipment. Teacher absence is a major target for lawsuits. Again, be where you're supposed to be.

Attendance

In Chapter 6, we explained the importance of keeping good records. We cannot emphasize this enough! In most cases, your grade book offers the final say in a legal conflict. In many districts, a computer monitors attendance and tardies. But many school computer systems contain glitches, and it won't be uncommon for an attendance officer or administrator to double-check with you. Keep your own accurate records. If the process of detention, expulsion, or loss of credit involves documentation, promptly fill out the forms. As annoying as it is, the paperwork is all part of what keeps you legal and accountable.

Conclusion

A phrase that often occurs in court cases and legal disputes regarding education issues is "reasonable and prudent." Paying attention to written policy and using common sense is "reasonable and prudent" and should keep you far away from what Jeff experienced. Twenty years ago much of what we have written in this chapter would have been scoffed at as paranoia. Today such caution is necessary to keep you in your job and out of court.

CHAPTER 8

Administration

Don't let the Administration or the
students wear away your Enthusiasm. P.S.
Don't pick on the kid drawing in the Back row... He is
listening.
                                    CHANCE D
                                         10TH

Administrators' Expectations

Administrators in your building had specific expectations when they
hired you. One of the judgments they made was that you had the
abilities and skills to fulfill these expectations. Administrators interested
in your success should be clear and candid about your responsibilities.
Administrators have common expectations of all teachers on staff
whether these are stated in writing or assumed.

Loyalty   Loyalty ranks high on the administrative wish list. All staff
members are expected to be loyal to colleagues, the principal, and the
school district. This means that you do not criticize teachers, administrators, or policies to students, parents, or others in the community. If you
have a complaint, talk to the person who can effect a change.

If a student complains about another teacher, do not get entangled
in the issue, even if you agree. Interject with, "Please do not complain
about other teachers to me. If you have a complaint, talk to that teacher.
If you talk behind your teacher's back, I wonder what you say to others
about me." Students then rush to convince you that they *adore* you and
never talk behind your back, but theyy get the point. Of course, students
will sometimes confide legitimate concerns to you—for example, problems concerning safety issues. Your job is then to take appropriate action
to protect the student.

Teachers complaining and whining in the lounge seldom effect any
change. At Ellen's elementary school, the principal announced an extensive series of meetings about curriculum and daily lesson plans. The
whining was loud and ardent in the teachers' lounge. Morale plunged.
Faculty attended the meetings sullenly. Finally, during a conversation in
the principal's office, Ellen said, "Mr. Roth, I feel that we work well
together and I trust you completely. Therefore, I would like to ask a
question for which I'd appreciate an honest answer. What specific goal
or outcome do you have in mind for these planning meetings? I'm feeling
anxious because I don't understand the purpose for them." Mr. Roth
explained his reasoning both to Ellen and to the rest of her faculty. He
was seeking complete and ongoing knowledge about what was happening in the classrooms of his school. He could then intelligently share
information with parents and provide stronger support for his teachers.
When the teachers understood the reasoning behind the project, the
whining ceased and the work began.

Disloyalty to the district is often reflected by staff members who complain to the general public about inadequate textbooks or poorly written curricula. You might hear another teacher talking down one school because of low test scores. Instead of complaints, administrators expect loyal employees to volunteer to join textbook and curriculum committees to improve existingg conditions. Administrators also expect employees to look for the good things that happen even in the low-achieving schools and to provide the best possible teaching situations designed to improve those scores. In other words, administrators expect you to work to remedy those situations you have control over and not whine about the rest.

Teaching Competency   Administrators expect you to arrive with a knowledge base in your subject area. They expect you competently to plan lessons that accomplish educational goals, appeal to a variety of learners, and fairly evaluate student progress. You will be expected to follow the adopted curriculum. If you feel the guidelines are restrictive or outdated, join curriculum-writing committees and participate in the revision.

Flexibility   You'll need to be able to both laugh and cry. You must communicate with students and enjoy the age group you work with. Administrators respect flexibility and the ability to adjust to surprises.

School Climate   Administrators expect teachers, both new and experienced, to contribute actively to the school climate. This contribution includes sharing extra duties, being supportive of all programs, participating in all-school projects and assemblies, and exhibiting a positive attitude. School climate also includes clear and honest communication between teachers and administrators. It includes sharing responsibilities when making decisions that affect the smooth operation of the total school program. School climate also means being socially cordial with other staff members and support staff. A positive school climate provides for a place where both teachers and students want to come every day to engage in mutual learning experiences. Whiners and complainers drag others down. Administrators appreciate positive people. Positive attitudes are infectious.

Community Awareness   Administrators expect their teachers to be sensitive to the community that populates the school. Is the community conservative, liberal, racially mixed, wealthy, or poor? You need to respond with dignity and compassion to diverse backgrounds. You might build lessons that teach about diverse backgrounds. Other lessons might center around open communication and tolerance.

Student Support   Administrators expect each staff member to do his or her part to develop a positive support network for the children in the school. Be aware of the resources and resource people in the building and how to access services. Appropriate use of library services, counseling, reading or music specialists, or even volunteers can provide a smoothly operating integrated learning climate that is tailored to the individual needs of students.

Classroom Management   Administrators expect all teachers to manage the classroom effectively. You must be willing to take appropriate steps to maintain a learning environment in the classroom. Administrators also expect you to follow the proper channels if you must take a management issue beyond your classroom.

Evaluation   Administrators expect all teachers to be able to take constructive criticism and compliments. They expect you to self-evaluate and grow professionally.

Open-Mindedness   Administrators expect teachers not to prejudge, but to view all situations and personalities as being part of a learning situation. When learning is viewed as changes in behavior, then all students, teachers, administrators, and support staff are capable of learning. Prejudgment does not leave room for learning and change. Don't assume the worst. Keep an open mind.

Health   Administrators expect staff members to maintain personal health—both emotional and physical.

When you are hired to teach in a specific school, you may have a clear idea as to that school's philosophy. Your school might be the most ethnically diverse in the city. It might be the richest or the poorest.

Whatever the "specialty" of your school, when you are asked to join that staff, you are also asked to support that philosophy. If you find that you do not fit in and are uncomfortable, you might consider asking for a transfer for the following year. In the meantime, do your job as professionally as possible.

The Role of the Administrator

School administrators, like teachers, exhibit a variety of styles while doing their job. Some guide their faculties; others lead. Some administrate from behind a desk; others can be found in classrooms, on the playground, or reading to students in the lunchroom while everyone else eats. Whatever the style, you should be able to expect certain things from your administrator.

Support   You can expect your administrator to provide the support you need for a successful teaching experience. This support needs to be tempered with a sense of humor and sensitivity. That person needs to be involved in conferences, help you with extreme discipline problems, and provide materials and assistance that will improve the classroom climate.

You need support from your administrator. If an irate parent storms into your classroom, you need your administrator to take that person to the office, calm him or her, and set up a conference time to solve the conflict. You should expect that your administrator will investigate all sides of the situation.

Your administrator should create an environment in the school that is conducive to learning. It is up to that administrator to make sure that the custodial staff, cooks, bus drivers, and other support personnel work to provide a safe, comfortable place for students and teachers. Effective administrating will produce a school day relatively free of interruptions, non-school-related campaigns, or surprises. This administrator should recognize your successes and inform the general public about the good things happening at your school.

Role Model   Ideally, you should be able to consider your building principal as your master teacher and role model—a positive instructional leader. She or he should both supervise and evaluate you. Supervision involves observing and providing suggestions for improving teaching techniques. Evaluation involves written summaries of observed classroom performance for your permanent records. Your principal should carry out this supervision and evaluation in a way that will improve instruction for students.

Many principals or otther administrators love to come into your classroom and participate. This is a good experience for you and your students. Brian's vice-principal occasionally teaches a lesson on archaeology for the sociology students. You could ask your principal to come in with a short piece of writing to share. In an elementary classroom, you might invite your administrator in to listen to students read. Robert's principal reads holiday stories to the classes. There are lots of creative ways to get administrators into your classroom to share in the learning process. It is good for your students to see their building administrator in this role, and it keeps that administrator aware of the good things that are happening in your classroom.

Involvement　　You can expect that your administrator will be interested and involved in the total school program. Through that interest, your administrator should focus on specific goals and help guide the whole faculty toward those goals. Your administrator should understand the scope and sequence of your subject or grade level relative to the total educational program in the district.

Professionalism　　You can expect your administrator to demonstrate a positive professional attitude. He or she should work hard and manage time wisely. This administrator should be able to make decisions and follow through on them, yet be able to admit mistakes and be willing to change.

Evaluations

Most schools have a regular program of formal evaluations. When you are evaluated, you can expect to be shown a written copy of that evaluation before it is put in your personnel file. Obtain a copy for your own file. Read each evaluation carefully before signing it. If you feel the evaluation misrepresents a situation, you have the right not to sign it. The administrator might then adjust the evaluation to your mutual satisfaction. Sometimes this is accomplished through additional observations by your supervisor. If something appears on an evaluation that you do not like, you need to explain your viewpoint clearly and calmly. Usually, the evaluator simply missed a verbal direction to the students or misinterpreted a class event, and the conflict is cleared. If the evaluation is not changed to your satisfaction, you are allowed to include a written explanation. Your professional association can advise you if such an uncomfortable situation arises.

Sometimes a chance remark might be included in your evaluation. Sharon was a new media specialist at a middle school. One day, in casual conversation, the principal asked her how much a certain art teacher used the library. Sharon commented that the art teacher did not use the media center often. That remark was used in a derogatory way against the art teacher in his evaluation. Sharon was horrified. The art teacher refused to sign the evaluation. Finally, the principal took the statement off the evaluation.

Years ago Betty was sitting in on a conference between her student teacher and the university supervisor. Betty had promised herself she would only listen. However, the supervisor started firing criticisms, leaving the student teacher speechless—frozen with dismay. Finally, Betty stopped the conference and explained that there was a huge misconception. Betty's student teacher had been following her specific directions. Betty's priority was to maintain a consistent learning situation, and Betty felt her student teacher was finding success in using her techniques. The supervisor looked at the teaching differently during the next observation and recognized the good things that were going on.

If you feel you are being harassed by an administrator, you need to begin documenting carefully and seek the advice of your association representative.

Many administrators drop into your classroom for casual visits that last 15 minutes and do not result in formal, written summaries. Whenever an administrator appears, be cordial. Some enjoy participating in class discussions, offering solutions in solving a math problem or sharing a memory from school years; others are uncomfortable with this. Be sensitive to individual administrators' personalities.

Administrative Styles

Just as students in your room have different styles of learning that sometimes are not compatible with your teaching strengths, your administrator may have a style that clashes with your approach. In your first year with this administrator, it's best if you go with the flow. Follow established rules even if they were obviously written in the Dark Ages, but also get involved in the process for change.

It is your principal's professional duty to know about different administrating and teaching styles. A top-notch principal will recognize and capitalize on the best of those differences. A rigid, inflexible principal may not acknowledge those differences; in this case, it will probably be easier for you to bend. Then you need to find a job the next year with a more compatible administrator.

Dealing with Principals

How you deal with your principal depends a lot on your teaching situation. If you are on a huge faculty, your meetings will probably be infrequent and formal. If you teach on a very small faculty and the principal also teaches part-time, your relationship will probably be more collegial. If the principal was a personal friend before you were hired, realize that your professional association in school is and should be different from the informality of your friendship out of school.

If you are on a fairly large faculty, new on the job, and need to see the principal, you don't need to stake out the parking lot at 7 A.M. to catch this person's attention. Leave a brief note or message with the secretary stating that you need an appointment, suggesting a time you can meet, and telling what you want to discuss. When you arrive, be prepared to tell what you have already done about the situation. Then state what information, help, or permission you need from your principal.

After you have received the information and resolved the situation, send a note of thanks to your principal for the advice and tell about your resulting success. This way the principal will be aware of your successes and be even more willing to help in the future.

Sometimes you can establish effective communication with your principal or vice-principal before you need his or her help in a specific situation by inviting him or her into your classroom to see a special presentation or personally present an award to a student.

If your principal is constantly critical and finding fault, you might need to begin documenting these events every time they happen in a journal that you take home every night. If the criticism is legitimate (for example, you need to keep closer control of tardies), make the effort to change your behavior. Such regulations can be annoying and time-consuming, but something made them necessary in the first place, so be loyal and supportive of your colleagues and do it right.

If the criticism seems aimed at getting you to resign, or is just harassment, document what is happening and solicit professional help from your teachers' association. If you are called in by an administrator on a serious disciplinary matter, you have the right to have an association leader or counselor with you. Whether you have this association support or not, make notes about what was said in the meeting and keep those notes with your personal papers. If the administrator writes a report about the meeting, you have a right to see that report before it is placed in your file.

Registering Complaints

Most building administrators dislike the complaining that often occurs behind faculty room doors. Since most administrators identify loyalty as an important trait in their staffs, some administrators perceive complaints as personal attacks; ill feelings can result. However, because all aspects of the school day are potentially volatile, teachers—like everyone else—have frustrations that need to be communicated.

Often anger builds because teachers aren't informed of some change in schedule or curricula. Perhaps the texts that were ordered haven't arrived yet, or the roof leaks. A casual remark about this at a faculty meeting may trigger hostility. An unpopular policy may create a tone that suggests mutiny. Most building principals recognize this, and the wise administrator will offer teachers an opportunity to express feelings of dissatisfaction and offer solutions. Sometimes a principal devises a special form on which the teacher can identify the problem and offer a possible solution. Some buildings have faculty committees designed to represent the staff in communicating problems to the administration. You will need to follow the chain of command that exists in your school. In larger schools, a department chair may be the liaison between you and the administration. In a smaller school, *you* may have to discuss the problem with your principal.

Sometimes, an unpopular decision may be made over which your principal has no control. If a school district has mandated a large renovation project, the principal's hands are tied. He or she will be just as frustrated as you are that the building is covered in plastic, paint, and plaster.

Whatever the means for venting such frustrations, it's critical that you don't become involved in whining; your goal should be to help solve the problem.

Several years ago, Sharon got tired of listening to the arguing that ensued over whether to make the one existing faculty lounge for smokers or nonsmokers. The principal, an amiable and equitable person, had not wanted to alienate either side. The faculty had to make its own decision.

Sharon found a small area hidden in the back of the media center that had been used for storing old magazines and newspapers. Sharon discussed the use of the room with other faculty members. She and a colleague proposed the alternate lounge to the faculty and administration. The principal allotted money for furniture and other amenities, and the faculty members spent several Saturdays cleaning and decorating their new space. The problem was solved.

The work world abounds with whiners and complainers. You don't want to join those ranks. When a problem exists:

- Think of how it can be solved.
- Consider to whom you'll address the problem.
- Think carefully how you'll communicate it. Know your building's policy for dealing with such problems.

Conclusion

Most of the time the administration's expectations of you will be clear. Loyalty is of paramount importance. You need to be loyal in your communications with others and in your behavior. Complete reports, attend meetings, and cooperate with your administrator. If you miss a meeting or a deadline, and you will, you will survive. Apologize, do what you need to do to catch up, and get on with your teaching. In turn, you should expect loyalty from your administrators. This mutual support and communication will help to create a positive learning climate in your school.

CHAPTER 9

Ancillary Personnel

. . . she did everything over and over until everyone of us understood completely. If you want to be a perfect teacher, then use Mrs. Young as a model.

Amanda
Grade 8

The support staff in a school includes all adults, both certified and noncertified, who often are not involved in teaching, yet provide support services that complete the educational plan of the school. Angie, the secretary at Robert's elementary school, is a combination of Mother Teresa and Lee Iacocca. She bandages knees, patches egoos, and soothes even the most savage of parents. The teachers and administrators have changed in Robert's school over the years, but Angie has remained and provided emotional and professional support for new and old teachers, principals, children, and parents.

Support staff members come with friendly, grumpy, hostile, cheerful, overbearing, energetic, lazy, supportive, resourceful, and unhappy personalities. When you stop to think about it, all these same personality types are also found among the rest of the faculty, but they stay in their rooms and teach their classes, seldom encroaching on your territory. When you work with a support person whose personality doesn't match yours, sparks can fly and utilizing this person's skills could become awkward for you and your classes. You can't do much to change the personality and moods of this person who may have been there longer than you. It is up to you to get along with this staff member.

Here are some tips for dealing with support staff and ancillary personnel:

1. Introduce yourself to them and ask about their responsibilities. Ask what services they provide for students and faculty members.
2. Be friendly and interested. Don't *tell* these people what you want—inquire if it's possible.
3. If these people meet with classes or individual students during the week, obtain copies of their schedules and keep these schedules in a folder in your desk for quick reference.
4. Discover what you can do for these people to help them do their jobs.
5. Ask how to notify them in case of problems, schedule changes, or needed repairs. For example, when Robert and Ellen exchange library time, one or both of them notify the librarian of the switch and check to see if the change is amenable. If applicable, ask how these people can be reached in an emergency.
6. Take time to build and cultivate friendships with ancillary personnel. They are often people with hidden talents and interests that can be shared in the classroom or simply be the basis of rewarding friendships.

Secretaries

These people are the heartbeat of the school. Watch them work at a peak time some day and admire their finesse in juggling ringing phones, managing student aides, answering parent questions, passing messages to teachers, applying bandages, and typing simultaneously. These secretaries choose to be there and are good at what they do. Cultivate good relations with them and be unfailingly courteous. If they ask you for a report, they probably needed it yesterday. If you have been friendly and polite, you will probably be able to ask for an occasional favor and will receive it. Teachers who are irritable toward the secretarial staff don't receive extra favors.

Know what the secretary's job is. The secretary is probably the support person for an administrator, while managing a busy, chaotic office at the same time. Some schools have a teachers' secretary whose main job is to duplicate bulletins, classroom sets of assignments, and transparencies. The teachers' secretary might also be responsible for such tasks as managing the mail room, answering the phone, and calling substitute teachers. When you ask this person to complete a copy job for you, give clear, readable written instructions and plenty of time to get the job done. Do not assume that the secretary will do your typing for you. Occasionally, you might be able to ask the faculty secretary to type a college recommendation for a student on school letterhead if he or she has time. When a secretary does type for you, turn in your rough draft in grammatically correct, legible form. Proofread the finished product. The letter will be sent out with your name, and any grammatical or typing errors reflect first on you and then on the rest of your faculty like a spotlight.

Custodians

These men and women often determine the success of your day. These are the people who have the tools to adjust your stubborn heater, the ladders to help you hang plants, and the brackets to attach the movie screen to the wall. They empty your trash cans and clean your chalkboards. Make a point of knowing the names of your custodians and compliment good work. Expect your students to pick up their own paper snippits—custodians are there for building maintenance, not maid service—and expect students to leave the room as clean as it was when they arrived. If you are doing a cut-and-paste project, stop for a

"Snippit-Pick-It" five minutes before the bell when everyone cleans. Never use cleaning for punishment unless it is a logical consequence for what the child did.

Find out what maintenance is done to your room on a regular basis. If your boards are washed nightly, clearly mark material you do not want erased and expect that once in a while mistakes will occur and you will have to rewrite material on the board in the morning. Building custodians are good people who have tons of work to do and not enough time to do it. If they occasionally do a less-than-perfect job, there is often good reason. If work is consistently left undone, drop a courteous note to the head custodian.

If you need room repairs, leave a note in the head custodian's mailbox and mention this. If nothing has been done in a week, inquire. Large districts often lose sight of a simple repair in a pile of paperwork because this job requires a specific crew. Sometimes you will get frustrated and do the repair yourself, but this offends custodians because it appears that you're telling them they aren't doing their jobs.

You will notice over the years that the people who get repairs done the fastest are those who are courteous and friendly to the custodial staff and keep their classrooms fairly clean. They thank custodians for their work and make sure superiors know about jobs well done.

When repairs are made, be aware that they are often made during class time. Paint crews may walk into your class on Tuesday and announce they are ready to paint; your class will need to meet elsewhere for a week. One hot, door-open spring day, a crew began drilling on the lockers in Betty's hallway. Complaining doesn't make such crews go away, and they can't see dirty looks. Getting angry only frustrates you and models ineffectual anger for the students. Laugh and throw up your hands—not showing the frustration inside—and adjust the lesson. You might have small group discussions with students about heavy equipment or how to deal constructively with inconveniences. Send a student to see if a certain room is unlocked and inquire if that teacher will let you "rent" during the remodeling. Show the students that when these annoyances occur, you need to think of viable solutions and then solve your problem. This is a good lesson in itself.

These same people who sweep and dust often have talents and skills to share with students. The custodian in Angie's school is well versed in mountain lore and helps stage a yearly rendezvous, to the students' delight. Another, now retired, wrote and directed the students in a yearly pageant, one highlight of that small community's holiday celebrations.

Librarians/Media Specialists

Depending on your state regulations, most librarians or media specialists are trained as educators with a teaching license and course work in managing media. Many begin with a subject area emphasis, gain teaching experience, then work for media certification. Yet, because they don't meet the same five classes every day, librarians ae not always thought of as teachers. They also are not formally in administration, although they manage library staff, the media collection, and the media budget.

One thing that is consistent among all librarians or media specialists is that each is concerned with doing a professional job. As our society grows at its current rapid rate, the place of the media specialist will become increasingly important. Students need access to current information, and the librarian can be the key. In the future, people with power won't necessarily know more than anyone else, but they will know where to obtain information. The media specialist's job, then, is crucial to student success. The librarian/media specialist's responsibility is to support the staff and teach and reinforce research skills for both students and faculty members.

The types and personalities of media specialists are as varied as those of any other staff member in your building. Some guard their collections closely and view each stolen book as a personal attack. Others look at their job as an escape from the classroom's continual pressures. Some can become an integral part of the school, arriving in classes with books, teaching minilessons in research techniques, and beating the corporate bushes for donations of needed equipment.

Utilizing your school's media center can provide support and enrichment for your teaching and give your students practice in using research and library skills. Make an effort to learn about offered services and solicit advice on integrating those services into your lessons. Here are some tips for using your media center effectively.

1. Get acquainted with the media center well before your class uses it for the first time. Spend occasional prep time in the library correcting assignments, reading the paper, or browsing through the collection. Attend any orientation sessions your librarian may schedule, or, if none are planned, ask for a personal tour. Ask, "What would you like me to know so that I can use the media center effectively?"
2. Know the procedures: How do you schedule your class into the library for instruction time? What is the checkout procedure for books, media,

and equipment for teachers? Is needed equipment delivered to the classrooms? What is the general checkout procedure for students?

3. When you schedule your class into the media center for a lesson, tell the librarian exactly what the assignment is, providing a brief lesson plan and any student handouts if possible. Tell the librarian what your student expectations are, and what she or he can do to support you. On your first day in the media center, you might ask your librarian to do a ten-minute review-tour of where everything is, then present your lesson.

4. Before the class even goes to the library, take time to work through your own assignment to make sure the collection will have enough information for all students to use successfully. On the day before going to the library, explain the overall assignment and give students clear behavioral expectations.

5. Make suggestions for book and media purchases that support your curriculum.

6. *Don't ever:*
   - schedule a class into the library when you know you are going to be absent unless you have cleared it both with the librarian and the substitute teacher.
   - send students to the library to sit and write an essay as a discipline measure.
   - send students to the library because they have nothing meaning-ful to do in your class.
   - speak ill of the librarian in front of students—the media specialist is a professional colleague.

7. Know what is *not* the job of media specialists.
   - They are not responsible for your class discipline when your students are in the library.
   - They are not usually too happy about running to your classroom to figure out why a projector is not working. It is your responsib-ility to check that equipment before class to make sure it is functioning and to keep student hands off the equipment during class. Tell students that you appreciate their offers to help and tinker, but if you accidentally damage the machine, you will be completely responsible. It is also someone's law that no matter what type of projector you know how to run, the library will deliver another brand that loads differently.

8. It is your responsibility to return the books you check out and to return rented films on time. Faculty members do not usually have a

due date on library materials, but it is courteous to return them as soon as you finish using them. Often students or other teachers need that same material.

Psychologists/Social Workers

If you don't find out during the fall orientation, inquire if your school has the services of a psychologist or a social worker. Ask if these people are in the building every day or on specified days. When you have this information, seek out these people and introduce yourself, asking about the range of services offered to students. Ask what procedure you need to follow to get help for a student and how to get emergency assistance in time of a crisis.

Maintaining a friendship with the school psychologist or social worker can be enlightening and good support for you as a teacher. These professionals often have a different perspective of a situation that helps you better understand what a student is doing in your classroom that might be driving you up a wall. These people know if a child has been tested for learning problems and can interpret the results for you. They attend most staffing meetings and may have met the parents or even visited the home. The information they share with you can help you understand learning patterns exhibited by the child and plan successful learning situations.

Sometimes you can lure psychologists or social workers into your classroom to help you teach. A social worker who wanted to try some techniques to raise student self-concepts in junior high classrooms joined forces with a teacher and a principal. Each believed in the value of a positive self-image. Their work resulted in the book *Building a Positive Self-Concept* (see the Bibliography). This book contains practical lessons that you can easily implement in your own classroom.

Other topics you might ask a social worker or psychologist to discuss with your class could include teen suicide, death, or dealing with difficult people.

Social workers and psychologists often hold support group meetings in school for anger management, substance abuse, teen parenting, divorce, and other topics important to the school community.

If you are aware of these support groups and know of a student who might benefit from membership, give the student's name to the adult in charge. Talk individually with the student and *ask* if he or she thinks there would be benefit in joining the group. Don't be surprised if the response is a violent "No!" You have fulfilled your obligation; let the counselors take the next step.

It is not your responsibility to attend or run these groups unless your training and background specifically qualify you to do so and the administration asks you to head such groups.

Often the psychologist or social worker can provide insight about a student who is returning to your class after suffering some personal crisis. Ask what you should say to the class before the student returns and how you should act and respond when she or he is back in class. Classmates need to think about what to say and what not to say. Often these professionals will come to the classroom to prepare students, answer questions, and rehearse appropriate responses. If possible, get these professionals to make contact with the student before he or she returns to classes. Ask how you can be most supportive.

It is risky to provide these kinds of services for a student yourself. It is not a good idea to get deeply involved with students' personal lives. Students can sometimes manipulate you into commitments you are uncomfortable with. Although Mary does not get especially chummy with her reading students, she always remembers the day that Bruce, in all seriousness, asked if he could move in with her. His mother had moved away and his father didn't want him. Her heart broke, but the answer was no. Instead, she talked with the school social worker, who investigated the family situation. These professionals are our legal protection from lawsuits. Refer such student problems to those specifically trained and authorized to deal with them.

Counselors

School by school, month by month, counselors have different jobs. Universally, they seem to be overworked and are caught in a multifaceted tug-of-war among the needs of students, teachers, administrators, and parents.

Introduce yourself to your school's counselor(s) in the fall and ask about their basic responsibilities. Some may be assigned to several schools. Some might see just juniors. Each secondary counselor is probably in charge of scheduling students, solving conflicts, keeping track of student credits, and coordinating standardized testing. Counselors also place students with special needs, facilitate conferences, and accomplish a myriad of other tasks. Seldom do they have undivided time to sit down, listen, and counsel their charges. There just isn't enough time in the day.

Sometimes you'll feel frustrated by counselors because they are usually busy when you need information on a student. At other times, you'll be grateful for their existence when they plan and run a productive meeting. Counselors can often make quick calls home to check on a sick student when you are in class, and frequently they are the people who gather assignments from six or eight teachers for home-bound students.

When you discover a student threatening suicide or obvviously crying for help through actions, words, or writing, go first to the school counselor. Inform the psychologist or social worker, too, but definitely tell the counselor. Which person makes the student contact then might depend on who knows that student and the home situation best. This is not your responsibility.

In less critical situations, counselors can lend you an ear and offer suggestions on how to handle difficult or troubled students. Elementary school counselors often present lessons in class about redirecting misbehavior or managing anger. When you think a counselor can help, call on him or her.

Security Personnel

Many urban schools employ security personnel. These people have been hired to supervise school parking areas, insure that people who do not have school business are not in the building, and write incident reports as necessary. In some buildings these people check the identification of every person who enters. Their job might involve challenging those they don't recognize and hurrying tardy students to classes. They might check restroom and locker areas to prevent vandalism. Their tasks are those that the administration identifies as necessary to provide a safe learning environment.

Introduce yourself to these people, register your vehicle for an assigned parking place if appropriate, and remain friendly and cooperative during the year. Security personnel are there to help you.

Resource Officers

The schools in some districts have available the services of school resource officers. These men and women are trained officers from the police department whose primary assignment is a specific school. They maintain an office in the school and deal with everyday problems from locker thefts and car accidents to substance abuse and truancies. They are also informed if students are involved in crime outside the school realm. On the positive side, resource officers chaperone school activities and speak to classes on student rights. They maintain high visibility to provide a friend and confidant for troubled students.

Students may relate to their resource officer because this adult is not a teacher and not part of the school establishment. This adult is a trained police officer who can advise the students about legal problems, be a friend, and also model the function of a police officer. One year at a large city high school, the resource officer was one of the volunteer targets for a pie-throwing booth at the school carnival. He also arranged for a car that had been involved in an alcohol-related accident to be placed in front of the school as a graphic example of the dangers of drinking and driving.

For information on the Resource Officers in the Schools Program, contact the Juvenile Department, Boise Police Department, 7200 Barrister Drive, Boise, Idaho 83706.

School Nurse

As in the case of most other ancillary personnel mentioned in this chapter, the schedule and job responsibilities of a school nurse are as varied as the number of schools that employ nurses. There are never enough nurses in our schools, and the needs of society have radically changed the role of the school nurse. In past decades, the school nurse's responsibilities included keeping immunization files updated, cleaning up skinned knees, screening vision and hearing problems, and sometimes dispensing a few aspirin tablets or cough drops. That image has changed!

School nurses today cannot dispense any medications without written parental permission. These staff members deal with lots of sick students but may invest much more time counseling pregnant teens, advising students who are suffering personal crises, and intervening between troubled students and their parents. These same school nurses often manage several of the support groups functioning in a school. Nurses don't have time to make enough home visits. They don't have enough time to teach wellness techniques in classes.

Introduce yourself in the fall and inquire about what student services the nurse offers. Find out the procedure for sending a sick student to the nurse's office. Review classroom emergency procedures with the nurse.

The school nurse usually (but not always) knows which students have chronic medical problems. Unfortunately, you do not always get that information. Sometimes the student or the parents do not want anyone to know about the problem for fear the student will be treated "differently." It is frustrating to find out mid-term that the student in the back corner of the room is nearly deaf in his left ear. It is frightening to find out in April that a very quiet, low-achieving student is heavily medicated for epilepsy and is having trouble regulating the medication.

You need to know how to recognize a child going into diabetic shock and what to do about it. You need to have current information on AIDS. You also need to notice when a child is squinting, continually missing spoken directions, or acting excessively drowsy in class. In these cases, ask the school nurse to call the home and check on the situation. Sometimes you might call home yourself and state that you have tried to help the student achieve success in the classroom but are stymied. Are the parents aware of any social or medical problems that might be blocking learning? If you learn of a medical problem from the parents, you need to then tell the school nurse and let him or her interview the student.

Your school nurse will probably make the following suggestions to you:

1. Trust your intuition on whether you feel a student is actually in need of a visit to the nurse.
2. Keep students accountable when they ask for passes to the nurse. Follow up at the earliest possible moment or require that your hall pass be returned.
3. Keep tissues and small bandages in your classroom. Don't dispense any aspirin, pain-reliever pills, cough drops, antacids, or other medication.
4. Watch for the following signs and symptoms in your students. Report any observations to your school nurse.
   A. Eyes
      1. Sties or crusted lids
      2. Inflamed eyes
      3. Crossed eyes
      4. Squinting at a book or chalkboard
      5. Bloodshot eyes, dilated pupils
   B. Ears
      1. Earaches and discharges from ears
      2. Hearing loss
      3. Obvious turning of the head toward sounds

C. Oral Cavity
  1. Inflamed gums or lips
  2. Faulty hygiene (halitosis)
  3. Toothaches or other problems
D. Nose and Throat
  1. Persistent mouth breathing
  2. Frequent sore throats
  3. Frequent colds
E. Rashes and Open Sores
  1. Impetigo
  2. Herpes simplex (cold sores)
  3. Ringworm
  4. Other skin rashes
F. General Condition and Appearance
  1. Failure to gain weight
  2. Excessive weight gain
  3. Listless, lethargic, pale
  4. Poor coordination
  5. Persistent poor posture
  6. Recurring headaches
  7. Speech defects
G. Behavior
  1. Emotional disturbance
  2. Persistent inattentiveness
  3. Twitching movements
  4. Shyness
  5. Excessive drowsiness
  6. Excessive use of the lavatory
  7. Personality changes
  8. Slurred speech
  9. Uncharacteristic jitteriness
H. Surgical Absences and Injuries
  1. Students returning to school from a hospital stay need to see the nurse before returning to class.
  2. Any injuries occurring on school property need to be reported to the school nurse and the administration. You may need to fill out appropriate reports.

Once you know your school nurse and the services he or she offers, you will be able to enlist help creatively in getting medical information that will help you build the most conducive learning situation for each of your students.

Volunteers

Volunteers, like all other people in the school structure, come in all shapes and sizes. Some volunteer on a regular basis to do specific, nonteaching chorres to free teachers and administrators for other tasks. Others arrive as guest speakers, in-room helpers working with groups of students, or presenters of special teaching units.

Take note of how other teachers around you utilize volunteers. If you feel a volunteer would enhance your program and you have a clear idea of the specific jobs you would like your volunteer to accomplish, contact either the person in your building who coordinates volunteers (the head secretary will know this) or the teacher you notice using volunteers most effectively.

Volunteer Presentations

When you have a volunteer scheduled for a class presentation, meet or speak with him or her several days before to give specific information: the exact time the class meets, the number of students, what they are currently studying, how the volunteer's information will fit in, and tips on what will appeal to the students. Volunteers are usually taking time from their jobs to work with your classes, so it is unrealistic to expect them to meet all your classes for an entire day. Solutions to scheduling might be for the volunteer to meet a different class every few days or engage several volunteers to speak on the same topic during the same day.

Bear in mind that, even if your guest speaker is a former teacher, she or he will be apprehensive about facing your class. (Remember your first day?) Do everything possible to prepare a successful experience. Explain to your students the day before what is going to happen and specify expected behavior even if the speech is Sahara Desert-dry. Provide a clean podium or speaking area along with requested supplies and equipment. Write the speaker's name clearly on the board, and consider having coffee or water available. Try providing the refreshment in a school-logo cup and then make the cup a thank-you gift. Volunteers often leave your class exhausted, wondering how you get through a full day in one piece.

If you have to be in the classroom when the speaker is to arrive at the school, send a student to greet and escort your guest. After the volunteer has been to your class, send a letter of thanks. Also send a letter to his or her supervisor acknowledging the employee's volunteer time supporting education.

The Partners in Education Program

There are people and businesses in your community who are more than willing to participate in the education process. You might locate these people on your own or by asking other teachers for resources. Some districts enjoy an organization called Partners in Education. Each participating school is linked with one community business and, sometimes, with one professor from the university in the city. Each partnership forms a committee of businesspeople and teachers to decide exactly how the business can serve the school and how the school cann serve the business. For the most part, direct contributions of money are avoided.

The business partners might provide:

- field trips, career guidance, career "shadowing"
- guest speakers
- large meeting space for PTO fund-raisers
- access to video equipment and operators when a school is planning to make a videotape
- advisers on operating new equipment
- access for teachers to company training meetings
- tutors for accelerated math or computer students
- classroom helpers who come on a regularly scheduled basis
- impartial judges for the school spelling bee or science fair
- organizers for a spring field day

In turn, the school might:

- stage band and choir performances during noon hours, meetings, and holidays
- provide coat-checking services for corporate meetings
- send student-made cards to all the employees involved in the Partners in Education project
- help decorate for a holiday or work on the company float for a parade
- join an envelope-stuffing campaign
- participate with the business in a community service project

compete with business teams at a community fun day
- provide complimentary tickets to the business for sports and cultural events sponsored by the school

The university affiliation might help the school by:

- contributing professional textbooks and research material
- providing tours of the university
- making appointments for students seeking admission to the university
- providing specialized resources and experts
- providing individuals to help with special in-class projects

The use of community resources can be as creative as the people planning the program. Small communities, for example, have embraced the Partners in Education concept but have modified the structure to include the whole business community and form a partnership with the town's one high school, one junior high, and one elementary school. The possibilities for the ways the various businesses can serve the schools, and the ways the schools can serve the community, are only limited by the imagination of the participants. You need only say, "Would it be possible . . . ?"

Other Volunteer Activities

Volunteer Listeners

Other volunteer activities or parent-generated activities in a school might include:

- arranging field trips to offices and manufacturing sites for career exploration
- collecting and delivering used books and magazines to supplement the library collection or to use for classroom enrichment projects
- handing out yearbooks at the end of school
- producing a parent newsletter
- planning and supervising the all-night, nonalcoholic senior graduation party
- planning an all-school field day in the spring

Aides

Adult Aides

Aides, unlike volunteers, are in school on a daily basis, are assigned to a specific teacher, department, or task, and are paid.

If your teaching assignment includes an aide, assess his or her abilities and utilize them. From the beginning have a clear understanding of what you expect the aide to do, what the aide sees as his or her job description, and the hours the aide is allowed to work. During Robert's first years of teaching, he was blessed with an outstanding classroom aide who supported his teaching. They became a teaching team. If your aide is great at grading and recording scores but can get snappy with students, you work with the students. Some aides will see what needs to be done and do it. Others will need specific directions. Make yourself knowledgeable about the legalities of having an aide. Can you leave this noncertified adult in charge of the class while you go to an in-school meeting? an out-of-school meeting? If an injury or accident occurs while the aide is alone with students, who is legally responsible? Maintain a clear message to your students and aide that you are the one in charge making the final decisions at all times.

A supervisor reports visiting a classroom for emotionally handicapped students in Mike's school. There were only 6 or 7 students in the room, but it seemed like 30. The aide sat at her desk at the side of the room with charts covering the desktop. Next to her desk was a student desk where individuals obviously enjoyed coming for tutoring and coaching. The teacher moved through the room, presenting lessons, using the board, sending a child to the aide for tutoring, another to the time-out area, a third to get a needed book. Sometimes the teacher would say, "Jon, that's a warning," and raise her hand. No matter how involved the aide was with a student, she would notice the signal and mark that student's chart without missing a beat with her own student. This teacher and this aide knew the secret of close teamwork in that classroom. The teacher was obviously in charge, but her aide had specific responsibilities, too. They shared in the academic duties, but the administrative structure was clear. Consequently, the students achieved in a tightly structured society with high but attainable expectations.

Student Aides

In some schools, students who have a study hall period in their schedules choose to function as office aides or teacher aides during that period. Depending on school policy, these students may or may not get a grade and credit for their work. Usually the individual teacher makes the choice whether to have a student aide or not. These students, depending on their skills, can provide a variety of services. They might create bulletin boards, file music or papers, wash desks, return books to the library, deliver messages, or type your study guides. Aides might be in charge of cleaning and storing equipment, textbooks, computer disks, or manipulatives.

Do not utilize student aides to type tests, discipline other students, or keep your grade book up to date. These tasks remain *your* responsibility. When training your aide, stress from the beginning that grades and other information she or he sees pertaining to your students is not to be shared with *anyone*. Insist on integrity and loyalty from your aide. If you do not get this loyalty, sign your aide back into the study hall and complete these tasks on your own.

Your aide should not cruise the building and wave at friends through open classroom doors. If you do not have a specific job for your aide on a particular day, have him or her bring a book and read quietly or do homework for other classes.

Conclusion

Your day in school runs more smoothly with the help of a variety of ancillary personnel. These people were hired for their strengths in supporting the learning goals of the total school program. These staff members are worth getting to know, both as potential interesting friends and as the providers of services that you are not in a position to offer to your students.

It is up to you to create a comfortable learning atmosphere when working with support staff and ancillary personnel.

CHAPTER 10

Parents

Many years ago Betty was sitting in the lounge with colleagues. Her principal walked in and asked what she was teaching in her fourth-period class. Because Betty had been thinking about her second-period seniors, her mind went blank. The principal said a parent had called and accused Betty of teaching the occult. Betty laughed in dismay and nervous confusion and mustered an uneducated, "Huh? I don't even know anything about the occult." Betty's dear friend rescued her and told the principal that all the junior classes were currently studying the same author with the objective of learning about writing that builds suspense through a series of small events tied to a surprise ending. The principal was satisfied.

It turned out that the parent had found a stack of books on the occult in his daughter's car. He was upset because many of them offended his religious convictions. The student had then explained that the books were being used to write a report for Betty's class. The parent called the principal.

This student had actually been working on a report that investigated haunted houses. Betty had approved this topic in relation to the author being studied in her class. After speaking with the principal, Betty immediately called the parent to clarify the situation.

During the call, Betty explained the assignment. She acknowledged that she had approved the topic, but that she had done so without knowledge of the parent's religious beliefs. Betty suggested that the report topic could have been one that was agreeable to all involved. She asked the parent to contact her directly if problems arose in the future.

Conferences

Sometimes communication with parents is best handled through a direct meeting. Conferences may be initiated by the teacher, the parent, or another staff member.

It's too bad that contact with parents occurs after things go awry, but that's often a fact of life. Only occasionally will a parent initiate a conference in order to give you information that will help you provide a better learning situation for the child. Usually a parent conference occurs after a severe disciplinary infraction or after repeated, frustrating attempts have been made to help the child academically. Even a meeting to plan a student's IEP (Individualized Education Program) can be a tense, unhappy encounter for the parents.

Many of the parents you meet at a conference have been there before. Many have unhappy or embarrassing memories that cloud their perception of the entire education process. Many feel threatened surrounded by educated people. Many arrive angry because they had to take time from work, incurring the boss's anger.

Managing the Conference

Any conferences you perceive as posing confrontation should take place with a counselor or administrator in attendance. Before you call a conference, you need to have already had parent contact over the phone. In the case of a sudden disciplinary infraction, an administrator may make that contact. Conferences work best in a room where everyone can be seated informally around a table. Many teachers prefer having the student at the conference, but that is not always done. Allowing the student to attend the conference helps him or her accept responsibility for past and future behavior and also be a part of planning the course of action for change.

When you walk into a conference, introduce yourself to those you do not know and greet those you do know (including the student) cordially by name. Stand to introduce yourself if you are in the room before the parent arrives. A conference should not be punitive; it is a time to look for solutions.

When the conference is ready to begin, outline the issue to be discussed. Check to make sure everyone understands and agrees on the matters to be discussed. Give everyone a chance for input into the discussion and the proposed solutions. Make a point of addressing the student and parent directly. Avoid using educational jargon. One of the most condescending things teachers can do is talk to the parent as though the student weren't there. Talk about the potential you see in the student and your hopes for his or her success. Ask the student how he or she feels.

Do as much listening and watching during the conference as you can. You will gain insight about your student's behavior as you watch the parent-child interaction. Sometimes you will discover that a student's behavior simply reflects what is modeled at home. This gives you a place to start. Make it clear what kind of specific behavior is acceptable and be ready to praise success and change as soon as you witness it.

You will understand why a student picks on others or has a low self-concept when a mother calls her offspring "Stupid" in front of teachers. Marc remembers a conference that was called for behavioral and academic reasons. Several teachers had been called in by an administrator to discuss with the parent and student solutions to the problem. The parent offered an opening remark that effectively illustrated the root of the problem: "You're not going to tell me anything I don't already know—I know my kid is stupid." While the girl squirmed uncomfortably, head hanging, the administrator quickly stated, "The purpose of this conference is not to attack your family. We are here to find some solutions to help Tina be successful in school." Often a parent will want to talk about personal school failures or problems rather than the child's situation. Sometimes you'll leave a conference marveling that the child is coping as well as he or she is in spite of the situation at home.

Parents may try to attribute the problem to anything else: the system, bad health, a divorce, another relative, or personality conflicts. You need to get the focus of the conference off blame-placing and onto planning solutions that satisfy everyone.

If the parent arrives angry and ready to scalp, draw on all your anger-management techniques: Listen attentively. Restate what you hear the parent saying. Acknowledge the anger, but don't let it control the conference. If the parent cannot get over being angry, suggest that the conference be continued when you can all talk constructively. If the conference does continue, you might ask the parent what specific things she or he wants to see happen: "What do you want me to do?" Then you can agree to the proposal, agree to parts of it, or state politely that you cannot agree to the solution because of (for example) curriculum restraints, school policy, or safety regulations.

Give everyone else at the conference an opportunity to relate their perspective and suggest solutions. Then, if the student is present, ask for his or her comments. Be sure the student agrees with the proposed solution. (The child often wants to cooperate and get back to class while the parent is the one being difficult.) Try to give the student as much dignity and control in the conference as possible. Afterwards, you might compliment your pupil on calm behavior and mention that it is not easy to sit in on a conference about yourself.

Unless it is a conference about grades, you don't need to bring your grade book, but you will want to have your written record of the student's behavior, class performance, and so on. Do think about the student ahead of time, and rehearse a list of positive things to say, plan a short list of concerns, and think about possible solutions. Try to emphasize student potential and possible solutions. Make it clear that you believe the student can be successful. At the end of the conference, thank everyone involved for their time.

Follow-up is necessarry after a conference. A contract is one way to insure understanding of expected behaviors and provide follow-up. Conttracts can be written and signed by the student, parent, teacher, and administrator. A behavioral contract will include expected behaviors and consequences for noncompliance. An academic contract will set realistic goals, including a time frame for completing missing assignments and improved in-class participation. A realistic contract length is two weeks. At the end of two weeks, you will review the contract and determine if there has been improvement or if a stated consequence will occur. When the contract is signed, mention to the student that you feel good about the process and anticipate success. File a copy of the contract in your folder of student records. Make phone contact with parents within two weeks, detailing student progress. Keep the student informed of progress as well.

Elementary Conferences

If you are an elementary school teacher, you will have regularly scheduled parent-teacher conferences in addition to those conferences called for special purposes. Elementary schools usually have conferences twice a year: in the fall after the first nine weeks, and in the spring after the third nine weeks. These conferences are held for teachers to share:

- student progress,
- goals for the year,
- areas of concern,
- ideas for working with the student, and
- concerns about curriculum areas.

Mike remembers his first parent-teacher conferences as stressful events. He was nervous and overwhelmed at the prospect of having to schedule, prepare for, and meet with all 52 sets of kindergarten parents. You'll be nervous too, at least in your early years of teaching, as conference time rolls around. Don't dismay. Everyone else is nervous too. Parents are usually anxious about what you are going to say. If you aren't feeling a few butterflies, you may not be prepared. The majority of your meetings with parents will be productive and go smoothly.

It is essential that you are prepared when you meet with parents. If questions come up that you can't answer, make a note of them and find the answer later. Get back to parents in a timely manner by writing a note or calling. If a parent disagrees with your observation, invite the parent to class.

Phone Calls

Rehearse phone calls in your mind or make some notes if necessary. When you call a parent, clearly state your name, school, and connection with a specific child. Then pause to make sure you have the correct parent and that person realizes who you are. So many parents have remarried that last names and relationships have to be clearly established at the beginning of a call. Ask if you are calling at a convenient time. State the reason for your contact and give specific details. If the call is about discipline, use the "I am concerned and I need your support" approach. If the parent is not supportive, simply restate what has happened and what will happen if the inappropriate behavior does not stop. Thank the parent for his or her time, and end the phone call. Document the conversation. Gary notes all calls made and keeps a list of dates in his grade book. Later, if he needs to refer the student to an administrator, he'll indicate he has followed through with the discipline steps and can give dates of parent contact.

It's best not to delay relating successes or asking for help and support in solving problems. Return phone calls from parents as soon as possible. If you return a call and find out a parent has left the office or is not at home, leave your name, a message that you returned the call, and a time when you will try again. It can be embarrassing not to promptly return a phone call when you've previously expressed concern about a student.

Since most parents work, it's best to try to make calls at a time when they may be reached at home. If you cannot contact a parent after repeated tries, leave a message listing specific times when you can be reached. Use discretion here. Some parents may not wish coworkers to be privy to their child's problems at school. A phone message from a teacher may imply that a problem exists. Often a phone message with no explanation may trigger immediate assumptions of misbehavior and can precipitate unnecessary conflict between the parent and child. If you feel that a message may cause turmoil, it is best not to leave one. You must use good judgment in contacting parents.

Mike looks for ways to make positive home contact. One Christmas, when an unexpected snowstorm closed schools two days early for vacation, he called each of his kindergarteners to wish that child a happy holiday and leave assurances that the class celebration would be staged when the students returned. Mike was a hero to his students and parents.

Report Cards

Messages to call parents right after report cards are issued usually do not yield words of thanks. Look over your grade book before you return the call. Recalcculate the grade just to double-check your math. Have the grade book with you when you call. Frequently a disappointing grade is a result of several missed assignments. Many students think if they forget several assignments, the bad news will simply go away. It doesn't. When you return the call, state the facts and comment on what the student can do to improve the grade. Mention the call to the student. Follow up with another phone call or note in several weeks.

Catching Kids Doing Something Good

Tell students that you are trying to catch them doing something good. You might tease, "Gotcha! I caught you doing something good." After acknowledging a positive behavior in class you might inquire, "Would you like a call or note to your parents?" Have the student write down a phone number, the parent's name, when you should call, and where you will be calling (home, office). Write the note or make the call that day if at all possible. "I'd like to share with you what happened in class today . . . ." You might consider mentioning to a class that if ever a student needs a positive call home, you will be glad to make one. Barbara got such a request years ago when the driving age in her state was 14. The student wanted her to report good grades in order to obtain parental permission to take driver's education. Barbara told the student she would call and report the grades, but she would not endorse driving at 14. Barbara laughs and tells her students she will make positive calls but won't promote their private agendas.

Publicity/Newsletters

Publicity can be defined as all the different ways teachers find to tell the public, parents, administration, fellow teachers, and other students about the successes of a student or a class. Every time you post a paper or project, you are publicizing student success.

If you have completed a project that involves student-choice awards, you might want to invite an administrator or a colleague with a free period into your room to view the projects and hand out the awards. Most get into the spirit of it and ham up the presentation, to the enjoyment of your students. One colleague from several school years ago staged an elaborate "Academy Awards" ceremony after her classes made their spring movies. Another holds an "Olympics Ceremony" celebrating students' accomplishments at mastering the multiplication facts. Parents should always receive special invitations to such events.

Your school or your parent group might produce a newsletter that is sent to all parents at intervals throughout the year. Make it a goal some time during the year to write a short article for this newsletter about an unusual project or one that enjoyed exceptional success. Include student names and even a photo or two if the reproduction process permits.

Another version of publicity might be the "Tuesday Folder." Each child in Kathy's elementary school purchased or was given a blue two-pocket folder. During the week all student papers went into that folder after marking. On Mondays, each teacher went through the folders and added sheets noting positive observations from the week, comments on papers that needed a parent signature or redoing, and any other necessary communication to the parent. Students took these folders home on Tuesday, had their parents look through the contents and sign the folders, and returned them on Wednesday. Although this was time-consuming, the teachers in Kathy's school agreed it was an effective method of communication with the home.

During an end-of-term review, Betty decided that her classes could produce a newspaper while studying for their semester exam. She divided her language arts classes into groups of three. The students brainstormed a list of all stories, skills, and concepts covered during the term, and each group chose one item from the list. After much discussion, each group prepared a short article reviewing that unit. The students shared the writing with other groups for additional information and editing help. Each article was then carefully rewritten. Betty pasted the three articles onto one sheet of paper and added the title each class chose for their "newspaper." She ran off a copy of this newspaper for each student to study and made sure the semester test reflected those units the students emphasized in their projects. While reading their creations, students discovered a coupon on the back that entitled them to 5 points on the next test if papers were taken home, shared with parents, and returned with parents' signatures. You could expand this news report to the parents into a more formal wrap-up project with more sophisticated reproduction techniques that provides a meaningful semester review.

Some districts employ a person to do schoolwide publicity in the community. If you are attempting to get television or radio coverage of a classsroom prooject, this person would know whom you should contact first. Then, this publicity person would be at your big event to get pictures, names, and the story for district publication.

Robert videotapes his class performing readers' theater and class plays. The class members then take turns checking out the videos and taking them home to share class activities with families.

Whether you choose a formal or informal plan to tell parents about what is happening in your classroom, the results will be positive. Students are pleased to have their successes made public, and parents become more supportive when they are kept apprised about classroom activities. Such an informed parent will also be a more motivated homework tutor who is supportive of the entire school process.

Accuracy in Correspondence

Any written notes, letters, reports, recommendations, or other papers that leave your desk must be accurate. Check for spelling and grammar. A newspaper columnist in Marc's community received a letter from a teacher that was, unfortunately, filled with careless spelling and grammar errors. That columnist had a heyday ridiculing the teacher; the embarrassment and shame reflected on every other teacher in the community. Take the time to be accurate; your professional image is worth it.

If writing isn't your strong suit, scribble out a rough draft; then recopy it. It is appropriate to send notes home to parents in your handwriting, but first do a draft. You might ask a colleague to proofread the message to see if it says what you want it to say. Then recopy it onto a fresh sheet of school stationery.

Keep a dictionary on your desk along with a basic grammar book or a copy of *Writers INC*, for quick reference sections on grammar, usage, and typically misspelled words. Those few minutes spent in correcting are worth the trouble and save you the embarrassment of sending out error-filled correspondence. Don't doubt for a minute that the general public will point out any written error they find in your correspondence. It is amazing how often, during a conversation, a parent will mention erroneous correspondence sent home by some other teacher or department.

When working with parents, try to avoid using current educational phrases. Most parents won't ask for a definition, but they may feel inadequate for not knowing what you mean. They may feel as if you're talking down to them. This is analogous to your physician or your mechanic using technical terms that leave you baffled. Use straightforward sentence construction. In the end your message will be clear, to the point, and appreciated by the recipient.

If the document requires it, type. In this age of spell-check machines, computers with spell-checkers, and printers that take school stationery, every teacher can produce error-free, professional communication. Learn how to use these resources. Letters to parents, recommendations for college applications, and material for publication must be sent error-free. Anything less diminishes your credibility.

The appearance and construction of the typed letter or handwritten note are like a photograph of you and your teaching. Make sure your hair is combed and your shoes shined.

Back-to-School Night/Open House

No matter how many years you've been in the classroom, you're likely to have butterflies before open-house night. Some secondary schools hold open house one evening early in the fall where parents follow their child's schedule and visit each classroom for 15 minutes. An all-school reception follows. Robert's elementary open house allows a short time for teachers to address parents followed by a time when parents look around the room and can ask questions about curriculum and programs.

The following tips can help you get ready for open house.

1. Make sure your room is neat. Wash desktops, and hang current student work on every bare wall. Have students help. Post your name and room number prominently outside your room and on your board. You could also post class lists by your door for parents to check to make sure they are in the right place. Dress professionally.

2. Type out an agenda for what you are going to talk about, and if applicable provide a copy of your class syllabus.
3. If you teach middle, junior high, or high school, write the names of the classes you teach and a brief outline of the curriculum you cover during the year.
4. Display copies of the texts and support materials.
5. Greet parents. It is amazing how many parents sit in or near their child's seat without knowing it.
6. Introduce yourself to the group and give a bit of background on the class. Explain your teaching and grading philosophy in relation to the course curriculum. Talk about the text. If it is a difficult text, tell the parents how they can help their child read it more effectively. Talk about your homework expectations.
7. Ask for questions.
8. *Do not* have your grade book out that night, because this is a get-acquainted time. If parents inquire about grades, tell them you will call them the next day, or suggest a conference.

Some of our colleagues use interesting techniques to inform parents about their program. Betty, whose classes are studying Emerson's and Thoreau's essays during the week before the annual school open house, has her students do research on a country they'd love to visit. She next has them create a large picture postcard on 8″ x 11″ paper from that country to their parents. The message is to reflect their understanding of transcendentalism. These postcards are delivered to parents at the open house.

Tami's open-house presentation includes a display of students' science lab projects in progress. Robert has his students direct their daily journal entries to their parents. He quickly glances at the writing (he doesn't need a surprise on this of all evenings). Robert then invites the parents to read and respond to their child's entry. He checks to make sure that all students' entries have comments. *He* fills in the voids.

Gerry's choir performs for the closing reception. Theater students may perform in costume or pantomime. The idea is to provide parents with a sample of what is occurring in the school.

PTO

Parent/teacher organizations can be found at every level of public education. Their function is to support the educational process. This

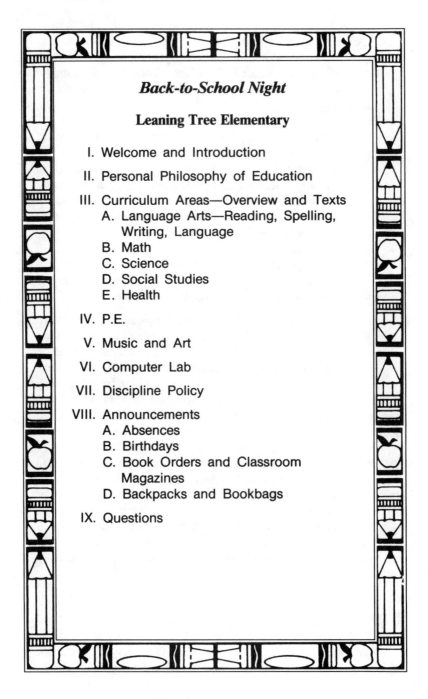

Back-to-School Night

Leaning Tree Elementary

I. Welcome and Introduction

II. Personal Philosophy of Education

III. Curriculum Areas—Overview and Texts
   A. Language Arts—Reading, Spelling, Writing, Language
   B. Math
   C. Science
   D. Social Studies
   E. Health

IV. P.E.

V. Music and Art

VI. Computer Lab

VII. Discipline Policy

VIII. Announcements
   A. Absences
   B. Birthdays
   C. Book Orders and Classroom Magazines
   D. Backpacks and Bookbags

IX. Questions

support might be in the form of volunteering, chaperoning, fund-raising, planning classroom parties, administering scholarship funds, or simply attending school functions. You might be expected to attend a certain number of PTO meetings a year. It is a good opportunity to meet and get to know parents, and you can gain some insight into their perceptions about what is happening in the classrooms.

Conclusion

It is always important for you to keep the lines of communication open. Involve the parents of your students in the educational process as soon as possible in the school year. Be prompt in advising them of any difficulty or success. Look for creative ways to celebrate the good things that happen in your classroom. Make any communication specific and accurate. Make sure that you have been heard and understood. Take time to listen to parents' concerns as well. In all communication, verbal or written, be respectful and aware of the needs and emotions of your audience.

CHAPTER 11

Wellness

Joe C.
p. 1
3-6-91

Beginning teachers need to be prepared for anything her/his crazy students might throw at her. They need to have great listening skills and great speaking skills. They have to be able to lay down the law. They also must have the skills of counselors.

Kendall A.   (11)

A few tips for beginning teachers that I can recommend from my years as a student are: a personal enjoyment when dealing with kids, an interest in people, the realization that the job goes much deeper than 9-5 hrs. in the class room, and plenty of patience.

Melanie, a first-year teacher, arrived in Betty's room with a gray face, wide eyes, and an anguished look that said, "I'm desperate; I need to talk."

In a shaky voice, she proceeded to tell Betty that she was doing the best she could, but in the course of the last two weeks she'd been fighting with her husband because she'd been up until 2:00 A.M. working on lesson plans, her evaluation from her principal had been disappointing, her toddler had been acting out at child care as a result of the problems at home, and the papers were multiplying faster than she could grade them. As the tears burst forth, Melanie looked at Betty through bleary eyes and said, "I left a job that paid me twice as much as what I'm earning now to become a teacher. I don't need this."

If this sounds remotely familiar, this chapter is for you. You will find that taking a few deep breaths, reevaluating priorities, and making some efforts to mannage stress will make life a bit easier. All people, at one time or another, feel frustrated and helpless for a variety of reasons. You are not alone.

Teaching certainly can be stressful, and your first years of teaching will probably be especially stressed. These stressors will come from expected and unexpected sources. You will become a juggler balancing school and home life, professional demands with personal needs. Unfortunately, when the "To Do" list gets long, the first things to be dropped seem to be personal plans: time with the family, exercise time, even sleep time. We urge you to think about making specific plans for your personal needs. It is too easy to neglect yourself, yet if you do, everyone suffers: your students, your fellow faculty members, your family, *you*. Then, besides taking specific steps to deal with these many life stressors, you must deal with how you *feel* about these situations.

If you allow excessive, inappropriate stress to rule your life, you will find that you catch colds more easily. You will snap at a student who needs attention. You will miss the teachable moment or the tiny learning step taken by your most troubled student. You will forget to turn in reports. The simplest reminder from a secretary will sound like a reprimand. Your students will not retain as much material when *you* are not enjoying teaching. You will avoid collegial contact and closet yourself in your classroom. At home, you will growl and look on a request for attention as a demand on your time. You will withdraw physically and mentally from friends and family because a mound of essays is spontaneously regenerating in the back room. Your sleep patterns will be interrupted. You will teach, scream, grade, and discipline in your dreams and wake up to find out you've put in an extra teaching day.

Fun? No. Controllable? Yes! Keep thoughts about personal wellness in your mind. There are ways to cope with the job and keep the stressors under control. Your physical and mental health is an essential factor in your teaching success, but other people will not usually be thinking about your personal well-being—you have to stick up for yourself on this topic.

Choosing Priorities

Reasonable levels of stress keep you motivated and eager to teach. Excess stress builds when you feel frustrated and out of control. Stress mounts when you have too many demands on your time. Setting priorities and sticking to them will help you stay in control. Answering the questions on the "Important-to-Me List" will help you set those priorities.

Important-to-Me List

- Are weekends exclusively for my family?
- Do my children need me after school?
- Am I going to participate in school activities and let church and community activities go?
- How many committees am I obligated to be on? When should I say no?
- What is more important—my teeaching or my coaching?
- Is the overnight return of papers more or less important than detailed lesson plans?
- Am I going to follow the curriculum to the letter or teach curriculum concepts based on student interest?
- Do I need personal time daily? weekly? When and where will it be?
- What kinds of things do I like to do to relax?
- Do I have to moonlight at a second job to make ends meet?
- Is this a good time to take a night class?
- I'm being evaluated. How can I demonstrate to the administrator that I'm competent?
- How do I regain control when I'm feeling stressed?

Stress Management

Years ago, when Allen was feeling particularly stressed, his doctor gave him some valuable advice. The doctor told Allen to list everything that bothered him. Allen was told to classify his complaints into three lists:

1. Those problems that he could not control or change.
2. Those problems that really didn't matter.
3. Those problems that he felt he could do something specific about.

Then the doctor told Allen to rip up the first two lists and work on those things he *could* change. It was a relief for Allen to throw away two-thirds of his worries!

You might also develop the habit of thinking about what is bothering you in relation to the question "Will this matter in five years? five days?" If the answer is no, then let it go and relax.

Betty has car-pooled for most of her professional career. Besides saving gas money, car-pooling has great stress-relief potential. Betty long ago found that her carmates provided sympathetic friends willing to participate in a rehash of the day's battles, trials, and victories. Those fellow riders experience the same stresses with the same students and staff members. The level of empathy is especially high. When Betty arrives home, the difficulties of the day have been aired and let go. She is able to walk in the door more relaxed and ready to focus on the needs of her family.

If you don't feel comfortable airing out your stress with fellow teachers from your school, or don't have the opportunity to do so, you could use your local teachers' association or subject-area organization as a support group.

If your stress reaches a level you can no longer manage yourself, seek counseling. Some communities and area school districts have worked together to create a program where a teacher can get counseling and professional help. Teachers who would not otherwise seek professional help can get advice through these programs on home problems, finances, marital difficulties, and other stressors. The consultations are confidential and are supported by the theory that a teacher whose personal problems are under control is more effective in the classroom.

Knowing Your Limits

A major component of stress management is knowing your limits. You need to be sensitive to the signals your mind and body send out when they are reaching the overload point. If you are aware of your physical and mental needs, you can make time for yourself to relax and rest, plan a change of focus or task, or consciously throw away a stressor you can do nothing about. A lot of dealing with your stressors includes forgiving yourself for what you can't control or what you simply can't get done. Use the following checklist to analyze your limits.

Adequate Sleep   How much sleep do you need every night? Occasional late nights won't hurt, but consistently losing several hours of sleep to work on school plans will not translate into better lessons. Begin to look for grading or planning shortcuts to gain sleep time. Get adequate sleep on the weekends, too. Reread the time-management hints in Chapter 4. Teaching demands an incredible amount of energy, and you often don't realize that fatigue is building a web around you until it's too late.

Prime Time   When do you do your best work? Betty (almost) never grades past 8:30 P.M.; when she does, she dreams about those essays all night. She tries not to grade on Sunday evenings—it makes her feel out of control and behind in her work. Betty often feels too tired to grade at her desk right after school, but if she exercises, then drives home (or vice versa), she can get some good work done before the evening meal. Some of her morning colleagues get up in the predawn hours to work quietly before the family awakens. Betty likes to write lessons plans Thursday afternoons. She gets assignments ready for the following week, orders films and equipment, and informs support teachers about upcoming deadlines. Betty frequently averages grades on Monday mornings and then prepares grade-check slips for her students. This grade reminder gives the students responsibility for their own progress during the week.

Saying No   The word is N-O. No. Practice saying it, because you just can't be on every church committee, attend every meeting, or be president of anything. Especially during your first years of teaching, give yourself the gift of time. Participate sparingly in projects outside of school and avoid chairing committees, if possible. You are in charge all day at school. If you must participate, be the follower and supporter for a change. Brian stuffs envelopes and nails yard signs together for political candidates. Choose projects that are personally satisfying for you. To the rest of the requests, calmly but firmly repeat that you need every minute to become the finest teacher possible. You might say, "I really appreciate you thinking of me, but I have a limited amount of time. I don't think I could do a satisfactory job at this time." Once you've settled into your teaching job and feel you do have some time to spare, you might offer some of your time in a support position.

Students will also ask you to sponsor, chaperone, or participate in their club activities. You will feel complimented, but do not agree without thought. Find out how much time you will be expected to contribute and if weekend or evening time is involved. If you have already been assigned to sponsor a club, you probably do not need to add any responsibilities to your day. If you are asked to chaperone a dance, ask who else will be sharing the duties. Ask an administrator about specific responsibilities before you accept. If the request is for you to participate in the school carnival as the pie target, think twice. If you look young or are having problems establishing your credibility with your students, placing yourself in a position of ridicule—even in the name of fun or fund-raising—will not help your classroom image. If what the students ask you to do will make you personally uncomfortable (being a candidate in the "Kiss the Pig" contest), decline politely: "No, but thanks for thinking of me. I don't do dunk tanks or windows."

Paperwork Relief   If the paperwork is about to suffocate you, look for a solution in Chapter 4.

Returning Assignments   Don't promise a specific date for returning assignments, but tell students how many papers you have graded and how many you have left to read. Set daily goals for how many papers you will grade. Share with your students how much home time you spend grading and preparing. It helps them get a sense of your job as well as appreciate that you are working hard in their behalf.

Doing Your Best   You must not allow school to dominate your every waking moment. If it does, you will burn out. You can't teach every item

Which Is the Most Important *Hat?*

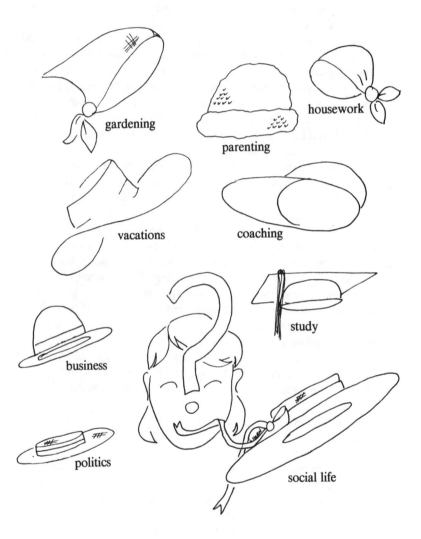

in the curriculum, reach every student, or make everyone happy, so don't feel frustrated when it doesn't happen. Decide what you can teach in the time allotted and do your best to accomplish this. How many times have you told your students, "Just give it your best"? They expect the same from you.

Outside Classes   Carefully consider the time you have outside the classroom. Taking any evening classes in your first year or so of teaching may overburden you. Classes take time you might need for schoolwork or for your family and usually include reading, paper preparation, or research time beyond the actual minutes in class. These classes meeet on a weekly schedule. You might find that you need your evening time unscheduled. On the other hand, classes you take strictly for physical recreation or to explore the arts might be a great release of tension.

Coaching and Club Sponsoring   Coaching and club sponsorships may be knitted into the fabric of your teaching responsibilities, especially in the early years. It is a sad fact that many beginning teachers get saddled with clubs, duties, and coaching assignments beyond basic teaching duties or as a stipulation of their contracts. Experienced teachers, too, may be called on to help with extracurricular activities. If your teaching assignment includes coaching, overseeing the school yearbook, or another time-consuming responsibility, be sensitive to the extra stress it will entail and work to manage that stress from the first day. If you're new at taking on these extra duties, try to cosponsor clubs with an experienced teacher so you won't have to find out the shortcuts to managing club activities after the fact. If you are the only sponsor of an activity, seek a mentor in a faculty member who previously worked with that group. If you are assigned a club that deals with money, introduce yourself to the person in charge of the school's business affairs and make an appointment to sit down with this person to learn about budgets, purchase orders, do's and don'ts.

Time Out   When you feel yourself losing the battle, catching cold, or getting angry too easily—get away. Don't do any school work for an evening or a weekend. Go away if necessary. Soak in a bubble bath. Walk, exercise. Call a nonteacher friend. Watch TV. Go to a movie or out to dinner. Cook a fancy meal. Go to bed with a good book and your teddy bear. Pamper yourself. Have some chocolate.

Moving On   If you do feel as if you lost, forgive yourself. Think about the limit you went beyond, and decide what you have to do to avoid that bear pit next time. Get on with life.

Feelings of Insecurity/Challenges

Insecurity causes stress. You may be highly versed in your subject area and haave gotten rave notices from your student teaching supervisor. You may have years of successful teaching under your belt. There are still many situations that leave teachers—especially beginning teachers—feeling out of control. This insecurity breeds stress and fatigue. If these feelings are not dealt with, health problems can result.

Student Challenges

No matter how many courses you have had in your content area, no matter how many degrees hang on your classroom wall, and no matter how thoroughly your lesson is planned, students will still challenge the whole process. "How come we have to study this stuff?" "We didn't do it this way with Ms.——." "I'm really not supposed to be in your class. I'm supposed to be in an advanced class." "This is stupid." "This is boring." "Why should I learn to type? I'm going to have a secretary." "I hate you." "History is stupid. I don't have to know any history to be a pro basketball player." "Everyone knows Mr.—— is the best math teacher, but his class was full when I registered." "This isn't fair!"

The last comment is absolutely right: It isn't fair—to you. Yet some students have always perceived that their duty in life is to challenge and harass teachers. They do it to novices and veterans alike, so take a little comfort in the fact that we all get those challenges every year. Don't take such comments personally. Students are challenging authority and power rather than you personally. It is important either to brush off these comments and keep on teaching or to pause and deal with them directly and firmly. Don't act flustered or allow yourself to enter into a verbal debate with the student.

One way to eliminate this verbal baiting is to structure each lesson so that it has a specific daily goal and write that goal on the board. Students are notorious for being concerned only with today. Point out that this one-day lesson is a step in a twelve-year continuum of math and thinking skills. The more you plan lessons that help students make connections between the learning and their personal worlds, the more they will be engaged in learning. Plan many activities that utilize maximum student participation. Students can:

- plan and teach a segment of the lesson.
- create visuals to represent main concepts.
- engage in cooperative group projects.
- tutor each other.
- gather research in the media center.
- share related personal experiences.
- participate in self-evaluation.

Challenges from Parents and Administrators

Unfortunately, students are not the only experts at rude remarks. Parental comments can be equally hurtful. "I was really hoping my Billy would get Mr.——for his teacher." "Are you sure that is the best way to teach my Wendy? Her teacher last year never asked her to draw what happened in a story." "What does my child have to do to get an A around here?" These remarks come more from concern for the offspring than from a desire to personally attack you. When talking to these parents, you might show them the curriculum sequence the class is studying or give them ways to double-check for learning. "Why don't you ask Wendy to retell her story to her younger brother? She tells the story using her pictures and is quite articulate." Make the parents your allies and partners in the learning situation from the beginning of the year by keeping them informed about their child's successes and needs. Make a point of sharing what is happening in your class through student-authored newsletters, phone contacts, brief conversations after school, or PTO meetings.

You will often feel anxiety when dealing with administrators. Betty once confessed to her administrator that she was upset with herself because she still felt extreme stress before every observation after so mnay years of teaching. Her administrator explained that stress is natural and a component of a good lesson. If you view your administrator as your master teacher, share what is happening in your classroom, and solicit advice when you need it, your administrator should become your ally and partner in creating a strong learning environment for your students.

Grading Challenges

Humans are not the only sources of stress. Grades often cause tense moments. Students frequently challenge grades on tests, essays, or report cards. They usually present the challenge in a strident voice in front of the whole class. "My mother wants to know how come I got a B when I aced the semester test." Mutiny can soon follow. Many teachers admit to giving in and not counting certain items because the nagging student simply wears them down. Students will even discuss which teachers on a faculty are easy marks for such manipulative behavior. You can forestall such confrontations.

1. Before you hand back a test or an essay, announce that you will not engage in a grade-debate during class. Tell students that you will gladly discuss the test or essay, but they must make an appointment with you for time before or after school. Remind them to bring along texts, notes, or essay drafts to support their inquiry. The interested students with legitimate concerns will do this.
2. Give students a short lesson in manners. Students who are respectful and listen get respect and attention from you in return. Students need to realize that rude and nasty behavior does not endear them to a teacher.
3. Return papers at the end of the class period so students don't spend the hour paging through notes or stewing angrily rather than focusing on your lesson.
4. Sometimes return the papers at the beginning of the period and use them as the focus of the whole lesson. Use the class time to reteach some concepts and engage the students in tasks that will help them strengthen the previously weak points in the unit.
5. Never set yourself up as infallible. All teachers sometimes write bad test items. There is nothing wrong with eliminating a specific test item after grading a test shows that your students misunderstood or otherwise were unable to answer that item.

As you deal with students, parents, and administrators on a daily basis, your personal feelings will be assaulted, challenged, and even ridiculed. You will feel rage, frustration, envy, and helplessness. You will feel alone and isolated. You have to consciously let those feelings go. You must focus on what really matters: teaching the lesson to the best of your ability.

Pacing

Thoughtful pacing of lessons can make a difference in your personal wellness, too. Some days you will be energetic, have tons of material to cover, and know exactly what must be done by Friday. The lesson plans will call for frequent change in activities to enable students to take notes, move quickly into groups, return to report back to the class, and perhaps take a quiz in the course of one class period. The pace of the class will be quick, energetic, and probably loud while students work on maps, short stories, newsletters, or skits.

However, other days you will want your students to proceed through the lesson thoughtfully, and on still other days you'll feel too tired or overwhelmed to act like a ringmaster. These are the days that call for a slower teaching pace. A slower pace doesn't mean that your lesson is underprepared or that your students will get out of control with boredom. Rather, it means that you have planned activities that engage students independently or in small groups. The class noise level should remain low. These activities will utilize past learning and expect students to process this learning into self-discovery and conclusions about the subject matter. This slower pace might be manifested in the form of project choices that appeal to student learning differences: drawings, reading quietly, or journal writing. This slower pace allows you to monitor individual progress. You might sit at your desk and consult quietly with individual students. Better yet, bring your desk chair into the center of the student work area or sit at a student desk. Some teachers sit on a low stool equipped with casters on the legs so they can roll between student desks. This proximity to the students is all-important to keeping the order and tone of the slower-paced lesson. So is engaging in the same activity as the students: reading, writing, or drawing. This proximity—being among the students and meeting them eye to eye on their level—is critical in classroom management whether you plan a slow- or a fast-paced lesson.

A slower-paced lesson might begin with you introducing new material to your students while they take notes. You might instruct them next to read related material in their text, give them a few tips on what reading skills to use, and remind them of the purpose for reading. Write several questions on the board that students must be ready to answer when they complete the reading. You might also read the questions at the end of the chapter aloud before the students begin reading. Allow class time for silent reading. You can then supervise and encourage individuals without using up a lot of energy. At the end of the class period, have students write reflectively in their journals, take a quiz and check answers with a neighbor, or draw a picture. You can glance over their shoulders and mark your grade book with a check if you wish. Students often welcome these slower-paced classes on those high-energy days: the day before a long holiday, the day of the pep assembly, or the day of a national crisis.

You can also pace your class with your voice. If you want to pick up the pace of a class—energize and speed up the learning process—you can do so by increasing the volume of your voice, raising the pitch slightly, and using the cadence of a game-show host. Without pausing for breath, you chant: "Okay, next we'll have the answer to question number 5: What is the atomic weight of copper [with a sweep of your arm], Barry?" After Barry's answer, you plunge on. "Right! And next we need to hear the atomic weight of aluminum from Mary." Clapping and finger-snapping also can be used to quicken the pace of the class. Student responses for fast pacing should require recall and not answers based on thoughtful contemplation. You might choose this faster pace during lesson introduction or review sessions.

To slow the pace of the class, you can slow the rhythm of your voice and lower the tone. Pause longer after sentences, take time to look students in their eyes, and frequently wait until you can see that everyone is listening. Reinstate the standard procedure for questioning and pause for think time before calling on a student. Accomplish any discipline in the same low voice tone. You can further slow the pace by asking that students all think of a response to your question but *not* raise their hands or shout out the answer. Then wait five seconds or more and quietly ask several different students to respond. You might have each student write a response on a flash card to hold up, or you might ask a question and wait until most of the students have raised their hands indicating that they have an answer. If you are doing mental math, students could indicate the answer on their fingers, but hide the answer until called upon. Other ways of keeping the students relatively quiet, yet all engaged in the lesson, might include thumbs up or down for agreement or disagreement, answers given in sign language, or written answers to be shared with a nearby student. This slower pace in a classroom allows time for students to think and contemplate connections between lessons and their personal lives. Encourage these connections.

You can use pacing, switching from energetic activities to quiet tasks, within one class period, too. This insures that you will not wear out before the day (or class) is over. Structure class discussions so that you monitor the activity while students take leadership roles. This appeals to both your impulsive and reflective learners. All you need to do is decide what objective you have for that day's lesson and decide how your students will show their mastery of that objective. Then plan a series of activities that reinforce that objective: some energetic and some reflective.

Getting Along with Others

There are plenty of stressors related to the daily work with students, parents, and administrators. You don't need to add any by getting tangled in uncomfortable situations among faculty members. No matter how well chosen, every faculty is going to have its differences, rivalries, and jealousies. Teachers who survive these complications without getting involved usually display a high degree of self-confidence and a ready sense of humor, while staying objective. You will quickly recognize the gossips, the complainers, and the trouble-makers. You can be friendly with these people, but beware of forming close alliances. Those alliances could be misinterpreted by administrators and other faculty members, and they certainly wouldn't help you manage your stress.

Be careful whom you talk about and what you say. You might make a comment about an administrator or another staff member, assuming that it will not be repeated just because your listener is your next-door neighbor. It would be uncomfortable to discover that this neighbor reported directly to the principal and often out of context. Especially during your first years at any school, practice patience. Watch for political affiliations, stay out of them, and keep your barbed comments to yourself. Figure out what the administration expects of its faculty and then work for that goal. If you are supportive of your administrators and colleagues; they will likely be supportive of you in return. This support can do wonders for your self-confidence and go a long way toward ensuring your personal wellness and satisfaction with your job. (If you find you are in a conflict with your administrators on some important issues, begin looking for a position elsewhere, but do not be insubordinate in your present job.)

Seek out positive friends. They will motivate you and share ideas. Listen to these wise colleagues. Surround yourself with people who make you feel good about yourself. These people will be happy to see you and interested in your success in the classroom. When you feel positive about your teaching, you will be happy and discover that you are growing professionally and developing a variety of interests.

Finding Your Mentors

If you are a beginning teacher, or an experienced teacher starting at a new school, you will often feel lonely, isolated, and overwhelmed. *This is normal!* Ideally, your building will have a mentoring network that will meet with you and other new teachers periodically. Many of these meetings could be informal and held after school or at a time when people aren't feeling rushed. Occasionally, breakfast or lunch meetings may provide some time for idea exchanges.

If no mentor comes forward to help you, speak to your administrator. Ask if such a program could be started. Make it a point to get acquainted with others.

In your first weeks and months of teaching, or of teaching at a new school, you will not know people well, nor will you know whom to trust. Don't get discouraged. You will eventually discover supportive colleagues to help you plan lessons and learn procedures. It may, however, take you even longer to discover friends who will listen compassionately, respond supportively, and keep your deepest secrets confidential.

Some people are not interested in your broken heart or home problems. Others will think less of you if they are privy to your personal affairs. Trust cautiously in the first months. You do not want some of your more candid remarks misconstrued or repeated out of context. This is a time to listen and learn.

People will probably not be willing to enter a trusting relationship if you complain voraciously or if you continually degrade your present teaching situation. Colleagues quickly tire of hearing about your practice teaching or previous classroom situations.

As you get acquainted with the faculty in your new school, you will begin to form friendships. These people will be your immediate support group. One may be formally assigned to you as your mentor; the rest may simply be kindred spirits. These are the people who will share your tears, frustrations, failures, and successes. They are the ones who make a simple suggestion that helps the lesson flow. Cherish these people, give support, and return the loyalty. You'll find that as early as your second or third year at your school you, too, will be mentoring.

Being Absent/Being There

It is a fact of life that if you are a normal human being, you will catch a lot of colds the first year you teach and every time you switch schools. Even as an experienced teacher staying at the same school, you will go through cycles every four or five years when you will be exposed to a lot of germs. Your first line of defense is to make sure your immunizations are up to date—for your sake as well as your students' sakes. Wash your hands frequently, don't touch your face, and drink lots of water. That advice is sound but not always possible based on teaching schedules, house rules, and distances to the restrooms. You will get sick. The debate is then whether to tough it out or stay home.

Don't be afraid to seek medical help. Teachers seem to get a mixed message on health. Because medical insurance costs are skyrocketing, groups like teachers are getting seminars on self-care and what to do for minor illnesses to avoid doctor's appointments. Often, teachers and students come to school too sick to be productive, or they self-treat for an ailment when they ought to be home or in a doctor's office. Teachers also find it frustrating and difficult to get doctor appointments after school hours, so the stress of waiting for help only adds to the frustration of being sick and makes the teacher feel less than effective.

Stay home!

Being in school sick often spreads your germs to the kids, and then you wrestle with their make-up work. Besides, if you go to school sick, you'll take longer to get well and often catch the next germ more quickly. If you are sick, stay home.

There are times when it is virtually impossible to be absent: a field trip, a guest speaker, or an assembly. If you are desperate, and know who your sub will be, you could be absent in some of these instances. If you are participating in this activity with another teacher and he or she feels capable of handling the situation with the help of your sub, you can be absent without worry. It would be courteous to let every adult involved know about the situation ahead of time.

If you are suddenly sick, you may need to get help quickly. Press your call button, summon your neighbor, or send a student to the office to let someone know you need help. If you must leave the room, be sure that a neighboring teacher knows you are out of your classroom. Your ill health may be the result of returning to work too soon after an illness. If you let students know that you are not feeling well, they are usually concerned and will be able to carry on with an alternate assignment that does not require your active participation. This may allow you to make it until you can engage a substitute or reach the end of the day. As hard as it is to believe, things can go on without you.

Substitutes

Planning for a Sub   It may seem like more work to plan for a substitute than it's worth. Using a substitute will be easier if you follow the suggestions about preparing a sub folder in Chapter 4.

Be sure you have a sub folder prepared with emergency lesson plans and that this folder is at school. Then stay home. This is the time when that rainy afternoon you spent writing emergency lessons you thought you'd never use and storing them in your sub folder will pay off. If you have a chance to write lesson plans before you go home sick, plan a single lesson or short unit covering several days that will enrich what the students are studying that grading period. Structure the work so that the sub has to collect, evaluate, or grade what the students do. Everyone must be held accountable for completion of the lesson.

Depending on your school district's policy concerning extra textbooks, you may want to have a copy of student texts or teachers' manuals at home. This can be a lifesaver when you are ill and at home for a few days. You can alter plans or talk with your substitute over the phone about what needs to be done and where to find information. This will also allow you to do planning at home when you aren't sick without having to lug all the books back and forth.

It helps if you can make up your mind by the end of the school day if you will need a sick day. This is an advantage for the person who calls substitutes, and you might get your choice of subs. Plan extra work for every class period with instructions to the sub to let you know how far the class progressed. Few subs can fill in extra time effectively. It is better to provide detailed plans for them. You might also tell a neighboring teacher that you will be gone and have that person check on your sub several times during the day. There are books of activities on the market that can help.

Sometimes you will get sick during the night and have to call for a sub early in the morning. If your lesson plans and seating charts are on your desk, you can simply notify the appropriate person and go back to sleep. Sometimes, you will need to get further instructions to your substitute. Your spouse or a family member might have to deliver plans to the school office. If you have a close friend in your department, a phone call to that person with lesson plans will solve your problem. You might ask that your sub call you after reading your lesson plans.

Returning After a Sub   Learning to cooperate with substitute teachers while coping with unexpected change is a good social skill for students to develop. Occasionally the diverse personality that covers for you in your classroom will be a real weirdo, according to the kids. Talk to students about dealing maturely with these kinds of people. You might explain why a sub might sometimes enter a classroom like a Sherman tank; try to help the students see the other side of the coin. More times than not, you will return to find that everything went well and the class had a great day.

It you return to a roomful of problems, have a meaningful discussion about behavior and responsibility. Make it clear all year that you expect your classes to be on extra-good behavior when you have a substitute, student teacher, or guest in your room. If a substitute hands out a justified punishment, hold the students accountable for their behavior. A phone call to parents will reinforce the point that you are 100 percent serious and that students' learning must proceed whether you are in the classroom or not. These parental calls serve as examples to other students.

One spring Barbara was gone for three weeks recovering from surgery. Although Barbara left detailed lesson plans, her substitute was a disaster. On the day Barbara returned, the students all wanted to tell her their side of the story, so she had them write about it. Then they talked about what they learned and didn't learn, what they did to try to make the situation go better, and what they probably shouldn't have done. The students didn't accomplish what Barbara had expected of them. However, she couldn't have avoided the surgery, and she had prepared for the sub as best she could. Beyond that, Barbara couldn't feel guilty about what happened. Neither should you in similar conditions.

Sub Survival Kit   One year Ellen, a fourth-grade teacher, and her husband went out of town on a long-awaited ski vacation over the Presidents' Day holiday. It was just the break Ellen desserved and needed during a busy second semester of her first year of teaching. Ellen was planning on getting home late Monday afternoon and spending some time preparing for class Tuesday. When she and her husband got up early Monday morning to load the car for the trip home, however, they couldn't help but notice that their car was missing! This changed Ellen's plans to have some extra time for planning before returning to school Tuesday. She also had to miss a day of school, as Monday was spent filing police reports and making alternate travel plans. On top of it all, Ellen had to spend time and money on the phone finding out whom she needed to contact to get a sub.

This incident convinced Ellen that she needed to have essential phone numbers handy for emergencies. Now she has a list of needed phone numbers that she takes with her when she's going out of town or has at home in case she can't return to work as planned.

You'll probably also want a list of the following phone numbers to have at home or to take with you when you are out of town:

- Sub call-in number.
- Special sub's number. (If you want a specific sub, have this number to call first. Then notify the sub call-in service so they don't waste time calling this sub for other assignments.)
- A colleague's home phone. This person could help the sub find needed materials or your sub folder. (See Chapter 4 about setting up a sub folder.)
- Your principal's home number.
- The school's phone number so you can notify the office when you will return or if you will need to retain the substitute for another day.

Fatigue

On many occasions you won't feel cold-in-the-head sick, but you will experience an overwhelming fatigue. Teaching demands huge amounts of energy, and even emotional fatigue can leave you feeling as if you have been filled with more lead pellets than that Jumping Frog of Calaveras County. Exercise helps. Go for a solitary walk. Fly a kite with the neighborhood kids. Walk to the post office rather than drive. Go down to the river with your children and feed the ducks. Sit on the porch and watch the sunset. Go to bed early. These simple actions can help you avoid full-fledged illness and the consequent absence from school.

IMPORTANT PHONE NUMBERS

SUB CALL-IN _____

SPECIAL SUB NAME _____

NUMBER _____

PRINCIPAL _____

SCHOOL _____

COLLEAGUE NAME _____

NUMBER _____

Renewal

One way to ensure personal wellness is to plan times of renewal. You might set aside this time daily for reading, writing, or exercise. The fatigue-relieving strategies mentioned above are minishots of renewal. This renewal might also be the weekends you spend on short excursions with family or friends. The time spent away from your busy, complicated job at school provides a chance to relax and rejuvenate. It is a chance to re-energize. Even if you feel in control of your teaching situation, you will be surprised how much more energy you will have if you give yourself time for recharging.

Joining an interest group outside the school community can give you short weekly shots of renewal. Seek out groups simply to have fun with people who are not teachers. You could try, for example, a softball team, a quilting guild, a book discussion group, or a church organization.

These groups will contribute to your positive self-image and feelings of well-being as a whole person, not just as a teacher.

Summer vacation offers several months for personal renewal. Many teachers take jobs in the summer to make financial ends meet. A non-education-related job can be refreshing because you are working with a group of people with interests different from those of your teaching colleagues. If you still want to work with youngsters during the summer, camps of every focus would appreciate your expertise. Working for the National Park Service might also prove a rewarding option.

If you do not have to earn money during the summer in order to keep ahead of the bill collectors, many interesting volunteer possibilities exist. The National Park Service will welcome you into their Volunteer in Park program. As a V.I.P. you might be a campground host, draw a plant map of the park, or write curriculum for science teachers who bring students to the park on field trips. Your expertise will be matched to your assignment and appreciated. State parks and state fish and game departments have similar programs. Writing to these organizations in the early spring will yield all sorts of interesting possibilities.

Some teachers peruse grant applications in the deep winter months the way others read seed catalogs. Grants and fellowships will pay you to attend programs at colleges around the world or close to your home. You can find lists of these programs in professional magazines or get them directly from the sponsoring organizations. One of the best ways to find out about these programs is to listen to colleagues talk about grants they have enjoyed. Many of these programs are specifically designed to increase your background knowledge and assist you in designing effective lessons to use in the fall with your classes. Others may attract you because they focus on a topic you have never had time to study before. On other occasions, your district may encourage you to go to a specific program to help you get ready to teach a new class.

The National Endowment for the Humanities sponsors institutes and seminars designed for teachers to study a specific topic and devote time to research on topics of choice. The NEH also sponsors grants for independent study. The focus of these programs is professional growth, with seminar directors seeking participants from a variety of teaching fields to create a diverse discussion group. Many applicants deliberately apply to seminars out of their teaching disciplines to add diversity and depth to their personal learning.

You'll find a list of sources for information on summer institutes and volunteer and paid summer positions at the end of this chapter.

Travel is also a tempting summer option. Teachers can get reduced rates on tours planned especially for educators. Other teachers lead groups of adults or students on foreign tours, often earning free passage for themselves. You can find information on these programs in professional magazines. Ask fellow faculty members if they have ever taken these tours and which were the most enjoyable.

Whether you decide to spend your summer working, doing volunteer work, or attending classes, view the summer break as a time to relax and regroup your energy. As the hot days swelter into August, you will remember the good times of the past year of teaching. The hard parts will not seem so bad now as they seemed at the time. You will also find that you have crystallized some ideas about how you want to structure your teaching during the coming year. You will find yourself looking forward to the next challenge—still nervous, perhaps, if you're a new teacher or started the year in a new situation, but a lot more self-confident now about your teaching.

Conclusion

Personal wellness is not given enough consideration. As you teach, always stay aware of your energy levels and make time for yourself, your family, and your friends. Find ways to separate your mind from the daily concerns of teaching. Take care of your mental and physical health. Accept the fact that you cannot be the perfect teacher and reach every student—no one can be that perfect. If another teacher tells you differently, you can be sure that some aspect of that person's home life is probably getting short-changed. Seek ways to keep in control of your health and your personal time. Seek support from colleagues. Your teaching can only benefit from your personal health.

When you *are* sick, stay home. If you plan ahead for substitute use, you can be away from school without undue stress.

If there is something that you didn't teach or handle to your satisfaction, or if there is something that you forgot to include in a unit, rather than stewing about it and feeling like a failure, write it down in your plan book or journal and include that material in the unit next year. Forgive yourself. This will go a long way to alleviate the stress of teaching.

Some Sources for Summer Opportunities

Education Week "Calendar of Events" column

Teacher Magazine "Extra Credit" column

Winter and early spring issues of magazines in your professional field

Local colleges and universities

Association for Supervision and Curriculum Development
(703) 549-9110

Phi Delta Kappa
(812) 339-1156

National Staff Development Council
(513) 523-6029

National Middle School Association
(614) 848-8211

National Endowment for the Humanities
(202) 786-0377

National Science Foundation
(202) 357-5000

Both Paid and Volunteer Positions

National Park Service
(202) 208-6843

State fish and wildlife office

State parks office

Local office of The Nature Conservancy

CHAPTER 12

Dispelling the Myths

Never give up. It ▬▬▬ will take a while to achieve the status you might like as a teacher. Try, experiment; and if you don't succeed, try again.
　　　　　　　　　　Jami　　　　　#10

Good Luck!

Brian W
Grade 4

If you're like most people, you left college in a glow of idealism. With your head packed full of teaching theory and educational jargon, you may have entered the profession with these ideas:

- All students will like you. (After all, you're nice to them.)
- Students will always be enthusiastic about you and what you teach.
- You can be your students' pal.
- There is no such word as *failure*.
- Master teachers are born that way.

Let's examine these teaching myths.

Myth #1: All Students Will Like You

For a variety of reasons, this won't happen. It's likely that with some students, no matter what you do, you'll be perceived as a villain. During these volatile times in students's lives, you may be perceived like the mother or father that the student, temporarily, can't stand. For some adolescents or children, anyone who represents authority, in any capacity, is suspect. If Jamie and her boyfriend have had a fight minutes before entering your class, you and what you have to say will bee as significant as a mosquito. Recognize and accept that you will not be a hit with everyone every day.

Myth #2: Students Will Always Be Enthusiastic About You and What You Teach

Depending on the grade level, the time of day, the season, and the weather, the enthusiasm of students is as predictable as a hurricane.

The day after Halloween or the day before vacation often guarantees that students will be giddy with enthusiasm. Homecoming games and athletic events spark similar excitement. Sometimes this vitality carries over into the classroom and enhances the classroom experience; sometimes it has the opposite effect—kids are too wound up to stay on task. Chapter 4 suggests planning high-interest activities that can channel the enthusiasm positively.

For most new teachers the realization that kids aren't enthused each day, and that some never appear to be, is devastating. Don't believe that all students will be motivated all the time. Too many factors prevent this, like home problems, health problems, and social problems.

Myth #3: You Can Be Your Students' Pal

Betty's father, a master teacher and educator for 33 years (though he's retired, he's still a master teacher), used to tell Betty that, ultimately, she was in control and that she could establish any type of classroom atmosphere she wanted. He also told her that subject competency would never be a problem—that classroom management would present the greatest challenge. He was right.

If any piece of advice in this book deserves the most emphasis, it's this: Do not be your students' buddy. Through your voice, dress, and expectations, remember that you are the teacher and adult role model. You want your students to respect and admire you, not think of you as one of their peers.

Myth #4: There Is No Such Word As Failure

You've been reading about tips for success. Many are formulas to help plan lessons, deal positively with human beings, and succeed as an educator. If only teaching were so easy.

What no one may have told you was that, unlike the salesperson, teachers don't always reap instant rewards. The test may measure the grasp of the information studied; the smile or nod may be merely a student's political tactic. Most teachers don't know the actual effect they've had on their students.

If daily lives ran according to formulas, students would express and feel regret when they had cheated, insulted, or lied. Ideally, the formulas would result in a classroom where all the students appreciated you being there and felt that learning was a privilege. These same students would be on time, always be present, and take pride in their work. Most teachers leave the university with heads full of knowledge, assumptions, and formulas and, fortunately, an agenda for success. However, as difficult as it is to accept, failures will occur, and nothing you can do will change this.

Because most teachers wish for success for their students, failures can be devastating. An explosive comment from an angry student, a failed test, a withdrawal from class or school, or a death or illness can severely disappoint you. Do not take these as personal failures. It's okay to feel let down, but if you've made students aware of consequences and expectations, you are not responsible if they choose not to comply. Don't enable students. If they have made choices to fail, do not feel that you have failed.

Lessons will flop no matter how well planned. It happens to all teachers every year. Analyze what happened and structure the next lesson to avoid these pitfalls.

Myth #5: Master Teachers Are Born That Way

A colleague of Robert's was once overheard to say to a beginning teacher, "I'm a master teacher because I was born that way." This statement might be humorous if it weren't such a falsehood. To be a master at anything takes years of trial and error, experimentation, and the ability to learn from past mistakes. Whether it be in classroom management or curriculum planning, master teachers continually encounter new students, material, and situations. Master teachers are not born as perfectly formed educators. They do not stagnate; they continually grow and improve.

The Truth About Teaching

Teaching is one of the most demanding and challenging of professions. After reading this book, you may even wonder about your career choice.

We'd like to leave you with some final thoughts about why, in spite of its challenges and demands, teaching is rewarding enough to attract millions.

Unlike the business world, there is no "bottom line" in teaching. You often don't know the impact your sales pitch has had on your clients, at least not immediately. What does make an impression is an occasional letter or note from a student that says, "You taught me so much. Your French class gave me the tools to study and gain this job that I love." "I never liked to read until I took your class." "The other students in my math class at college were lost, but thanks to you, I know this stuff!" "You were the best teacher I ever had!"

Sometimes you'll hear about your successes in a most unconventional way. An acquaintance of Barbara's had been seated on a plane next to a former student of Barbara's. During the 800-mile sojourn the young lady revealed to Barbara's friend that if it hadn't been for Barbara, she would never have written well enough to give her the confidence to apply for the position she held.

The impact of a teacher may last a lifetime. Rarely can other professions make the same statement.

Teachers have a great deal of autonomy. What happens in the classroom is largely up to the instructor. While others in the work world complain about having so little control—deadlines, phone calls, and sales calls—you, for the most part, plan your day.

You have an opportunity to see human beings at their best. The enthusiasm and honesty of kids is often a treat to witness. While adults often have their beliefs carved in stone, young people are still developing their own values. Your role as a model has a major impact on this.

Elbert Hubbard once said, "If you want to learn something, teach it." Teaching offers an opportunity for continuous growth and enlightenment. Each new prep, collegial chat, or article provides new information. Nowhere except in the field of education are you daily in the company of so many experts on subjects ranging from science to Spanish. You have a wealth of knowledge at your fingertips because of the environment you work in.

If teachers feel frustrated about salaries and benefits, there is comfort in knowing that time is money. The time teachers have for renewal and growth is precious. The teaching profession allows opportunities for travel and continued education. Few careers offer a period for such renewal and growth, providing a chance for a clean slate each year.

The responsibilities of a teacher are mind-boggling. As you embark or continue on your journey, we'd like to leave you with a thought: The effective teacher trains students to surpass his or her own capabilities. May you, like Mentor, influence those who follow.

Professional Associations

American Alliance for Health, Physical Education, Recreation and Dance
1900 Association Drive
Reston, VA 22091-9989

American Association for Counseling and Development
5999 Stevenson Avenue
Alexandria, VA 22304

American Association of Physics Teachers (AAPT)
5112 Berwyn Road
College Park, MD 20740

American Association of Teachers of French
57 East Armory Avenue
Champaign, IL 61820

American Association of Teachers of Spanish and Portuguese
Box 6349, Mississippi State
Mississippi, MS 39762-6349

American Classical League
Miami University
Oxford, OH 45056

American Council on the Teaching of Foreign Languages (ACTFL)
6 Executive Place
Yonkers, NY 10701-6801
(914) 963-8830

American Federation of Teachers
555 New Jersey Avenue, NW
Washington, DC 20001
(202) 879-4458

American Home Economics Association
1555 King Street
Alexandria, VA 22314

American Vocational Association
1410 King Street
Alexandria, VA 22314

Association for the Advancement of Computing in Education
PO Box 2966
Charlottesville, VA 22902

Association for Educational Communications and Technology
1025 Vermont Avenue, NW
Suite 820
Washington, DC 20005

Association for Supervision and Curriculum Development
PO Box 27415
Washington, DC 20038

Council for Exceptional Children
1920 Association Drive
Reston, VA 22091-1589

Council for Learning Disabilities
PO Box 40303
Overland Park, KS 66204

International Reading
  Association
800 Barksdale Road
Newark, DE 19714-8139

International Society for Technology in Education (ISTE)
1787 Agate Street
Eugene, OR 97403-1923
(503) 346-4414

Music Educators National
  Conference (MENC)
1902 Association Drive
Reston, VA 22091-1597
(703) 860-4000

National Art Education
  Association (NAEA)
1916 Association Drive
Reston, VA 22091

National Association of Biology
  Teachers (NABT)
11250 Roger Bacon Drive
Reston VA 22090

National Business Education
  Association
1914 Association Drive
Reston, VA 22091-1596

National Council for the Social
  Studies
3501 Newark Street, NW
Washington, DC 20016

National Council of Teachers of
  English
1111 Kenyon Road
Urbana, IL 61801

National Council of Teachers of
  Mathematics
1906 Association Drive
Reston, VA 22091

National Education Association
  of the United States
1201 16th Street, NW
Washington, DC 20036

National Middle School
  Association
4807 Eva
Columbus, OH 43229

National Science Teachers
  Association
1742 Connecticut Avenue, NW
Washington, DC 20009

Bibliography

Annotated Bibliography. Jamacia, NY: Center for the Study of Learning and Teaching Styles, St. John's University, 1990.

Bracey, Gerald W. "Looking to the Experts." *Phi Delta Kappan*, March 1990; pp. 559–60.

Dunn, Rita, J. Beudry, and A. Klavos. "Survey of Research on Learning Styles." *Educational Leadership*, June 1989, pp. 50–58.

Dunn, Rita, Ken Dunn, and G.E. Price. *Learning Style Inventory*. Lawrence, KS: Price Systems, 1989.

Glenn, H. Stephen, and Jane Nelsen. *Raising Self-Reliant Children in a Self-Indulgent World*. Rocklen, CA: Prima, 1988.

Glennon, Karen. *Miss Eva and the Red Balloon*. New York: Simon and Schuster, 1990.

Guild, Pat, and Stephen Grager. *Marching to Different Drummers*. Alexandria, VA: Association for Supervision and Curriculum Development, 1985.

Harp, Bill, ed. *Assessment and Evaluation in Whole Language Programs*. Norwood, MA: Christopher-Gordon, 1991.

Hoban, Russell. *Best Friends for Frances*. New York: Harper and Row, 1969.

Jacobs, Marjorie, Blossom Turk, and Elizabeth Horn. *Building a Positive Self-Concept*. Portland, ME: J. Weston Walch, Publisher, 1988.

Johnson, D. W., and R. Johnson. "Classroom Conflict: Controversy Versus Debate in Learning Groups." *American Educational Research Journal*, Summer 1985, pp. 237–56.

———. *Learning Together and Alone*. Englewood Cliffs, NJ: Prentice-Hall, 1975.

Kagen, Jerome, and M.C. Madsen. "Cooperation and Competition of Mexican, Mexican American, and Anglo American Children of Two Ages Under Four Instructional Sets." *Developmental Psychology*, May 1971, pp. 32–39.

Kirby, Dan, and Tom Liner with Ruth Vinz. *Inside Out.* 2nd ed. Portsmouth, NH: Boynton/Cook, 1988.

MacLachlan, Patricia. *Sarah, Plain and Tall.* New York: Harper and Row, 1985.

McCarthy, Bernice. *The 4MAT System: Teaching to Learning Styles With Right/Left Mode Techniques.* Barrington, IL: Excel, 1987.

Molloy, John T. *Dress for Success.* New York, NY: Warner Books, 1976.

Routman, Regie. *Transitions.* Portsmouth, NH: Heinemann, 1991.

Sebranek, Patrick, Verne Meyer, and Dave Kemper. *Writers INC.* Burlington, WI: Write Source, 1989.

Sharmat, Marjorie Weinman. *I'm Terrific.* New York: Scholastic, 1977.

Student Learning Styles. Diagnosing and Prescribing Programs. Reston, VA: National Association of Secondary School Principals, 1979.

Ulrich, Cindy, and Pat Guild. *No Sweat! How to Use Your Learning Style to Be a Better Student.* Seattle, WA: The Teaching Advisory, 1986.

Index

W